Attention Dynamics

By Ade McCormack

The Digital Life series:

Attention Dynamics: High Personal Performance in the Digital Age

Beyond Nine to Five: Your Career Guide for the Digital Age

Also by Ade:

The IT Value Stack – A Boardroom Guide to IT Leadership

*The e-Skills Manifesto: A Call to Arms ***

* This book is available as a FREE PDF download from

www.ademccormack.com

where you can also access Ade's blogs

Digital Life

Digital Strategy

ATTENTION DYNAMICS

High personal performance in the digital age

First edition

Ade McCormack

Published by Auridian Press
www.auridian.com
Enquires: info@auridian.com

First published in Great Britain in 2017. Issue 1.0

ISBN 978-0954765149

British Library Cataloguing in Publication Data

A CIP catalogue record for this book can be obtained from the British Library

Auridian Press is a division of Auridian Consulting Ltd.

Dedication

This book is dedicated to my parents, Gabriel and Sarah Mary McCormack. Thank you for providing me with a stereoscopic perspective on how the game of life can be successfully played. I love you both.

Contents

Table of figures

Preface

Here's the premise. Attention mastery is critical to life mastery. Inattention could well lead to:

- Getting eaten by a predator.
- Seeing your life partner 'walk out the door' for the last time.
- Missing the train, and so missing the career-enhancing job opportunity.
- Waking up one day in an intensive care unit.
- Having your 'lunch' eaten by a competitor.

Understanding the dynamics of attention will help you 'optimise' your life. That is what this book aims to do.

I am conscious that life optimisation, as a topic, is not a recent trend. Ancient philosophers have laid the foundations on which the modern personal development industry is based. My justification for taking on such a bold theme is that I wanted to pull together the various drivers / levers that impact our personal performance into one cohesive approach. My premise is that attention is the most critical of the levers. It sits right up there with food, sleep and oxygen, as being critical to both survival and a purposeful life.

Professionally, I am a former technologist who today advises on the near future, particularly on how both people and organisations can thrive in it. Human performance is a key element of this.

Personally, I am a former track athlete (sprinter), who today practises a variety of martial arts. From the age of twelve, I have been fascinated by human performance, and have studied it assiduously throughout my life. Not least, because I needed, and continue to need, to optimise every element of my performance, given that I was gifted with a particularly average set of physical attributes.

Like many people in the second half of their lives, I reflect on the meaning of life, and what one might have done differently with a different testosterone-to-wisdom ratio.

Again, as someone who has practised martial arts for a significant period of my life, the concept of attention is quite important. Mulling over an altercation at work, whilst a sword is heading rapidly towards your cranium, can seriously impact how the rest of your evening pans out. I have experienced something similar firsthand. The encounter culminated in my right forearm snapping in half. The punctured artery and the hemorrhaging added further grit to the experience. And yes, my evening plans changed substantially. Martial arts, practised properly, require one to be extremely 'present'. Off the mat, they often inculcate philosophical curiosity and reflection on how these martial principles could be applied to less violent situations. But again, this is nothing new, or exceptional.

My ability to explore this theme through the lens of digital transformation is perhaps where I can add something new to the existing body of knowledge. This transformation from the industrial era to the digital age is seismic in nature, though many of us are too busy to notice. Again, my professional focus is on helping individuals and organisations thrive in this post-industrial age. My work takes me all over the world, advising and speaking on the changing nature of work, people and leadership. So, I am well positioned to see these tectonic changes from a global perspective.

The digital era is sometimes referred to as the digital economy, social economy and even attention economy. These terms all serve to highlight specific elements of post-industrial life.

In writing this book, I am endeavoring to show the importance of attention in respect of living your life in this age of distraction. Most importantly, it is a workbook with actionable guidance on how you can harness your attention to make the most of your precious time here on Earth.

Now, please, pay attention!

Ade McCormack, 2017

How to use this book

Attention Dynamics is a reference book, and so does not require you to read it as you would a novel. That said, it is structured in a logical order and, attention permitting, I would encourage you to read it, from start to finish. Thereafter you can dip in as your personal objectives dictate.

Structurally the book has three sections.
- Orientation.
- The problem.
- A solution.

Expanding on these sections:

Orientation

In this section, we explore how the shift to the digital era is changing our outlook, and impacting our attention.

We look at the key elements of modern life, along with an associated framework for showing their interrelatedness. We also explore our key relationships. Influential concepts such as willpower, motivation, values, kindness and courage, amongst others, are also covered. The notion of mastery is also introduced.

A guided tour of your mind is provided, along with a framework for how you might best manage it. Or at least gain an understanding as to why your quality of life differs from that of other people.

The problem

In this section, we explore inattention, and its pernicious impact on all aspects of our life. We also 'call out' the attention thieves, and explore the consequences of living an inattentive life.

A solution

Here, I present a framework to show how the 'working parts' of attention interact.

There is an opportunity to establish, through a simple exercise, where you might best place your attention in respect of improving your life. Given that many of us might need improvement across a myriad of domains, for example, work, health and social life, this book will help guide your priorities, and so avoid becoming overwhelmed.

We also explore some practical approaches for tuning our attention. Many of these are well established, but are distributed across a variety of sources. Thus, until this book, making it difficult for people to acquire a holistic approach to self-development.

You might say that this book aims to provide a 'unified theory' for self-improvement. It can also be considered a gateway to further exploration. Appendix D provides a bibliography of the referenced sources.

In writing this book, I have pulled together many themes, to provide a holistic framework for living an attentive life. These themes, habits being just one, are well covered both academically and in 'easy to assimilate' mainstream texts. Again, I have endeavoured to corral the disparate elements that impact attention, and thus impact living a meaningful life.

The challenge with pulling together many themes is that it places a burden on you, the reader, to keep track of them all. To alleviate that, I have included a glossary (Appendix B). I have also included a categorisation section (Appendix C) to show the interrelationship of the themes. Please make use of them should you become disoriented at any point throughout the book.

But first, let's check that this book is for you.

Calibration

Do any of the following apply to you?

- You are frustrated by your general lack of time.
- You are not fully convinced that your investment in your career is paying off either financially or in the overall quality of your life. Others, perhaps less determined than you, are making better progress with seemingly less exertion.
- You are an athlete operating at the top of your capability, but are looking to improve your performance by making some 'marginal' gains.
- You are sometimes a little snappy with those close to you, and that saddens you.
- You have a sense of emptiness despite having acquired all the badges of success in the modern world.
- You are bewildered as to why some people are so cheerful, despite the hardship of their lives relative to yours.
- You spend a substantial amount of your 'thinking time' focused on your shortcomings.
- You are conscious that your life is out of balance, eg., spending too much time on your career, at the expense of your family.
- You feel physically lethargic, and your thinking is somewhat foggy.
- You can't help but feel there is more to life than what you are currently experiencing.
- Your goals are constantly thwarted by reality.
- You are excited by the possibility of discovering your true potential.

If any of these apply to you, then I think you will find this book worthy of your attention. But if you haven't given this much thought up until now, then here is a little exercise to focus your thinking. You are attending a funeral. The eulogy is being read by someone you know very well. This is not a surprise, as it is your funeral. What would you like them to say about you?

Many of us in the developed world are on a path where our eulogy will be littered with references to our attainments. "She was HR director of a Fortune 500 company", "He was a first-class pub landlord", "He was a very capable triathlete", and so on.

But what about references to our character? Is this something that the eulogiser glosses over, because at the end of the day, your attainments came about through, for example, single-minded self-centredness?

Of course, there are people who attain great heights, and are great people too. They are life's masters. But those people have simply worked on their character with the same dedication that they have pursued their career / sport / art.

I am all for pursuing genuine greatness. Watching talented people perform is to watch nature at the top of its game. As is engaging with those of great character.

In writing this book, I am encouraging you to live the best version of yourself, whether that leads you on a path to being a world class professional or to simply being one of life's good guys. Or both.

Ultimately, this book provides you with a path to life mastery, as defined by you. One that is paved with good decisions, and not just good intentions.

Next up, I will briefly make the case for the importance of attention management as we enter the digital age.

Orientation

1 The Age of Distraction

Overview

In this chapter, we take a brief look at how the world is changing, and its impact on our attention.

The shift

The digital era is not just the industrial age on 'tech steroids'. There are some fundamental attitudinal shifts taking place. Those brought up in the industrial era were primarily focused on money. Money could buy you a lifestyle. Money would keep you out of poverty and thwart the threat of destitution. World wars have played their part in this preoccupation with money.

Those brought up in the digital age have noted the extreme actions taken by their parents to acquire money. Not least in the amount of time they spend on it. Often doing work they don't like, to acquire goods they will never have time to enjoy. Young people today appear to be more time than money-focused. This is manifested in many ways. For example:

- A greater focus on acquiring experiences over material goods.
- Greater impatience. If the page does not download instantly, or the app doesn't allow a transaction to take place in three or less taps, then it is abandoned with the callousness of an in-demand assassin rushing off to the next job.
- An almost pathological need to let others know how their time is being used, often through social networks.
- An overwhelming desire to consume experiences in parallel. Think multiple screens.

One might argue that this is a middle-class phenomenon, backed by the 'Bank of Mum and Dad'. Such young people can afford to choose time over money. Personally, regardless of class, I think this reassessment of money versus time is long overdue. We were never meant to 'live to work'. Many of us could improve how we make best use of our time. Or more specifically, where we place our attention.

Not all young people have an optimised 'work – life – money – experience' index, so to speak. Conversely, many older people do. But optimising our own lives is not enough. I am sure that a significant percentage of those who have chosen a career in the public or voluntary sectors recognise that there is more to work and life than making money and acquiring experiences.

Attention please

Before the digital age, there was a time when the detection of a slight movement, or an unfamiliar sound, would trigger a survival response. A lack of attention could have fatal consequences. Such events might happen a few times per day. Whilst this scenario might come from a prehistoric era, our brains remain wired for such scenarios.

Today, if the film you are watching isn't triggering a similar response every few seconds, you will likely change channel. Back then, it was the snapping of a twig. Today it is a super large comet, roaring in Dolby surround sound, hurtling towards millions of people, gathered around the world's most iconic human constructions, topped up with a blossoming young romance, which may / may not survive the impact.

Given the length of blockbuster films today, this equates to well over three thousand survival responses you put your body through, with only popcorn as your primary form of protection.

But, it's not just the impressive computer-generated imagery that is bombarding our nervous system. Every camera angle change, or scene change, has a similar effect.

But we crave more.

There was also a time when:

- You might have had <u>one</u> favorite TV programme, and each week, just after it had finished, you entered a mild depression, as you knew the next episode was a whole week away.
- The chances of keeping in touch with all but a handful of your school friends after the last day at school were very low.
- Your ability to listen to music on your commute to work would have involved hulking a gramophone with an extremely long lead.

Again, today is very different. We are living in wonderful times. The rate of technological innovation is growing exponentially. Access to friends, family and work colleagues is '24-7'. We can consume content when and where we want.

It would appear that everybody is vying for our attention. The content providers, the retail stores, and even teachers are having to raise their game in terms of attention-grabbing tricks.

The beauty of having so many people and organisations vying for our attention is that we can simply drift between 'attention magnets', with little mental effort.

The big downside of this existence is that you literally stop thinking for yourself, and spend your time 'thinking for others'. That said, you would be wise to pay attention to your boss, partner and children.

Whilst being constantly distracted can make for a stimulating life, it can also serve as a means of avoidance in respect of addressing important matters, such as, resolving relationship issues with people close to us, or addressing the problem of spending more than we earn. Such matters feel painful to address because we know their resolution will be cognitively and emotionally costly.

Be aware that many of these attention-seekers want your attention because they can exploit it, directly or indirectly.

Direct approaches include:

- Come into my store and buy something.
- Watch this film, for a fee.

Indirect approaches include:

- Gorge on our free online content, whilst we 'sell your eyeballs' to our advertisers.
- Subscribe to our free newsletter, and we will sell your email address to any spammer with a budget.

Of course, not all attention-seekers with an agenda should be considered our enemy. Context-relevant attention-grabbing, whether commercial in nature or not, is often valuable. If I am stuck up a mountain with a broken ski, I would be grateful to hear from an app that has detected my lack of motion in the last few hours. To hear they have an operative in the area who can help me get down the mountain is great news. In fact, in what could be a life or death situation, I might even be a little price-insensitive.

Focus?

But why attention and not, say, focus? Focus is a form of attention that is essential for many tasks. However, we need to pay attention to how we feel, and our environment, regardless of what we are doing. We could call this 'soft focus'. But I prefer the term 'attention' as it embraces both the qualities of focus but also a preparedness for the unexpected.

Focus and attentiveness are both key to life mastery. Focus enables us to zoom in on what needs to be done at any given moment. Attention provides the 'zoom out' needed to ensure we focus on what is most important and / or most urgent. Focus enables us to withdraw money from a cash machine. Attention ensures that we keep it, if opportunistic criminals are loitering nearby. Most people 'get' focus from a conceptual viewpoint. I don't think attention is so well understood. In what is often called the Attention economy, not understanding attention can have serious economic implications.

In summary

Young people are perhaps seeing their parents more as cautionary case studies than role models. Spending inordinate hours at the office, and being on 24-7 corporate stand-by when at home is not for them.

However, if having acquired more free-time, it is squandered because of poorly managed attention, then today's youth will be their children's cautionary tale.

My reason for writing this book is to alert you, the reader, that as we enter the digital age, there is a danger that we are losing the ability to manage our attention. The consequence of which is that we fail to think and act in our own best interests.

We already know that in today's world there is infinite choice as to where we place our attention. We will now narrow this down to eight areas.

2 The Life Stack

Overview

In this chapter, we look at the key elements of an attentive life. Inattention in any of these areas will lead to a suboptimal existence.

Please note, the elements that comprise an attentive life are not truly discrete. Your physical wellbeing impacts your emotional wellbeing. Your social wellbeing impacts your career fulfilment, and so on.

So, whilst I am providing distinct descriptions of the key elements of an attentive life, be aware of their interdependence. The interrelationships between these elements will be covered in the Solution section.

I have chosen these elements because they are the ones we are most likely to experience in life. You may feel that my approach has gaps, or has coalesced elements that should be treated separately. This is an evolving model. In any case, if tuning it makes it map better onto your life, then please do what is best for you.

Here are the key elements / layers:
- Physical.
- Psychological.
- Emotional.
- Social.
- Financial.
- Career.
- Lifestyle.
- Spiritual.

Figure 1 - The Life Stack

Think of each element as a layer in a stack. Like most stacks, the sturdiness of the lower layers will determine the sturdiness of the higher layers.

You might say that these are the martial arts belts in the path to life mastery. Novices (white belt holders) will be preoccupied with their physical circumstances. Those preparing for black belt (life mastery) will place much greater emphasis on their spiritual lives, as they have no need to be mentally preoccupied with acquiring the skills of the lower belts. Though, like serious martial artists, they should be maintaining and refining all the skills they have learnt.

How you match belt colours to each layer in the Life Stack is, of course, entirely up to you. Keep in mind, that even if you have gained great mastery in, say, your career, and financial matters, if you do not have mastery in the physical domain, you are still a white belt. There are no short cuts.

Let's look at each layer in turn:

Physical

This element covers all aspects of our own physicality, and the physical environment in which we live. If we are physically fit and can live our lives without being in a constant fearful state, then we have the basis for living an attentive life. NB. My definition of physical is a little stretched. Strictly speaking the term physical, in a biological sense, relates to the body. However, I am also including physiology, ie., the functioning of the body, along with the environment in which we live.

Broken down, the Physical layer embraces our need for:

- Air.
- Sleep.
- Water.
- Nutrition.
- Sex.
- Clothing.
- Home / shelter.
- A safe environment around where we live, work, and generally spend much of our time.

These are critical factors. The extent to which we have a robust Physical layer will be determined by the extent to which these needs are met.

I have placed them broadly in descending order of importance. Some fashion magazines might insist that clothing be ranked higher. The counter argument is that after a day or so without water and sleep, one's interest in tracking what's next on the Paris catwalk diminishes significantly.

An absence of shelter is the cause of great stress, particularly as we are vulnerable when we sleep in an insecure location. And even if we do have shelter, living with violent occupants / neighbours will keep us in 'survival' mode, where concerns over the late delivery of your jasmine pearl green tea order from the recently opened delicatessen is low down your priority list.

Military, social and emergency services are three notable categories where the personnel, through their career choice, expose themselves to physical harm. Living under a cloud of danger has a cognitive overhead, on top of the physical risks. However, as we will see, this cost can be offset by the knowledge that one is acting for the benefit of others. From a life mastery perspective, what we lose from the Physical layer, we gain in the Social and Spiritual layers.

As a species, we have developed complex social structures and produced great art. Some might say we are the most evolved species on the planet. Given the relatively short time we have been here, I would say that the jury is still out on whether we have made it past the feasibility stage of this particular biological experiment. Apparently, ninety-nine percent of species that have ever existed are extinct. So perhaps, we must consider our existence a privilege, rather than an entitlement.

In any case, like all the other 'less sophisticated' species we share the planet with, we fundamentally have the same drives and urges, including the desire to reproduce. It is important that when we reach sexual maturity, we channel this energy, otherwise it will play havoc with almost every other aspect of our wellbeing.

Psychological

Psychology is a broad church, covering many topics including brain function, the mind, emotional behaviour and personality, amongst other disciplines.

For the purposes of living an attentive life, we will limit the term psychology to matters concerning the mind. There have been great advances in this area, particularly in neuroscience. Old beliefs are being dismantled. Apparently, old dogs can be taught new tricks, thanks to neuroplasticity.

However, there is much we have yet to learn, and so much of what we know today can be considered a 'work in progress'. Whilst we are not even clear whether the mind is even 'contained' in our body, we can still benefit from some of the current cognitive models.

The attentive life framework I propose later in this book, calls upon concepts such as cognitive control and working memory. Over time, these concepts may prove to be incorrect. However, like Newtonian physics after the discovery of relativity, these concepts are still useful for most day-to-day purposes.

In respect of my Life Stack model, I will subdivide the Psychology layer into three elements, namely:

- Perception.
- Thinking.
- Memory.

Looking at each in turn:

Perception

Making sense of what our senses tell us is critical to our existence. Understanding that what stands before us perceives us as lunch is critical to our survival. Our senses are inundated with data. Our ability to extract a signal from the noise is an important skill. Perception is a key driver of where we place our attention. As we will see, where we place our attention determines the quality of our lives.

Thinking

Thinking would appear to be a unique human characteristic. All animals have pre-programmed instinctual responses to certain stimuli. But we humans can reflect and consider our actions. Unfortunately, our thinking can get in the way of reality. We gather the flimsiest of evidence to make a mental case for why our partner doesn't respect us, or why a work colleague got the promotion.

Whilst daydreaming has its uses, missing the signals that someone finds you very attractive, because your mind is elsewhere, makes thinking, if not properly managed, a barrier to an attentive life. Though in fairness to daydreaming, neuroscientists are starting to conclude that it is a useful tool for problem solving and creativity (ref. The Organised Mind).

Our own internal chatter can often create noise that fogs our perception of reality; again, causing us to misdirect our energies. The Chimp Paradox, by Professor Steven Peters, eloquently contextualises this chatter by referring to it as an undisciplined chimpanzee. More importantly, Peters' book guides us on how to 'manage our chimp'.

Thinking is a key element of decision making. As we will see, decision making has a cognitive overhead. Thus, we want to avoid making decisions unless it is necessary, unless we are happy to spend much of our waking hours with our willpower tank 'running on empty'. Whilst not all thinking leads to making a decision, there is some correlation between time spent thinking and cognitive expenditure. So, the message is, choose what you think about with great care. Keep in mind, that our brains are primarily designed for movement, rather than thinking. We need to reflect that in how we live our lives.

Memory

The analogy of our brain as a computer is a useful one. Our senses provide the inputs to the computer. The actions we take can be considered the outputs. Our brain processes the incoming data in a manner similar to a computer. Our brain needs somewhere to store the recently acquired input until it gets around to dealing with it. This temporary holding bay is called short-term memory.

Once the brain is ready to deal with the recently acquired input, it is loaded into working memory. This is the brain's worktop. As well as fresh data, the worktop will also hold data retrieved from long-term memory. So, for example, you have just noticed a crawling furry insect on your shoulder. In turn, you now retrieve everything you know about such creatures.

Your working memory is comparing what you are experiencing with what you know. It may conclude that you are playing host to a tarantula. It is likely that such a stimulating realisation will firmly embed itself in your long-term memory. If all goes well, you will be able to share your tarantula experience at dinner parties for years to come.

So, short-term and working memory can be thought of as computer RAM (Random Access Memory). They are simply forms of temporary storage. Whereas long-term memory is like a hard disk / USB memory stick, in that the data is permanently stored for possible future use. Though strictly speaking, working memory is a little more than just a holding bay for your current thoughts. The cognitive psychologists also think of working memory as the place where the processing of those thoughts takes place. The thing to keep in mind is that we have limited capacity in respect of working memory.

As we will see, working memory is of particular importance to us when it comes to living an attentive life.

Emotional

In much the same way as physiology and psychology influence each other, our emotions influence our physiology and psychology, and vice versa. Again, like psychology there is still much to learn. But it is safe to say that emotions are driven by our nervous system. We feel emotions.

Standing in front of a sabre tooth tiger feels different to strolling in a bluebell-coated forest. Emotions help us to prepare for what our senses are telling us.

Our emotions thus enable us to react swiftly to the environment. As we have evolved socially, our emotional behaviour enables us to be accepted by the pack, and in some cases, be feared by the pack.

Emotions might be considered a neurological mechanism to optimise our relationship with our environment.

Emotions thus help to:

- Extend our life.
- Improve the quality of our life.
- Create further life.

The problem in the digital / attention economy is that those who crave our attention have become adept at manipulating our emotions. That hunk of metal in the showroom is not just a mode of transport, it is a statement of your social status, and perhaps even your sexual desirability.

Hollywood is adept at triggering your neurotransmitters. Whilst 'gorging' on YouTube, you might as well be in a Google laboratory, where the scientists are injecting you with dopamine, serotonin and oxytocin, as needed, to keep you glued to the screen.

Living in a world where our emotions can be exploited, reacting to what our emotions are telling us can lead to a suboptimal life. Unless of course, it is your desire to sleepwalk through life, donating your attention to those who can turn it into profit.

In the digital economy, we need to respond, rather than react to our emotions. One such response could be to recognise you are being played, and so resist the urge to behave as the attention-grabber intended.

The problem with having to override our natural / manufactured urges is that there is a cognitive overhead. As we will learn, if we are not careful, there comes a point in the day when our ability to 'defend' ourselves evaporates. At which point we become attention economy 'sitting ducks'.

In our fast-paced world, frustration is becoming an increasingly common emotion. Often, we become irritated that things are not as they should be. We are frustrated when the traffic is bad, or when the kids are noisy. Frustration is draining. It largely comes about because of our inability to deal with reality. And reality never takes a day off.

Fundamentally our emotions need to work for us and not for those who do not necessarily have our best interests at heart. Better self-awareness through better attention management is required.

Social

We are social animals. Being part of a pack gave us all sorts of benefits, not least security. As cities emerged, people left their villages for the security and convenience on offer. As societies became more sophisticated, one could opt for being a farmer or a soldier knowing that, if you chose farming, there would be others who would take care of your safety.

Those who could not get along with others would be drummed out of the group. Life expectancy was low for those who had to go it alone. Our ability to be social is an increasing requirement for our economic wellbeing. Irritating the boss, colleagues or clients through social clumsiness is not the path to career success.

The digital economy is the social economy. As we move online, we become part of much larger social groups, unconstrained by geography. In fact, we move from being people to being brands. So, like the predatory attention-seeking organisations I have mentioned, we too seek to be noticed. In respect of professional networks such as LinkedIn, we hope to influence others to engage with us and / or employ us.

It has never been easier to have access to so many people. However, unless you manage your brand carefully, you could find that, in the extreme, you are banished from the network. You may not necessarily have your membership declined, but those who don't know you, who are considering engaging you, will withdraw once they have done their social due diligence, ie., asked mutual contacts about your character and capability. Conversely, our ability to build, and maintain, strategic alliances will have a career-boosting impact.

Of course, social is not just a professional concept. The quality of our lives will be determined by the quality of our relationships with key people such as partners, family and friends (actual, not Facebook-grade).

Relationships, professional or personal, require investment. In our quest for professional greatness, we might take our personal relationships for granted. 'Successful and selfish' doesn't make for a great epitaph.

Financial

It is unlikely in these modern times that you will get very far without money. Bartering might work to some extent, but the extent to which you can pay for dental work with livestock will significantly limit your choice of dentist.

Songstress Liza Minelli was indeed correct when she stated that "money makes the world go around". If you are struggling to make ends meet, your attention is going to be largely focused on your financial predicament. Thus, to live an attentive life, we need to have sufficient income to survive. We also need the certainty that our current source of income will not dry up.

Many people have created financial problems for themselves because they didn't pay attention. They buy goods they don't need, with money they don't have, to impress people they don't like. Their craving to socially climb has been exploited by the attention-grabbers.

Thus, we can find people with impressive incomes, who are living above their means and are thus suffering similar financial stress to those with no money. Their career decisions become focused on feeding their 'social' habit.

"Annual income twenty pounds, annual expenditure nineteen [pounds] nineteen [shillings] and six [pence], result happiness. Annual income twenty pounds, annual expenditure twenty pounds ought and six, result misery." – Charles Dickens, David Copperfield.

The Financial layer is not about amassing untold riches. That is a matter for the Career and Lifestyle layers. This layer is focused on financial health. In other words, living a life where you do not have to worry about money because your income exceeds your outgoings. Thus, allowing you to build a cash molehill to buffer you in periods when you are without income.

It is not about how much you earn, but about how much you keep. If your outgoings exceed your incomings, you have a problem. One that, as we will see, will financially and emotionally drain you.

Career

For most of us, the concept of paid work is very important in respect of our financial wellbeing. Some of us look beyond the concept of work and think in terms of career. As we get deeper into the digital age, people will increasingly design their own careers that follow a path where the end of the journey barely reflects the outset. I cover this in my book: Beyond Nine to Five: Your career guide for the digital age.

Given that retirement and work-life balance are becoming outmoded concepts, it is important that we pursue a career that not only meets our financial / lifestyle requirements, but also feels like a worthwhile use of our limited time on this planet. In the traditional capitalist model, your career choices and career success have a large bearing on your social status. Salary being a strong indicator of how well you are playing the capitalism / career game.

The problem comes when one's career becomes an obsession. Rather than working to live, we end up living to work. Whilst this may be financially rewarding, it can have negative implications for our health and relationships. So, the layers associated with physical, psychological, social and emotional health start to crumble. No doubt financial health will likely topple in turn.

To live an attentive life, we need to manage our career carefully. We need to ensure that there is a strong balance between our capability, our passion and market demand.

In the digital age, market demand is somewhat volatile. Imagine training for a decade to become an architect, only to discover that a group of experienced architects have developed an app that encapsulates all their wisdom and skill; and costs the user ninety-nine cents. Career management in the digital age requires a degree of paranoia, where each day we wake up and consider whether we are still economically relevant, along with what we can do to remain so.

But again, we need to ensure we don't overly invest in our careers to the detriment of the other key elements that make up an attentive life.

Lifestyle

If you were unfortunate enough to have a series of misfortunes that led to you living penniless and rough on the streets, your decision making will likely not include the following:

- Pilates or yoga.
- Prokovief or Mahler.
- Asian fusion or a paleo lunch.
- Cancun or Cannes.
- Town or country.

It will be one hundred percent focused on where the next meal is coming from, regardless of the number of Michelin stars. We each have a lifestyle, though many of us have acquired it by default. Some people just go with the environmental flow, eg., do a job they dislike, self-medicate in the evening through alcohol and video binging. Subsequently they wake up, with self-loathing being the first thought of the day, before repeating the cycle.

Lifestyle reflects our sophistication, in that it reflects that we have cultivated a life that gives us both discretionary spending power and discretionary time to enjoy it. Keep in mind that there are many high-income people who do not have an enviable lifestyle. They have acquired the toys, yet have no time to enjoy them, or to enjoy the company of others.

By the same token, there are low-paid people who do meaningful work, spend less than they earn, and thus have both the time and money to socialise, smell the flowers, appreciate art, pursue hobbies and take modest vacations.

Lifestyle, in many respects, reflects who you are as an individual. As such, it is our art. An expression of who we are. That said, it should reflect your individuality, and not your desire to socially impress, or please your parents.

Many people in the world have little choice over their lifestyle. So, it is even more important that we don't squander the capacity to design ours.

Lifestyle can be considered an element of our personality. But beware. Along with our attitudes, opinions and interests, it is an element of the discipline of psychographics. Lifestyle can thus be thought of as a marketing tool by vendors to manipulate people into saying goodbye to their hard-earned cash.

Living an attentive life means designing your own lifestyle, rather than having it subliminally programmed into you.

Spiritual

Spiritual development may not be something you give much thought to, given we live in a world where we are encouraged to work hard, play hard and consume hard. These are willpower-taxing pursuits. Possibly by the end of the day, many of us have little capacity left to reflect on spiritual matters.

Spirituality is a delicate subject, given the general rule that one should avoid, in conversation at least, topics such as religion.

In my view, organised religion might be considered as the 'off the shelf' section of the 'spirituality catalogue'.

Religions generally hit the three key notes of spirituality, ie:

- Your relationship with yourself.
- Your relationship with others.
- Your relationship with the cosmos.

Often, we are born into our religion. But for those looking to embrace one, the choice might be based on the extent to which you value each of the above. Some religions seem harsh on the individual, but kind on others. Harsh is probably the wrong word. Discipline might be better. And as this book implies, the secret to a purposeful life is discipline.

I like the idea of organised religion because it gives the adherent a playbook for how to live a purposeful life. Those that sign up do not have to spend their lives trying to find out what their purpose in life is, because the wisdom of many generations is embedded in the associated doctrine.

Culturally, we may find the practices of some religions distasteful. Or we may despair over the degree of suffering resulting from religious fanaticism. Some cultures encourage individualism (read narcissism) to the extent that a concern for others becomes almost a source of amusement. Such cultures struggle with religiosity.

In any case, religion, done properly, has love and kindness at its core. Onlookers may say that religion exists to keep the ignorant masses under control. Whether you are religious or not, or ignorant or not, if you choose to live within a society, you are to some extent subjugated. Kindness, compassion and love were, and are, key elements of what makes for a stable society. In theory, at least, societies should be better off where religion and the state are aligned. Unfortunately, in practice, there are quite a few exceptions.

If you cannot find something to suit you 'off the shelf', there is no reason why you cannot create your own religion. Not so much a cult, but a set of values that you personally adhere to. These values should again embrace the way in which you treat yourself and those around you. As you get older, and start to consider your post-life options, you will likely reflect on what this gift of life is all about.

You might marvel at human capability and the magic of nature. You might also think that given our universal footprint, in the grand scheme of things, we are insignificant. You may wonder whether God has limbs and a head, whether there is more than one God, whether everyone is God, or whether God is a collective term for dark energy.

I regard spirituality as the most important concept in living a purposeful life. Though it becomes increasingly difficult, though not impossible, to be truly spiritual if you are fixated on your career, beat yourself up over your perceived shortcomings, blame others for your plight, or are in a permanent state of fear brought about by living on the streets. Returning to the eulogy theme, the quality of our spiritual life will have a bearing on the quality of our eulogy.

Keep in mind that there is no correlation between wealth and spirituality. But wealth enables your spiritual influence to extend beyond those around you. The charitable endeavours of Bill and Melissa Gates being an example of using wealth to change the world. In their case, to improve global health.

Whether you have signed up to an organised religion or not, if, in your final days, you can say that you have made a positive impression on those around you, and perhaps even further afield, then you can say you have lived a purposeful life.

Making a positive impression requires significant attention. Attention that could be used elsewhere, frivolously, or otherwise. A purposeful life thus requires spiritual attention. This attention can range from praying / meditating, via smiling at others, through to eliminating global poverty.

Some might say that spirituality is just a variant of being social. I would argue that sociality is a tool for avoiding ejection from the tribe. Spirituality is a means for making all tribes better.

It would be a shame to lie on your deathbed and think of what might have been, if only you had made better decisions. Judgement aside, you might be remembered for one or more of the following:

- Your lifelong dedication to hedonism.
- The total number of hours you spent in the office.
- The volume of people you managed to 'bring down' by your insensitive downbeat world view.

If that was the plan, then you can tick the final box on your to do list and pass away with a smile on your face. I am certain that for many people, this wasn't the plan, but that's how it ended up.

Spirituality requires mental effort. Inattention to one's spirituality could well lead to your final breaths being ones of regret.

Summary

In this chapter, I have presented the Life Stack, a schematic of modern life. Some will argue that I have left layers out, or that one or more of my layers are sublayers of a more accurate model. That may be true, so think of this as an initial prototype.

The Life Stack simplifies the challenge of optimising our lives in respect of where we need to place our attention both today, and in the future.

Its simplicity enables us to immediately draw such inferences as, mental health is more important than, say, career advancement. Some might say, isn't that obvious. It is, but simply knowing it is not enough.

The nature of attention is such that we need to be conscious of everything that may impact the quality of our life, from a falling tree to a job advert. The Life Stack enables us to take a more asymmetric approach to attention in that we do not, for example, need to concern ourselves with Lifestyle matters, when we do not know where our next meal is coming from.

Working from the bottom, we can get our life in order layer by layer. At any one time, our attention will largely be on the layer we are currently working on.

Once we have addressed the issues at that level, we can move the bulk of our attention up a layer. Keeping in mind that we must always be paying some attention to the lower layers, given how easy it is to revert to the old habits that led to problems in these layers in the first place.

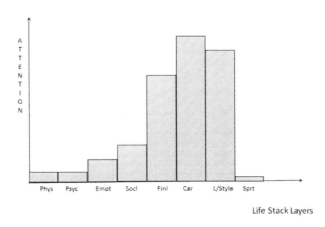

Figure 2 - Attention profile example

Think of the Life Stack as the X-axis of a histogram. With the Y-axis being the level of attention. The peak value needs to be in the layer that you are addressing. And most importantly all layers below the layer you are addressing need to have been addressed prior to this. Otherwise you are building your life on sand.

Figure 2 shows the profile of a typical person in the developed world. Their attention is largely focused on career and lifestyle. The relatively high level of attention on the Excessive financial leverage necessitates significant attention on the Financial layer. Social activity is mainly for business purposes, with little attention given to family and friends. The lower layers are perceived as too mundane, or simply unessential to their career success. Spirituality is perceived as a career option for the likes of nuns, monks, priests, rabbis and mullahs.

But let's imagine that you have worked diligently to address all the layers of your Life Stack. What happens when you make it to black belt? Is your mastery programme complete? In keeping with the martial arts theme, serious practitioners tend to practise every aspect of their skillset, including those they learnt on their first day as a white belt.

With years of practice, the black belt becomes frayed, and over time becomes white. The implication of this being that we must always maintain the humility of the novice, and never take the view that we are the 'finished article'. Plus, we must continuously return to the basics to ensure that the foundations on which our current skills are based remain strong.

If life mastery was medicine, it would be a daily tablet, rather than a one-off inoculation.

3   Your 4 Key Relationships

Overview

Having looked at the key elements of our lives, and pondered on our final minutes, I now want to explore several important relationships, namely with:

- You.
- Those you know.
- The world.
- The Cosmos.

Some may argue that their relationship with their key possessions, such as their home, car or the family cat should be included here. I would accept that if the cat is considered a member of the family then it could be bundled in to those you know.

I would contend that inanimate possessions are not key relationships. As much as you love your home or sports utility vehicle, it simply doesn't love you. But if this is a deal breaker for you, then by all means add personal possessions to the list of key relationships. However, the wisdom of the ages, tends to lean away from this notion.

The key relationships I have listed, will serve to help us understand how we relate to both ourselves and beyond. These relationships have a significant bearing on our attention and thus the quality of our lives.

Making sense of your relationship with yourself, the world at large and even the universe, helps us to live our limited time on the planet with a greater sense of purpose.

There are those who do have a plan, those that have lofty plans, and those who are successful in their lofty plans. I don't want to knock a life of attainment. Striving gives us a sense of purpose.

In eulogy terms, attainment might be considered the facts of your life. These might include:

- Received a Nobel prize.
- Built and sold a series of high value companies.
- Was the first member of the family to go to university.
- Never got caught.
- Ran a sub-four-minute mile.

But if we consider your eulogy in terms of your relationship with others, for example:

- Had time for everybody.
- Was a self-centred materialist.
- Was a devoted mother.
- Was an asset to the community / planet.

These hit an emotional chord. People tend to remember how they feel more so than what they heard. If you intend to leave an indelible legacy through those you leave behind, you need to ensure you devote sufficient attention to your relationships.

So, let's look at these four key relationships.

You

You are a very delicate instrument. Whilst you are awake, you are constantly receiving sensory data that over time shapes who you are because of the way you interpret it, and subsequently act on it.

At one extreme, if you do not make the fast-approaching car a priority, your life will end abruptly. More subtly, your parents might refer to you as the 'sporty one' and your sibling as the 'bright one'. Such parental classifications might have been constructed solely for the purpose of superficial social pleasantries. Even so, it may well have burnt deeply into your psyche, ultimately giving you a complex in respect of your, say, intellectual capacity.

As children, we cringed at this stereotyping. Witnessing one or more parents locked in a sibling-rivalry competition with one of your aunts or uncles was to see this in its rawest form. This can leave us with deep scars. But in fairness to our parents, they too carry the scars of stereotyping / compartmentalisation.

Such compartmentalisation may well be accurate, but it is often only relative (no pun intended). You may have won the national schools one-mile track championship, but your sibling may have finished second. To the outside world, you are both brilliant athletes.

Our perception of ourselves is also shaped by those whose opinions we value, such as school friends, partners and work colleagues. They may choose to 'manage us' by exploiting our high opinion of them. Any lack of self-esteem you suffer today may be the result of simply accepting and internalising their perspectives with little scrutiny.

I am taking a very negative path here to make a point. Our environment plays an active role in programming us. When we include the incoming barrage of advertising messages, all designed to inform us that we are in some way inadequate, unless we make a purchase, it is a surprise that smartphones don't come with a dedicated therapist quick-dial button.

The key point is that you, or more specifically your perception of you, is critical to the quality of your life. Many of us carry an idealised version of ourselves around in our heads. Such a model might include:

- Ownership of a 'six pack'.
- Being a polyglot.
- Acquiring a qualification.
- Owning a larger home.
- Playing for the A team.
- Never eating chocolate.

In fact, the list might be much longer. Throughout the day, little reminders of your inadequacy erode both your confidence and your enjoyment of life.

There is absolutely nothing wrong with having an idealised version of yourself, and striving towards it. That is what this book is about. However, if you have acquired these 'future you' goals through inattention, then you have set yourself up for misery. As is the case when you have too many such goals, some of which might even be conflicting. What often happens is that you become totally self-centred, as you try to engineer this ideal you, and become despondent in the process. 'Miserable and self-obsessed' will certainly challenge the writer of your eulogy.

In what we might call the attention economy, through a lack of attention, we subconsciously acquire such goals. For example, your desire to have abdominals of steel, has come about through the constant media depiction of heroic and beautiful people appearing to have chiselled torsos, as standard. Even the cartoon character, Sponge Bob, Square Pants, dons a six pack. Now, even a negative body image is accessible to toddlers.

Also because of our inattention, we focus on the outcome, "wouldn't it be cool to speak five languages!", but fail to grasp what a significant investment of time and lifestyle is required to achieve this goal.

Many of us would like to be a famous actor or top athlete because we only see the glamorous end of their lives. They did not become the best in the world without making sacrifices. Or without discipline.

You are encouraged to reassess the ideal you. Why do you want to acquire these skills and attainments? Do you truly understand the level of sacrifice required? And who are you trying to impress? Could this be traced back to an insensitive comment by your aunty, when you as a child, witnessed your mother and sister launch into one of their alcohol-soaked one-upmanship contests?

I encourage you to scrutinise every corner of your brain and build an inventory of the mental baggage you are carrying in respect of this idealised you. Work through it, discarding the stuff you weren't even fully conscious of, or have acquired through inattention. Ultimately you need to be left with a set of goals that reflect the idealised version of you. A version which you are genuinely happy to pursue. George Mumford in his book, the Mindful Athlete, covers this poignantly.

Please do not interpret this as implying you are less than perfect in your current state. If you are as happy and healthy as you feel you need to be, then you are in great shape. Many of us, through our circumstances and inattention, need a goal audit.

'Spring cleaning' your head and setting carefully considered manageable targets in terms of your personal development will energise you. It will make you kinder to yourself. And perhaps, just as importantly, you will in turn be kinder to others.

Ego

You may be aware that you have an ego. You will almost certainly be aware of the egos of others. Our egos cause us to strive, be proud and take unkindly to the disrespectful acts of others. Disrespectful acts also include those that merely insinuate that we are inferior to those seemingly attacking us. As an aside, this is more generally known as the false attribution error.

Our ego is also the cause of anxiety that comes about through our actions not living up to our expectations. Finely tuned athletes crumble on the day, if they mismanage their own egos.

We all have egos. The extent to which we manage them or they manage us will have a significant bearing on the quality of our lives. Egos are neither good nor bad. They are no doubt built into us to ensure the propagation of the species. You might say that the size of one's ego is proportional to our sense of entitlement when it comes to securing the most virile / fertile mate.

This inbuilt sense of entitlement battering against the hard wall of reality is the source of much stress. You may believe you are superior to others, and live your life accordingly. But in this day and age, particularly in cities, you are likely to encounter similar folk, giving rise to road rage, trolley rage and the occasional beating.

Modern societies have created concepts such as civility to encourage us to manage our egos and thereby 'rub along' with others. The problem is that civility places a cognitive burden on us. And in this world of distraction, where our cognitive capacity is already allocated to, for example, our Twitter feed as we walk through a shopping precinct, there is very little capacity left for civility.

This is less a rant at the demise of society and more a recognition of the consequences of a poorly managed ego. Again, with an unchecked ego, disappointment, frustration and worse await.

With a well-managed ego, it is possible to make great things happen because you truly believe, for example, that the world you live in should not contain poverty. Plus, with well-managed attention, you might even secure that 'trophy mate'.

Your relationships

As discussed, your ego has consequences for those around you. Poorly managed, you will be a source of misery. Well managed, and you will be a charismatic and graceful energy beacon.

If you study the animal kingdom, specifically those species that have been around longer than us, you will notice that those that are particularly impressive tend to operate with relatively sophisticated social models. Ants, who unlike us are not planetary-arrivistes, demonstrate that social cooperation trumps individualism.

As a species, we are still trying to find a model that works well for us. Capitalism has increasingly encouraged us to be more individualistic. There is no shortage of such people in Western economy cities.

This 'every man for himself' approach seems to cut across the social contract that underpins society. 'If you agree to protect the city, I agree to grow the food'. Societies work because the members have a shared and interdependent interest in their survival.

Today it would seem that we can forget about the issues facing others, and just act in our own self-interest. Such a state is, in my view, the sign of imminent societal collapse. There comes a point where the divisions between the poor and the rich become so large that the poor take it upon themselves to redress this. Possibly the Internet and drugs are useful governing tools to ensure that nobody has the cognitive capacity to work out what is happening. And even if someone does, planning and coordinating a coherent response would be impossible.

This is not a call to arms, but a call to acknowledge that the quality of our relationships with others ultimately impacts the quality of our own life.

Close friends and family are often quite testing in terms of relationship management. Our ego may have expectations in respect of their behaviour that do not reflect that they, like us, are imperfect irrational humans.

We didn't choose our family. Coming from the same DNA pool, with common environmental experiences, it is likely we will often behave very similarly to our loved ones. Sometimes the manifestation of our own faults in others can be a source of irritation. A shared 'interest' in stubbornness does not seem to encourage closer bonding.

Perhaps this is an inbuilt DNA dispersal mechanism. Those that are genetically similar are designed to repel each other. This makes reproductive sense, but I am merely speculating.

At least we have some influence over our friends (friend (noun): an apology from God for one's family). Sometimes friendships evolve simply through shared experiences and interests. Sometimes through the need to address gaps in our own personalities, for example, their upbeat manner is the perfect antidote to my maudlin disposition.

But again, even close friends are subject to human frailty. When the value proposition is too one-sided, then friendships crumble. We need to remember that to maintain friendships, we need to invest as well as withdraw.

Work colleagues, like family, are often not chosen by us, and perhaps wouldn't be chosen by us if we had a choice. So, the concept of being professional has come about to encourage us to rise above the petty squabbling that, by default, we might revert to, particularly when feeling the heavy burden of commercial pressure.

Acquaintances are somewhat easier to get along with. Usually there is not enough familiarity to breed contempt. Often, we encounter them when pursuing our hobbies. They may well be of dubious character, but you will likely get along like a house on fire, if they provide you with sound advice on how to raise your game in your shared hobby. The fact that they can also show you how to burgle luxury apartments is simply a conversational path you choose not to go down.

And then there are strangers. And within this group there are strangers who are not like us. Through stereotyping, useful when facing something salivating with big claws, we assign them a set of characteristics that reinforces our differences. Differences that may give rise to scorn or fear. Given we don't in any case know them, it is not so difficult to give them a wide berth.

But thanks to the laws of entropy, the chances are that the strangers you encounter will increasingly be different to you. You can choose to adopt a siege mentally and thus self-incarcerate yourself for your remaining days. Or you could see this as a great opportunity to expand your worldview and gain access to the wisdom that lies beyond your original tribe.

The bottom line is that if you want to live a purposeful life, you need to get your act together in respect of your relationships with others. Whilst this will initially draw down on your cognitive capacity, it will over time replenish it in respect of the richness of your life.

Showing kindness to a self-centred sibling or helping a boss that appears determined to thwart your career is a big ask. But the consequences of doing so are likely to lead to a much more positive outcome than bearing an 'always-on' grudge.

What if your ego can't take this level of beneficence? Then think of it as playing around with your target's head. I cautiously suggest this in the hope that you subsequently discover the power of kindness, rather than set you on the path to being a world-class sociopath.

For those that do not have to be sold on the notion of kindness, you might try to up your game, by advancing to invisible acts of kindness. No special cloak required. You simply commit an act of kindness where the recipient cannot easily identify you as the source.

I started doing this some time ago. After everyone had gone to bed, I would wash any remaining dishes. It took quite some time for my wife to realise it was me. Her suspicions became aroused once she had ruled out our Shetland sheepdog as a possible suspect.

Most people realise that life is better when we have strong relationships and can broadly live in harmony with those with whom we come into contact. The problem is that in the digital age there are many attention-consuming distractions, thus diverting our energy away from relationship building and general civility.

The World

We are not destined to meet most of the world's population. So perhaps we should not waste precious energy considering how we might help them, let alone take action.

Our current nation-state model tends to make us see those from another nation as a different breed. Even though we are perhaps happy to trade with them, or take vacations within their borders, we fundamentally do not trust them.

Those of us who take little interest in world affairs, perhaps because we have enough to think about in our own little world, may take the simple view that our country is best and the others are to be viewed with suspicion. The reality is that most people on the planet simply want to lead fulfilling lives, where they and their families do not have to worry about persecution and starvation.

Those of us who live in the developed world generally don't have such issues to worry about. Most of our concerns are affluence, rather than poverty-related.

My slightly longwinded point is that we are all the same in many respects, and therefore our interests are best served by looking out for each other as a species.

One can easily counter argue by stating that it is in our nature to form tribes and fight for territory and resources. But what if the arena on which we are fighting, ie., the Earth, is becoming permanently damaged by our behaviour?

Nature doesn't really care if:

- We introduce so many antibiotics into the food system that we create resistant bacteria that will make routine surgical procedures next to impossible.
- Through use of pesticides, we cause bees to stop pollenating the plants, thus causing us to run out of food.
- We continue to produce greenhouse gases that cause the icecaps to melt and, in turn, submerge currently inhabited land masses.

As mentioned, given our short time on the planet, Nature still considers us as something of an experiment. If it doesn't work out for us, Nature will happily watch us become extinct, as it has done for ninety-nine percent of all species that have ever existed. Whether human life goes on, or not, is a detail for Nature.

Nature is even less fussed about the fact that developed nations think it is in the best interests of developing nations that they import the cultural and economic practices of their 'economic superiors'. Or whether obesity is cured by cross-training or a staple gun.

Forgive me for talking about Nature as if she is a deity, rather than just a convenient biological / ecological catch-all term. But hopefully, you will see beyond this to the point I am making.

Imagine that we all live on a boat way out in the ocean. It is better that we cooperate in terms of reaching dry land, rather than squabble and fight, and thus risk tipping the boat over.

Thus, I believe that if we are to live a meaningful life, we need to allocate a certain amount of attention to what we can do to stop the boat from rocking.

This of course, is not top of mind, if:

- You are on the verge of being evicted.
- You are a junior on the fast track to partnership at an international tax law firm.
- Every free moment you have is spent 'troughing' in an 'all you can eat' media buffet.
    - There was a time when you would have to walk to the TV to start the gorge fest. Soon it will be a simple voice command to your glasses.

We live in a world where it is increasingly acceptable to step over a dying person in the street, if you are late for a meeting. Or even to stop and record their death on your phone, as that will have more social value when uploaded onto YouTube than you being of assistance. Maybe it even represents a chance to catch a 'selfie' to share at the office.

I don't think that such people are necessarily bad. They have simply lost the ability to pay attention to their own humanity. I think this is, in part, a consequence of an increasingly digital society, and in part because parenting in the digital age is ill-defined. There is currently no digital parenting playbook.

Ultimately, if we regard the concerns of the wider world as, at best, a form of entertainment served up through a myriad of media channels, then we will have lost our humanity, and nature will not stand in our way as we career towards our own self-created demise.

This can be addressed, but only if we regain control of our attention.

The Cosmos

Many people do not have a worldview. As mentioned, their interests lie closer to home. However, organised religions have generally recognised it is important to consider the biggest view one can take, that of the cosmos / universe / everything.

These religions recognise that we, as humans, have a deep-seated need to understand the very big picture. Who created the universe? How old is it? And how heavy it is? Religions tend to abstract the details in terms of who / what was responsible for its creation.

Humanity spends an inordinate amount of money on space science. Not all of it is directed to adult content communications satellites, space weaponry, or which planet is best suited for a reality TV series. Countries spend billions on space science projects that could otherwise be used to feed the poor. Admittedly, some of these projects are of a natural resources exploration nature. And even if the projects appear to be nothing more than man's curiosity in respect of the heavens, at least some of the technological innovation by-products will eventually find their way into the mainstream economy.

It is in our nature to wonder how we fit into the grand scheme of the universe. Some maintain that we are the most important species in the universe. Others feel we are just a slightly evolved form of bacteria that has taken root on an insignificant planet revolving around an insignificant star.

So, it may be that we are divine and/or we may be somewhat pointless. Many of us are too busy to give this much thought. Some of us have mental / spiritual frameworks that we accept, and thus can live our lives on this planet as it hurtles around the Solar System, without suffering any existential crisis. Religions, by addressing this, help us make sense of our place in the universe, along with what happens once we shuffle off our mortal coil. The rest of us must build our own cosmos-view and come to terms with it. Failing to do this will eat away at you. Unless some form of self-medication is taken, this matter will grow in prominence as we approach life's 'departure lounge'.

Summary

This chapter details the significant relationships that make up our life. They have been presented as standalone elements for convenience. We know that they are, in reality, highly interdependent.

Understanding each of these elements is necessary to appreciate the nature of the framework I will present in a subsequent chapter.

Now let's look at the key drivers that determine the quality of our life.

4   Life-Enhancing Concepts

Overview

In the absence of attention-grabbing events, where we place our attention is a matter for our mind. Understanding the factors that influence the mind will enable us to harness them to steer our mind along a purposeful path.

Meet the key factors:

- Mastery.
- Attention.
- Willpower.
- Motivation.
- Habit.
- Energy.
- Values.
- Purpose.
- Goals.
- Positivity.
- Kindness.
- Confidence and courage.

Let's look at these in turn:

Mastery

The term mastery can be viewed in a negative light. It can suggest that we have control over others, a master-slave relationship. It can suggest an air of superiority; if I am a chess master, why would I want to play against a novice.

In the context of this book, mastery means self-mastery. In fact, if you bought this book with the specific intention of universal dominance, or simply to belittle people at social events, then you will find little of value in this book.

As mentioned, we see mastery being used as a term in pursuits such as chess and eastern martial arts. Sometimes the title of master is bestowed on an individual because they are exceptional in their field. Sometimes there is a set standard for being awarded mastery status.

In medieval Europe, associations known as guilds were formed around specific trades such as stone cutting, baking, brewing and carpentry. To become a recognised tradesman, you needed to initially serve an apprenticeship under a master craftsman. During this phase of your career, you learnt the trade. The next step was to become a journeyman, whereby you could charge a fee for your work. This usually entailed travelling around the country, gaining further experience from other masters. Eventually, the guild would elect you to become a master. At which point, you could set up your own workshop and employ others.

Becoming a master required the acquisition of skill and experience. It also required the approval of senior figures in your trade. This model is still in operation to varying degrees. We are seeing a resurgence in the notion of apprenticeships in the world of work. But there is little talk about mastery. Yet.

Author Robert Greene has written the definitive mastery book, conveniently entitled 'Mastery'. As such, it is well worth reading, if you are serious about mastery in general. He recommends that the following steps are taken:

- Observe how the 'game' is played.
- Learn to play the 'game'.
- Change the rules of the 'game'.

This is not unlike the Guild model. The first two steps are essentially suggesting that you find a great teacher. Imagine trying to learn to play the piano or master karate without an instructor.

You will waste a lot of time discovering what doesn't work. You may even develop a degree of competence, but find that you hit a platcau from which you can never leave because, for example, 'seek and peck' one finger piano playing has its limitations. Anders Ericsson and Robert Pool in their excellent book, 'Peak – Secrets from the New Science of Expertise', are strong advocates of having an experienced and capable teacher. Only experienced teachers can design exercises that move the student from what might be called rote learning to what they describe as deliberate learning; an approach that fundamentally (neuronically) sculpts your brain.

Changing the rules of the game can be considered as weaving your character into the accepted standard for good work. In turn, it might mean that you have in fact raised the bar for what is considered great work in your field. You are now reshaping the domain in which you are a master. In fact, you are redefining what it means to be a master.

This might be considered extreme mastery. Such a level of influence would likely make you one of the best in the world. As, I have written in my book, 'Beyond Nine to Five', from a career perspective, this will increasingly be necessary in a highly connected global marketplace.

But Attention Dynamics is not about being the best in the world physically, mentally and so on. I am proposing that you operate at a performance level that gives you comfort, or a gentle stretch. A level that does not cause the undue expenditure of your cognitive capacity. Worrying about your weight, or searching the dustbin for remnants of chocolate, detract from endeavours that lead to a purposeful life.

I am not saying that you should not endeavour to be Ms Universe or be capable of memorising long strings of numbers. But these are more career / life style matters than peak performance at the physical / mental levels of the Life Stack.

By all means be a peak performer in one or more aspects of your life. Just keep in mind that becoming the best in the class, country or world only make sense in the Career and Lifestyle (ie., you have a hobby that you pursue competitively) layers.

Being world class in respect of the following sounds ludicrous:

- Physical: Your ability to stay healthy and secure.
- Psychological: Make better decisions.
- Emotional: Manage your emotions.
- Social: Have great friendships.
- Financial: Be financially secure.
- Spiritual: Live a spiritual life.

If you are uncertain, try this experiment. Occasionally drop into your conversations that you are considered by many to be world class emotionally / socially, and so on, and see whether your declaration is greeted with awe and respect, or sniggers and derision.

So again, for the majority, if not all the main aspects of our life, as defined by the Life Stack, mastery needs to be tempered. Think self-mastery, rather than global domination. Again, if you can happily go about your life without worrying about any of the Life Stack layers, you have indeed achieved life mastery.

Self-mastery can be achieved in each layer of the Life Stack. I might have mastered the Physical layer because I am healthy and feel physically secure, and have the skills to remain so. You might have mastery in the Social layer. You have good relationships with family and friends, and you are skilled enough to retain those relationships no matter how much they are tested.

The reality is that we each have our own unique profile, and goals, in respect of our degrees of mastery for each of the eight Life Stack layers. The aim of this book is to identify where improvements are needed, as defined by you, and in what order these improvements should be addressed.

There is no United Nations approved standard for life mastery, so we need to develop our own. You might decide that emotional mastery is being able to smile serenely, even though the shopping mall you are in is under terrorist attack. I might regard emotional mastery as the ability to walk past McDonalds without the uncontrollable urge to charge in and join the shortest queue.

Life mastery is thus to some degree subjective. If over time, you spend less time in your head, worrying about various aspects of your life, and more time engaged with the world living your life, then you are making great progress.

Attention

Attention is both a noun and a verb. As a noun, it can be considered as a resource. So, we possess a certain amount of attention capacity, and we can use it as we, or even others, see fit. As a verb, it is a mental act. For us to pay attention to something or someone, we need to commandeer our senses and redirect them towards the object of our attention.

The problem with this verbal definition is that it suggests that we redirect all our attentional capacity on the 'target'. One might regard such attention as focus. In other words, focus is a subset of attention. Focus is good, but focus to the extent of complete inattention elsewhere can have negative consequences. The bomb disposal expert, who whilst diffusing an improvised explosive device doesn't sense the approaching tiger, may not get to finish the job.

Perhaps, more mundanely, when we overly focus on our career, we may inadvertently neglect our loved ones, or our own health. Thus, there are times when focus is as detrimental to our quality of life as inattention. Ultimately focus generates inattention, elsewhere, as a by-product. And inattention can have serious consequences.

We should never be so focused on something that we blank out everything else. But even this is an oversimplification, as this implies we only can exert attention consciously.

The reality is that much of our attention is unconscious; we pay attention without judgement or introspection, or even consciousness that we are paying attention. Hypnotism, autosuggestion and subliminal messaging capitalise on this.

But keep in mind that the conscious mind has limited bandwidth. It can only ever focus on a small subset of the data that is hitting our senses. Our unconscious mind is akin to broadband and thus can deal with large torrents of data.

Living an attentive life needs to reflect our unconscious attention. Our unconscious attention is a powerful asset. Sleeping on a problem to wake up with the answer is just one example. Conversely conducting your life in an environment where you are engaging with toxic people, unless you are exercising your willpower at full throttle, and have an inexhaustible supply, which by the way you haven't, will pull you down to this toxic level.

Some of us are fortunate enough to control our environment, and with whom we engage. However, we are still exposed unconsciously, if we consume life-negating media and / or life-negating food. Our bodies tend to follow our minds.

Beyond reflex responses, we need to think something to make it happen; I am going to walk to the shops, or I am going to raise my hand. Therefore, it is critical as to what we expose our mind to. An inattentive mental diet will lead to unpredictable outcomes. Some of which may have a significant bearing on the quality of your life.

I have chosen to make attention the central theme of this book. Others will say it is all about body posture, or a paleo diet, or getting up early each day. I am not suggesting they are wrong. I just take the view that if we manage our attention effectively, we will be in a better position to explore these other recommendations.

Attention, unlike focus, enables us to be aware of everything around us. It's like having a zoom camera, telescope and microscope all operating in parallel. Driving is a useful analogy here. Spend too much time monitoring the petrol gauge and you will eventually have an accident. Spend too much gazing into the horizon and you may find that you are breaking the speed limit.

So, is attention multi-tasking? Sort of. The difference being that multi-tasking involves what computer scientists call context-switching. Traditional computers can only do one thing at a time, but they swap between tasks so rapidly that it appears to us that they are performing tasks concurrently.

There is an overhead in switching between tasks, as it requires us to clear working memory of the data associated with the current task and then replace it with the data for the next task. If we are not careful, and take on too much, we spend all our time context-switching, rather than getting things done. This is wasted brain power.

Whereas multi-tasking can be thought of as rapid episodes of laser focus, attention can be thought of as a continuous state of soft focus. Laser focus sends the data directly to our brain, where it is evaluated, and then a suitable response is recommended before we act. Soft focus allows us to bypass the brain so that the incoming data does not have to undergo the 'slow' process of evaluation and recommendation. With soft focus, the data immediately triggers a muscle memory response.

Laser focus is required from time to time. But it must be used for specific purposes, and even then against a background of soft focus. Street fighters know that laser focus can have deadly consequences. Rarely do attackers work in isolation. A soft focus enables them to pick up on incoming signals beyond the immediate threat.

Perhaps a better analogy is to see attention as more akin to being an air traffic controller. There are a lot of planes in the air. You need to be aware of them all, but be constantly scanning for those that appear to be veering off the flight plan or getting too close to other planes. And even where an issue does appear to be emerging, you are still required to monitor the wider picture as you deal with this issue.

Over the last few decades the notion of Continuous Partial Attention has emerged as a concept. In part, to warn against the dangers of being overwhelmed by too much input, or of living a life of extreme superficiality, never totally engaged. I think that whilst it captures an important concept, it is an oxymoron. Continuous Partial Focus would be more accurate.

In the digital economy, we are faced with an incredible level of distraction. Most of which will erode our ability to focus on what is important in respect of our lives.

Being hit by a car, or mugged, because of the inattention brought about by our impulsive desire to respond to a noise made by our phone is both embarrassing and potentially dangerous.

In this attention economy, unless we get our 'attention act' together, we will increasingly be the 'star of the show' in such scenarios, which from time to time might be captured on video and shared via any number of social networks. Your inattention might thus create unwanted attention. Such is the attention economy.

The path to life mastery requires you to be attentive to all aspects of your life. Unlike worry, attention is a detached, almost third party observance of how you are performing at each layer of the Life Stack.

In a world designed to redirect your attention to the agendas of others, your ability to maintain attention on your own wellbeing becomes increasingly challenging.

Willpower

Willpower plays a very significant role in what we think about. If we turned off our willpower, we would be faced with a life driven by comfort and pleasure, which on the face of it, doesn't seem like a bad option.

Unfortunately, pleasure requires feeding. And unless we manage our pleasure intake carefully, we will find ourselves with an addiction. With an addiction, you now work for your nervous system. Your primary task being to source whatever it takes to satisfy your nervous system's cravings.

Willpower:
- Stops us overindulging.
- Enables us to delay gratification – Save today to avoid a destitute dotage. Or study hard today to enjoy a rewarding career tomorrow. "Today, I will do what others won't, so tomorrow I will accomplish what others can't." - Jerry Rice, NFL Hall of Famer.
- Enables us to engage in social niceties with people we do not like.
- Overrides our tendency to react 'in kind' to road rage combatants.

Unfortunately, we do not have an infinite supply of willpower. A stressful day will result in us abandoning our diet come the evening.

It appears that we are given a daily allocation of willpower at the start of the day. And once it has run out, we are at the mercy of YouTube videos and junk food.

Willpower also gets expended when, for example, we read something that doesn't make sense, or someone in your presence makes a controversial comment. In the former case, you have the cognitive burden of trying to make sense of what is written and whether to press on or give up reading. In the latter case, you must decide whether you let the comment pass or respond to it. You must also consider how you respond in order to avoid a tense escalation.

There are various schools of thought on willpower. Some believe that it is a marque of your character to tame and exert your willpower as needed; those that succumb to desire being of weak character. I would contest that once your willpower battery runs flat, you are at the mercy of your desires, and the wiles of the attention grabbers. The true measure of character is the extent to which you have developed habits that consequently reduce the day-to-day burden on your willpower reserves. Such habits are perceived by others as discipline. But the very nature of habits, as we will see, once acquired, require no mental effort. Again, once acquired, there is no actual discipline needed.

Willpower might be considered a daily gift, designed to protect us from ourselves and those, skilful in neural manipulation, who do not necessarily have our best interests in mind. Because the daily supply is limited, we must use it with care, if we are to live a purposeful life.

Motivation

Motivation defines the connection between what we do and why we do it. Olympians do the most unappealing of activities in pursuit of gold. Why would anyone get up at 5am to head to a chlorine-filled swimming pool, or sit in an ice bath post-workout in order to shorten the time to the next punishing workout?

Motivation is a useful resource because it in effect tops up our willpower. After a stressful day at work, one might be tempted to hit the junk food and the TV clicker (post-industrial irony at work here). But just before you raid the pantry, you remind yourself that you have a trophy to defend in the summer. So, you step away from the pantry, grab your kit bag and head off to training.

One could argue that this is simply another example of a habit. It is, but it goes deeper than just a reflex to a given stimulus. It is a conscious desire to do something now because of the potential reward.

Motivation can be intrinsic or extrinsic. By intrinsic, we mean that the motivation comes from within. You have decided that you want to explore your capacity to learn foreign languages. You do not need anybody to cajole, charm or bully you into practising. Making a deep connection between who we are and what we want to achieve is essential to intrinsic motivation.

Extrinsic motivation, on the other hand, requires the stimulus to come from an external source. Possibly your parents pushed you to study, against your wishes. Maybe you want to learn languages to impress on people that you are a global citizen, or to be more attractive in the labour market. These stimuli lie beyond you, and so can be considered as extrinsic sources of motivation. Intrinsic motivation is seen to be a better form of motivation.

A variant on the extrinsic motivation theme is temptation. This might be considered a type of motivation that drives us to take action that we will later regret. Attention grabbers are temptation peddlers. They coax and manipulate their victims into taking actions that are not in the interests of the victim. Such victims are drawn in by curiosity, social pressure and the fear of loss.

Not all temptations are bad. For example, I might be tempted to join a gym or try a new multivitamin tablet. But without a deeper motivation, it may be that the gym membership quickly becomes unused and the tablets remain in the bottle, indefinitely.

Motivation again enables us to get things done without overly taxing our willpower. It can be thought of as a willpower turbo-booster, ie., we are getting an improved return on our daily allocation. So, to lead a more purposeful life, we need to dig deep in order to establish why we would want such a life, when the alternative of a hedonistic lifestyle seems quite appealing (bar the addictive consequences).

An important overlapping concept is desire. You might say desire is the bait that causes you to be motivated. You want that Olympic gold or that new shiny car. Desire is thus the motivation for our motivation.

If we are to fulfil our ambitious dreams, we are going to need it underpinned by a burning desire.

Habit

Habits are a powerful toolset for living a purposeful life. Whereas motivation boosts our return on a unit of our limited willpower, habits obviate the need to even use it.

Habits turn conscious behaviours into unconscious behaviours. Thus, the associated actions happen without any cognitive burden, and so willpower is not expended.

Habits can be classified as good or bad. Examples of good might include:

- Tidying your desk at the end of each working day.
- Getting your creative work done before you attend to the administrative work.
- Thanking those who have helped you in some way.
- Not using electronic devices prior to going to sleep.

Bad habits might include:
- Never walking past a MacDonald's without popping in.
- Gossiping about colleagues.
- Working through your social media feeds each time you turn on your smartphone or tablet.

But if you think thanking people is a sign of weakness, or bypassing McDonalds is 'dissing' Ronald, then by all means recategorise my examples.

One might argue that a life based on habits is a life lived on autopilot. This is true, to some extent. But if we consider our lives to comprise two categories:

- Doing the things, we like.
- Doing the things, we dislike or are indifferent about.

The things we like to do generally do not overly burden our willpower. If they are challenging, they might dig into our willpower reserves, but because we are gaining enjoyment from the activity and / or are highly motivated to do it, it doesn't have such a draining effect.

The extent to which we can do the things we like is largely determined by the amount of time we spend on things that we do not like (eg., personal tax finances), or are indifferent about, but must do (eg., shaving).

The more efficiently we work through these unattractive activities, the more time we will have for what we enjoy. The more mentally automated these activities are, the more willpower we will have available to expend on fun / exciting things, eg., asking your future partner to go out on a date.

Habits are a form of mental automation. Once established, we can rely on them to get the job done. Some habits have come about without us consciously building them, eg:

- "I recall nothing of my drive home from the station".
- "Where has my lunch gone?", as you look at your empty plate whilst watching TV.

Habits might be considered a form of mindlessness (sic). As you will read later, the concept of mindfulness is growing in popularity. This is a concept highly related to attention and so we will come to it later in this book.

Again habits, particularly good habits, have a direct bearing on the quality of our lives. Habits determine our productivity. Writers create habits that enable them to produce a certain number of words each day, come what may. Writers that prevaricate, using avoidance tactics, such as checking email or the news online, tend to be less prolific and the quality of their work is thus not reflective of their true potential.

Energy they could have directed into the creative process has been expended elsewhere. Their subsequent guilt and introspection in respect of their lack of writing discipline simply consumes more of their willpower, and in turn consumes their confidence.

Some habits arise because of our parents. Potty training being a socially significant one. Our parents, as important role models, by their very actions can generate lifelong habits in their offspring. Exposure to kindness and assertiveness in the appropriate situations often leads to the children behaving similarly, because for a very formative period of their lives that is all they have been exposed to.

Cultivating a habit

The interest in habits has grown significantly in recent decades. Many of us, through living inattentive lives, want to create a better version of ourselves. This might relate to our dietary, exercise or relationship habits. In effect, we already have habits in place, it's just that they are counterproductive.

The discipline of neuroscience has come to the rescue. By using increasingly refined brain scanning tools, they are unravelling how habits are created and how they can be replaced, if required.

The topic of habits is almost a book genre today. There is a market for people who seek to remove destructive habits and replace them with something more beneficial to both themselves and to those around them. Habit books tend to be very popular around February, when, in some cases, our self-loathing at our inability to stick to our New Year resolutions becomes apparent, and we conclude that we are weak-willed, possibly even defective in some way.

Poor willpower is not the sign of poor character, but a sign of poor attention management and a lack of skill in cultivating good habits.

The former is what this book covers. The latter is covered in many well written books, including 'The Power of Habit' by Charles Duhigg.

Duhigg suggests there are three elements to our habitual behaviour:

- Cue.
- Routine.
- Reward.

So, if we take the scenario of being at a family celebration, where there is an open buffet. You are attentive enough to spot the chocolate cake, which appears to comprise chocolate of various densities bound together in a 'come hither' manner.

Unbeknownst to you, you have dribbled. Like Pavlov's dogs, the cue of the chocolate cake has triggered the salivation routine. In a social situation, you cannot simply dive face first into the cake, so you try to be more discrete about your interest in the cake. You might even sample some of the main course dishes and engage in some chitchat. But your eye is on the prize. And before long, as you so routinely do, you have helped yourself to a generous portion of cake. You are devouring it as if there was a risk that it might evaporate or disappear before you had wrapped yourself around it. It feels good. Your body is lighting up. You feel in the zone. Life doesn't get much better than this. These represent significant rewards for your behaviour. The habit is thus reinforced and it will happen again and again.

However, this reward is short lived. Your young nephew is looking at you as if you were an oversized blue-bottle fly. He has witnessed your behaviour. Shame kicks in. Further self-esteem eroding thoughts enter your mind, as it dawns on you that your self-centred behaviour has, for at least a period, diverted you from being truly engaged with friends and family, some of whom you rarely get to see.

As this scenario suggests, cue, routine, reward is the habit sequence. The reward tends to be delivered immediately and so little attention is given to the longer-term implications.

Cues such as the ping of an arriving email, the smell of cigarette smoke or the detection of chocolate-based offerings at social occasions will not go away. Often, we cannot avoid the cue that triggers a bad habit. However, we can change the routine, ie., the way we respond to the cue. This is difficult because the habit has been engraved into our nervous system, thanks to the powerful hits delivered by neurotransmitters such as dopamine (euphoria), serotonin (wellbeing), adrenalin (excitement) and oxytocin (love).

Thus, in the event of being unable to sidestep the cues, we will need to invest considerable willpower to embed substitute routines that are better for us and deliver a positive short-term reward.

Of course, chocolate cake may not be your thing. It might be shoes. It might be abusive men.

People we admire, people who get things done, people who get the results they seek, are not superhuman. They do not have an infinite supply of willpower or a character made of granite. They simply have good habits.

They might have acquired those habits unconsciously from parents and friends. They might have been implanted through schooling, work environment, or even through military service. They might have been consciously acquired through paying attention to what works and what doesn't work in respect of achieving one's goals / living a purposeful life.

Some of us, through our fortunate life journey thus far, have acquired a set of largely empowering habits. Some of us may not have been so fortunate. In either case, the point is that we need to be attentive enough to our own behaviours to see what is and isn't working, and to then take the appropriate action. The problem for most people is that their mental bandwidth is consumed with other thoughts, such as:

- Picking over the remains of an acrimonious argument with a loved one.
- Fantasising about torturing an obstinate work colleague.
- Lamenting about how your life is spent either working, or travelling to and from work.
- Envying your more successful siblings.
- "I can't believe I spent that much last month".

Thus, there is no room to reflect on the quality of your life and what you might do to enhance it. This becomes more acute the more your thoughts become preoccupied with survival and wondering where the next meal is coming from. This is an issue for a significant fraction of the world's population, and not just for those in developing economies.

Meta habits

Meta habits are habits we have acquired that are used to cultivate habits. They are not true habits because they operate in the conscious part of the brain and thus consume willpower.

They might be thought of as habits of mind. They are the discipline you bring to acquiring good habits.

Such habits of mind might include:

- Being crystal clear as to why you want to acquire a new habit. Why do you want to give up chocolate biscuits / Tinder?
- Creating new responses, and rewards, to triggers that have previously resulted in undesirable behaviour, which in turn lead to outcomes in terms of the life you would like to live.
- Making a commitment to consciously embed the new response and rewards, despite the allure of the old habit. Perhaps coupled with minimising the likelihood of the trigger occurring through better environment management.
  - o Eg., No chocolate in the home.
- Aligning your new habits with your goals. Wanting to become a professional bodybuilder is a non-starter, if your diet comprises nutritionally-dead food washed down with significant volumes of alcohol. Believing that you can maintain your consumption habit and achieve your goal will lead to mental disharmony, and over time a decoupling from reality.

This book is strongly in favour of positive habit formation. But you may well be overwhelmed by the number of habits you feel you need to acquire. The Life Stack model will help you to prioritise your habits. Again, career habits are less important, if you still have physical habits to acquire, such as those related to quality sleep. As we will see, both you and your environment have a significant influence over your ability to form good habits. In this respect, we are not born equal.

Energy

Our energy levels are critical to the quality of our life. Low physical energy restricts our ability to explore and engage with the world. Low mental energy in effect reduces our mental bandwidth. Rather than work through our finances, we feel just about capable of booting the tablet for some sofa-based boxset action.

Poor eating habits, for example, lead to lower energy, which leads to reduced mental bandwidth, which leads to further poor habits. Consider whether you have entered this tailspin. Exhaustion and an inability to concentrate are just two of the symptoms.

But our energy levels, physical or mental, are not just a matter for us. They affect those around us, and in turn those around them. Our energy levels ultimately affect the world.

An argument at work creates physical tension. This pent-up tension gives rise to an altercation on the train. It stresses out some of the onlookers. One onlooker in particular is struggling to make ends meet. She takes her raised anxiety, triggered by the altercation, and when she arrives home, she is less than attentive to her young child. If that happens with sufficient regularity, then the sum of all these indirect stresses will lead eventually to another stressed adult with mental baggage entering society.

Whilst this is not exclusively a metropolitan issue, the fact that in cities we are more closely packed together means that our energy levels have a greater chance of impacting the energy levels of others.

It takes great fortitude to remain positive and kind when those around you appear to have no consideration for others. There is a great temptation to develop a similarly hardened shell and just charge through the crowd with disregard for the needs and feelings of others.

There is a link between our physical energy and mental energy. The Roman poet Juvenal stated "Mens sana in corpore sano" – A healthy mind in a healthy body. Whilst it is not fully understood as to what our mind or our consciousness really is, it is likely that their development is in some way related to our energy levels. That is not to say that if you stuff yourself with high carb confectionary you will become Mother Teresa or Mahatma Ghandi.

It could be that whilst a chocolate biscuit binge might give us a temporary physical high, it may result in us mentally being somewhat inwardly focused. So, any energy we may have unconsciously allocated to civility is now directed to concerns over our digestive system.

Our mental energy is typically measured by the extent to which we can solve problems or make good decisions. But there is also an aspect to mental energy in terms of our social behaviour. Looking at this as a scale:

1. Self-centred.
2. Awareness of others.
3. Consideration for others.
4. Prioritising others over oneself.

Thus, those that are community-oriented are operating at a higher consciousness, ie., energy level, than those who see the world as revolving around them.

I believe that the more of our energy we can direct towards others, the greater the quality of our lives. Self-centred individuals often do well in the game of modern life, particularly in respect of career success and material acquisition. But it is a somewhat empty outcome, if you cannot share your success with others, or you are in a constant state of anxiety because of a concern that those you abused/deceived on 'the way up' are actively plotting your downfall.

Thus, energy is an important element in living a purposeful life. From a physical perspective, at the lowest level we are comatose. At the highest level, we are like highly curious spring lambs. Mentally, we can extend from bewilderment through to crystal clear lucidity. Consciously we can be self-centred or society-centred.

I am on slightly unsteady ground here in trying to isolate our physical, mental and consciousness dimensions. Science hasn't quite bottomed this out yet. But I think it is fair to say that, regardless of how independent or interdependent these aspects of us are, operating at a higher energy level is preferable to the alternative when it comes to leading a purposeful life.

Thus, we need to pay attention to our energy management. Inattention to our energy will impact our physiology, psychology, emotions, relationships, finance, career, lifestyle and our spirituality.

In this respect, we can see attention as a form of energy. This is very significant. I am sure that someday an Einstein equivalent will develop an equation to show the relationship between energy and attention $(E=Ac^2)$.

Values

Values can be thought of as a filter that shapes our decision making. In other words, our values instantly rule out certain behaviours and thus reduce our cognitive load, eg., under no circumstances must you kill your neighbour's wife. Similarly, values ensure that there is only one action we can take in each circumstance, eg., help rather than avoid a distressed stranger.

The terms morals and ethics also come to mind. Values can be considered as your personal rule book. Morals can be considered the societal rule book. Values can be considered as coming from within, whereas morals are taught.

Ethics tend to be more a professional code of practice, or a rule book laid down by a professional body. For example, doctors will be ethically bound to treat people of all ages equally in the event of a major disaster, rather than focusing on those that are most economically valuable to the society concerned.

Values, morals and ethics, once internalised, become a set of habits. Thus, they facilitate decision making. What is a quandary for others, is less so for those who have values, morals and professional ethics frameworks in place.

Again, the beauty of organised religion is that these are 'ready to wear' frameworks. There is no need to spend a life discovering what is right and wrong, if it is inculcated into you at the outset of your personal / professional life, and / or by the community within which you live.

Such resolved quandaries include:

- I don't eat animals, so I won't opt for the half pounder cheeseburger with shiny bun.
- Despite the provocation of my sister, I will not kill her.
- I haven't met my sales targets for the month, but I will still tell these prospective buyers, that this property is lying squarely on the proposed route for the next intercontinental high speed rail link.

Purpose

Many aspects of our life are driven by purpose. We are seeking an outcome in respect of the activity we are undertaking. Shopping, visiting the cinema or finding a cure for malaria all have a degree of purpose. Though without a shopping list that you rigorously adhere to, your purpose may well become blurred. Similarly, you might change your mind as to which film you will watch when you get to the cinema.

The decision to go shopping may well be made in the spur of the moment. Similarly, your urge to watch a film may have been triggered by a chat with some colleagues at work. However, the decision to eliminate malaria will typically have required a traumatic trigger, eg., witnessing its impact. This will lead to some introspection, coupled with some planning around how you will approach this, along with how you will adjust your life to accommodate your goal.

I personally like to be amongst people who have a sense of purpose. They seem to have high energy levels and are typically very positive. Their enthusiasm and intention infect me like a 'benign virus'.

Through my work over the years, I have engaged with many sales people, primarily in the technology sector. Their goal isn't to save the planet, but to hit their sales targets for the quarter. If they don't, then they are out on the street, if they do, they can look forward to financial abundance.

In my personal pursuits, I engage with athletes. Over the years, I have met some who are looking to improve on their 5K time, whilst others are looking to win gold at the Olympics.

I often reflect, as a 'past the sell by date' sprinter, as to why I get such satisfaction from trying to run fast, despite knowing:

- I am past my peak.
- My peak was okay, but not exceptional.
- There are other species much better adapted to speed than I am.

My point is that having a sense of purpose gives our life meaning, even if on the grand scheme of things, the purpose is pointless. Such purpose drives the sales person to make one more call, and the athlete to head off to the track on cold, wet and miserable evenings. They have a vision of their future selves and are willing to invest in it today.

Purpose is thus important, if only to provide us with a personal growth path. It needs to be woven into our day to day activities. We need to regularly remind ourselves as to why we are doing what we are doing. It may transpire that the work you are doing at this very moment is less than aligned with your purpose. At least being aware of this will enable you to consider more purposeful options, even if you are trapped by your current economic circumstances.

Imagine you are a Nordic skier in a long-distance race. It's a real grind. You grit your teeth, and with your head down you drive forward, despite every muscle in your body telling you to stop. After an hour, you look up to discover you are lost. You become highly anxious, plus you realise that at least some of your limited energy has been expended wastefully.

Compare this to the skier who looks up every ten metres or so to ensure she is on the right path. You both have a purpose in that you both want to win the race. But you have focused on the process, and whilst you might not have mentally lost sight of the goal, you certainly have physically.

I don't want to send out the wrong message here. Scientific experiments have shown that those who visualise their goals are less successful than those that visualise the process of achieving their goals.

In any case, in our daily life, we need to keep one eye on the task at hand (laser / focus) and one eye on our purpose (soft / attention).

Those of us that develop a sense of purpose will have a more fulfilling life. No matter how pointless the goal, if it doesn't negatively impact ourselves or others, it will lift us to perform at a higher level.

Better still if your purpose positively impacts others, whether that be your family, humanity, or the planet. Pursuing such a goal, and its associated sub goals will, I believe, lead to a life lived on the highest plane. No longer are you just on the planet to eat, mate and die. Leaving the planet / humanity in a better state than when you arrived is both noble and inspirational.

But beware. We have never been exposed to more choice in respect of purpose. Life itself has become an infinitely-stocked app store of purpose options.

When I look at the social profiles of friends and business acquaintances, I am both inspired and overwhelmed by the good causes they are committing to. It is not dissimilar to walking down the street and being accosted by a continuous torrent of charity representatives. All worthy, but where do you allocate your limited charity budget? Your purpose will guide you as to where you devote your limited resources.

After a typical day in the digital economy, you lie in bed mulling over the thoughts that passed through your head during the day. You reflect, wouldn't it be great if:

- You had a six pack like the model on that health magazine cover.
- You built a property empire like that entrepreneur on TV.
- You wrote a series of books on a theme similar to 'Game of Thrones'.

- You were the 'best' parent in your child's nursery class.
- (Having watched 'Air Force One'), you became US President.
- You went on a two-week detox juice diet.
- (Having watched the gymnastics on TV), you became an Olympian.

Some of these were just fleeting thoughts. All of them require lifestyle changes of varying degrees. You will wake up having forgotten most of them, until the various attention economy triggers bring them back into focus.

Such triggers do create Olympians, and bodies of steel. The trouble is that today:

- We get an overwhelming number of triggers.
- We are prone to forget the level of investment required.

We live in a world now where fame can be almost instant. And where fame itself is the goal. Some despair at the lack of substance underpinning the celebrity status of some people. But those 'famous for being famous' people know that in the attention economy, it is less about your unique capability, and all about your ability to hold the attention of the masses. And, ironically, they know that such seemingly vacuous fame can be applied for the greater good of mankind, if they use their attention garnering skills to draw attention to, say, injustice.

Finding our true purpose, even if only for the next few months, is quite a challenge, given the number of options available to us. Choice anxiety is not confined to the supermarket aisles. Finding our life purpose is even more challenging. Many of us are oblivious to the need to find a purpose, until some seismic life event sets us on our path, eg., the death of a loved one.

Some of us spend most of our lives trying to establish what our purpose is. Establishing our purpose lies at the heart of living a truly meaningful life. To achieve this requires diligent attention in respect of what is happening around us, and how it makes us feel. The chances of making such a discovery, when soaked in alcohol and / or glued to stimulating content is low.

Equally so when we are engaged in seemingly more constructive activities, such as preparing for an exam or a sporting event, where our laser focus on the task at hand blinds us to the broader realities of our environment.

Some genetic biologists will argue that our only purpose is to maximise the likelihood that our genes will survive beyond the current generation. And that attempting to win an Olympic gold is merely an indirect way of increasing your chances of making that happen. The medal in effect being a symbol of your biological attractiveness, which in turn provides you with more procreation options. I would tend to agree. But clearly, some people have a sense of purpose that goes beyond their personal genetic agenda. Endeavouring to cure cancer or eliminate malaria come to mind. But even these may be driven, deep down, by self-interest. No harm in that, particularly if society /mankind is in credit because of your fleeting existence.

Goals

Please note that I have used the terms purpose and goal interchangeably. They are very similar. Strictly speaking goals come to an end. I win the gold and now I am on to the next thing, which may be to find a high paying job in the media. Purpose is more about who we are and how we live our lives.

If your purpose is to be successful in everything you apply yourself to, then your goals are strongly aligned with your purpose. One might say that goals are the stepping stones to a life of purpose.

Goals are very useful because they act as a decision-making filter. Once you have decided to become an Olympic track athlete, suddenly life's little dilemmas evaporate:

- Should I go training, considering how bad the weather is?
- Should I meet up with old school friends for a drug-fuelled all-nighter?

Should a colleague at work, ask you to attend a charity fun run at the weekend, you can say no because it will interfere with the Olympic heats taking place on the same weekend.

Goals exploit the Reticular Activation System (RAS) of our brain, which is designed to filter out data that is not relevant to our survival, or just uninteresting. Hearing our name mentioned in another part of the room at a lively party would be an example of the RAS in action.

Once we have internalised our goals, the RAS will flag to us when something relevant to our goal is detected in the incoming torrent of data we continuously receive through our senses. If you are looking to lose weight, you will notice magazine covers that are covering weight loss. If you are planning to buy a specific car model, you will start to notice the car you have in mind more often when you are driving. So, whilst goals help us to reduce our decision-making quandaries by filtering out dilemmas, they also help us by filtering in environmental information that will propel us towards our goals.

The beauty of goals is that they provide us with clarity. Albeit until they have been achieved. The challenge of setting goals is that they can interfere with life's small pleasures. Losing weight is not compatible with a chocolate doughnut binge.

And if your reason for losing weight is not because the doctor told you that you will be dead in two months, if you do not act, but because you have a vague intermittent dream of having a 'Hollywood body', then you are going to fall at the first hurdle. Goals need to be underpinned by a burning desire. A desire that overrides your primal mis-programmed urge to eliminate those doughnuts. Goals that are aligned with your definition of what it is to live a purposeful life are a powerful toolset in your life armoury.

Goals are at the useful-end of self-belief. "I intend to achieve this". At the other end are the almost imperceptible messages that we continuously relay to ourselves. Such chattering self-talk has the same impact as our goals in terms of how our reality is filtered. Tell yourself often enough that your boss has it in for you, or that you are not good enough, and the evidence will show up. In effect your thoughts drive your reality.

With this in mind, we should be very careful about what we wish for. Or even think about.

A word of caution

The danger of being too goal-driven is that we miss out on what life has to offer, in particular, what life has to offer in respect of alternative and even more rewarding paths.

Let us imagine you are determined to win an Olympic gold medal in your favourite track event, the four hundred metres. You are an excellent runner, but not a prodigy. A track coach one day notices that you have excellent hip mobility and suggests you try the four hundred metres hurdles. You ignore the suggestion as you are focused on your goal. But the reality is that you have a better chance of winning gold in the hurdles. If your goal is to acquire an Olympic gold, then it would make sense to swap events. But often people feel too invested in their current goal, to reset the target. Even though a reset will increase the chance of success.

This is at the extreme end of goal setting. Nonetheless many of us set goals and ignore the cold winds of reality. Business leaders press on with their strategic intentions, despite market disruption. Medical students continue with their desire to be a heart surgeon, even though robotics and 3D printing will turn the role into something akin to a car tyre fitter.

A more radical approach is to have no goals. You start each day with a keen sensitivity to what feels like the right thing to do, based on the opportunities and obstacles you are facing. Your decision at each point could be based on a hedonistic 'follow the pleasure' rule. It could equally be based on what moves you, no matter how insignificantly, towards being a better violinist, business leader, or simply a better person.

In East Asian philosophy, this approach is often referred to as Dao or Tao, meaning 'the way'. In essence, the approach is to avoid fighting reality as you move through life.

You are seeking, as much as is possible, to harmonise with the obstacles and opportunities that occur along your path. This doesn't mean that you must be a passive victim. It means that once you harmonise, you have a better chance of influencing the outcome. Dancing is Daoism in action. Arm wrestling isn't.

Should you find that your path is continuously blocked by insurmountable obstacles, it might suggest that you are on the wrong path. That is not to say you should thus abandon your goal, though that should be considered. It might suggest that you are not going about your goal in the most optimised way.

My aim here is not to knock goal-setting, but to develop a more flexible approach to how you achieve them. And to be open to the reality that the goal you are currently seeking might be causing you to deviate from reality, in respect of how you and the world have changed since you set the goal.

Positivity

Positivity might be considered an outlook on life where everything is possible, obstacles are simply learning opportunities, and in any case, it will all turn out for the best.

Mass genocide, cruelty to children and the Ebola virus might suggest that positivity is a naïve perspective to take on life. Positivity will not halt an incoming tsunami. But a positive mindset may well provide the conditions for you to act in a manner that will increase your chances of survival, or of finding a lost loved one.

Negativity narrows your life options. It is a self-constructed form of helplessness, and thus a means of shirking responsibility / avoiding action. "People like me never get jobs like that, so why should I apply?" Negative people are, in the extreme, 'killers of buzz'. More often it is their resigned sighs, and utterances of 'hey ho', that have a deflating effect on those around them. After an unexpectedly large clang, 'hey ho' is not something the astronauts want to hear from the head of ground control, as they spiral into the abyss.

Positivity is not just about seeing all people as being good. It is about seeing the specks of goodness in people, whilst paying attention to how their less benign characteristics might make them a 'carrier' in respect of disharmony cultivation. The mugger in front of you may well be focused on acquiring your wallet to pay for their next fix, but they might just have the humanity to let you keep the pictures of your loved ones. The associated short dialogue might highlight that the mugger is in fact high and unsteady on their feet. Your solution-oriented mindset may be to throw her ten dollars and just trot off for fifty yards or so.

Martin Seligman in his well-researched book, Learned Optimism, has found that both optimism and pessimism can be acquired in childhood through those whose opinions we value, for example parents and teachers. Thus, we need to be positive, if only to avoid turning the next generation into pessimists. Pessimism being closely linked to depression. The good news is that optimism can be learned. If this is an issue for you, I encourage you to explore Seligman's book.

As with goals, positivity programmes your RAS. You will consequently receive information from your environment, and yourself, which will reinforce your positive world view. This will be empowering and will act as grist to the mill in respect of the quality of your life.

Kindness

Today, it is possible to get by without wasting energy on being kind to others. Some societies have become so 'evolved' that there is now no longer a need for kindness. You can simply act in your own self-interests, within the law, and do what you need to do to in respect of swapping your value for money, without diverting any of your limited cognitive capacity to acts of benevolence.

This was not always so. Back in times when survival was at the top of most people's agenda, circa 100 years ago for developed economies, a lack of kindness would ensure social isolation. Once 'decoupled from the herd', your chances of survival dropped drastically.

Sitting outside of society meant you had to focus your day on foraging for food and being continuously on guard in respect of threats. You now had to rely on the benevolence of others. Kindness, back then, was an important social skill.

I am pleased to say that kindness is making a comeback. Possibly we have new technology to thank for that. Social media / networking sites are encouraging us to share and help others. No longer is it simply value for value. People and organisations are increasingly giving away value for free. In part, this is a marketing move to enhance their branding and marketing reach, in part it simply feels good.

Kindness also provides a form of sensory filtering. You are more likely to spot, for example, a person struggling to get their large suitcases / pushchair down a flight of stairs. Or you might pick up a piece of litter and put it in the bin, or even wash the dishes after a meal your friend just cooked for you.

People remember acts of kindness. However, some might take the view that kindness is a useful tool for triggering the reciprocation impulse in others. For example, I send you a link to a website that focuses on a topic of interest to you, because my underlying goal might be to make you feel inclined to buy my books in large volumes. This would be more of an investment act on my part than an act of kindness.

The best forms of kindness, in my experience, are those where the recipient is unaware that you are the source of the act. Anonymously sponsoring someone's education in a developing country is an example. Or making anonymous donations on the sponsorship pages of strangers raising funds for good causes is another.

You can enjoy the glow of anonymously being kind to people you do not get on with. This is not easy, but it can have the impact of diffusing the disharmony that exists in your head, which may well diffuse the tension between you both.

Choosing not to respond aggressively to challenging behaviour is a form of kindness, in that by not escalating the situation, you are saving the other party from an eventual beating (from your exhibitionist mixed martial arts pal who has just returned from the wash room).

Or from an assault charge (as your so-called MMA 'pal' spotted what was brewing, and left by the nearest exit).

'Paying it forward' is a great concept in respect of kindness. A good deed done to you, is repaid by you doing a good deed to someone else.

Kindness was once the glue of society. Today, at least, it is starting to become a cool thing to do.

Confidence and courage

"Faint heart never won fair lady" and "Who dares wins" strongly allude to the virtues of courage. We have all experienced uncertainty, when the stakes are high.

- Should I hand over my wallet or take on the mugger?
- Should I apply for the promotion?
- Should I join the conversation or die a slow, painful and lonely death at this networking event?

We perceive the consequences of failure to be significant, and so deliberate over taking action. Traditional Hollywood action films rarely showed the hero prevaricating, or even losing control of their bowels. Courage and confidence were one and the same thing.

Of course, they are not. I might be able to take the knife away from my attacker and hand it back to her. She may well reinitiate another attack. We repeat the process until she gets bored, and then we both head off for a coffee. There was no courage involved on my part. I simply knew how to handle the situation. In fact, my mind might have been more drawn to the special clothing offer advertised in the shop across from where this scene was playing out.

My fantasy aside, confidence is important. It generally requires competence. This implies that we may be confident in one aspect of our life, but not in another.

Confidence obviates the need for introspection. You observe the situation. You decide on your course of action. And then you act. You are not reckless; your cold computational decision-making weighed up the benefits against the risks.

1. I notice a future mate.
2. I approach the person.
3. "Hi, my name is Clark Kent…"

Of course, what I have also described is the internal processing of a psychopath. Observe. Decide. Act. In that sense, they make great role models.

Self-doubt feedback loops lead to inaction and missed opportunity. But the corollary is that if a big challenge, with significant consequences, does not at the very least generate 'stomach butterflies', you might well consider a neural check-up.

Think of the path to a meaningful life as one superimposed on a complex map where there are many options to go off track, but also many options, to get back on track. In fact, there are many meaningful paths you could take. But at each junction, you must decide which route you take. Many of us opt for the easy path, or the most appealing path. Each path requires a decision. Your confidence and courage will determine the path you take. Your attention will determine whether you realise there is a decision to be made, and options are open to you.

The problem with courage is that it draws heavily on your willpower reserves. Triple-chocolate muffin or the difficult conversation with your boss? Confidence requires little cognitive burden. I can do this. Done. The more we can work on our confidence the less we must call on our courage. Initially, this does require courage, but it can be considered a life investment, rather than just inattentive frittering away of your limited willpower reserves.

We approach hundreds of these junctions every day. Without a sense of purpose and confidence, underpinned by some well-established habits, we are likely to dissipate our willpower reserves and thus veer off track as the day goes on.

In summary

We now have a sense of the variables that will determine the quality of our life. We can see there is some interrelationship between these variables. Attention today benefits your life today. Attending to sound habit formation today, will benefit your life tomorrow too.

How we score on each of these variables will give us strong insights into our personality. How we present ourselves to the world is an indication of the maturity of the quality of our life. Purposeless, miserable and low energy is neither an attractive combination for you as an individual, or those who are exposed to your presence.

A lack of confidence, or even courage, can, sometimes, be traced back to a lack of attention in an earlier part of your life. Your conservative approach to life might have led to little use of the 'explore, fail, learn, succeed' cycle, which is a critical loop in developing competence, confidence, and even courage.

But not all cases can be attributed to inattention. Adults who have suffered abusive upbringings might point out that their constant state of fear, and an inevitable high-level of parental dependence at the time, gave them little spare mental capacity to consider their options. Survival being their priority.

Even as adults we may have developed a lifestyle that in effect protects us from exposure to 'testing' events. We become expert in our work, we avoid anything that exposes our physical weaknesses. We perhaps also choose to socialise with those who will not challenge us intellectually. Pad this out with attention-consuming diversions, and you have a life that feels pretty good. Until of course, the day your industry becomes a 99-cent app, or your diminutive partner decides to enrol on a special forces hand to hand combat programme.

Self-mastery means that we are making the best use of our limited mental bandwidth, and time on the planet, to live our lives by design, rather than having it consumed by worry and the agendas of others. We all worry to some degree.

Those of us who choose to act, rather than simply ruminate, are the ones who are moving forward on the path to mastery.

We will look at a framework for addressing this later in the book. But first I would like you to meet your mind.

5   Meet Your Mind

Overview

In this chapter I present an overview of how our mind works, so that we understand to what extent we can tune it for an optimised life.

The model presented is not a physical representation of the brain. It is a schematic, which identifies the important functions of the brain, as far as attention is concerned.

It is worth highlighting that whilst neuroscience is making great advances in respect of our understanding of the brain, there is still a lot we do not understand. This model brings together what we do know in respect of the functionality relevant to attention.

Literature on the mind broadly focuses on its conscious and unconscious aspects. However, you will see references to the subconscious mind. It has various definitions based on which psychoanalyst is using the term. It has also found its way into New Age thinking. For the purposes of this book, I have bundled subconscious into unconscious.

Let's look at the main elements in turn:

Triggers

Triggers can be thought of as stimuli that have the potential to elicit a response. Sometimes the response will save our life. Sometimes it will simply distract us. The voice of the school bully is an intense trigger. The slight fluctuations in the air conditioning, less so.

Whilst environmental triggers play a role in determining what we think about, so do we. We can actively choose to dwell on an argument we had some time ago. Or it may float uninvited into our head. Sometimes this mental noise can impair our connection with our environment. Under these conditions, we are said to be 'in a world of our own', or even, 'away with the fairies'.

Environment

The environment we operate in, as mentioned, has influence over our thoughts. Noisy neighbours are an example. A family home stocked with demanding children, or the factory workplace are further examples.

The weather, the lighting, the view, and a fellow passenger's ringtone can all impact our attention.

Our ability to choose or shape the environment in which we live has a significant bearing on the quality of our lives.

Consciousness

Our consciousness is that part of our mind that gives us awareness. Decisions get made here. Interruptions are processed here. Urges are approved / suppressed here.

In our consciousness, we develop a sense of self and our relationship to the wider world. It is in this conceptual region of our brain where we conduct such activities as:

- Being aware.
- Paying attention.
- Focusing.
- Noticing.

These terms are used interchangeably by most people. If you are trying to get an introverted psychologist, cognitive scientist, neuroscientist or educationalist to chat at a social event, you may want to suggest they explain the difference in these terms. In fact, you could go off to another party and return later to find they are still in full flow.

I believe attention is the most critical conscious activity for living a purposeful life. Hence this book!

Willpower comes into play in respect of our consciousness. Though, as we will see later, self-discipline doesn't.

We will look at the unconscious shortly. But, to make a comparison in terms of our processing capacity, one might say that the conscious mind is equivalent to dial-up networking, whilst the unconscious is equivalent to broadband.

In respect of our conscious mind, we are constrained by our awareness of ourselves and our environment at any given point in time along with the experiences, knowledge and skills that we have acquired and can recall.

There are several important elements to our consciousness. Let's take a look:

Short-term memory

Our conscious minds have the capacity to retain a very limited amount of data for the purposes of making decisions. The 'location' for this data retention is referred to as short-term memory. Whilst it is an essential element of our decision-making process, it is a bottleneck in terms of what we can attend to at any given time.

The common belief is that we can retain seven plus or minus two elements in our short-term memory at any given time. Like many 'facts' related to the study of the mind, that may not be definitive. Though most people would find that trying to retain a random combination of circa seven numbers and letters in their heads, whilst trying to read a map to be mentally very challenging.

Short-term memory is quite a constraint in terms of our capacity to think.

Long-term memory

Long-term memory is, as the name suggests, where our memories are stored indefinitely. In computer terms, our long-term memory is persistent, ie., the data is stored in such a way that it can be retrieved in the future. Whereas, short-term memory storage is temporary in nature, with the data being retained for a just a period of seconds.

All our conscious experiences are captured in long-term memory. These can include:

- Things we have learnt.
    o A person's name.
    o How to solve simultaneous equations.
    o What things mean.
- Experiences we have had.
    o Our sixth birthday.
    o The first time an adult shouted at us.
- Skills.
    o Tying shoelaces.
    o Dancing.
    o Tying shoelaces, whilst dancing.

These can all be brought to bear when engaging with the world at any given moment. Whilst our long-term memory holds everything we have ever consciously experienced, it is not a given that we will be able to instantly recall, eg., the lead actor's name in a film we recently watched, even though we know we should know it. This is why successful students look at their course work more than once. Each revisit deepens the learning and entangles it, so to speak, with other memories, thus providing other access points in respect of memory recall. It thus might be argued that long-term memory is not totally conscious memory, particularly the things we cannot recall when we need them.

Also, long-term memory fades over time. This is part of the aging process. Some memories, through lack of usage, will naturally fade. Neurodegenerative diseases can also cause long-term memory loss.

Long-term memory is of great interest to learning specialists. Calling on all the senses when learning, including our emotions, appears to increase the effectiveness of our recall.

Whilst we don't fully understand sleep, it is becoming clear that sleep has a major role to play in respect of our long-term memory. Imagine that each thing you have experienced, or learnt, or recalled during a day is documented in their own notebook. And you have been so busy that you have left the books lying all over the library. Well when you go to sleep, the nightshift librarian gathers all these books and puts / returns them to their rightful places in the library. So, sleep has a role to play in both encoding our memories and filing them.

Working memory

This is where our thoughts are processed. And this is where we decide our next course of action. Thus, this is the part of us where we build our lives. As life coach Anthony Robbins points out, our destiny is defined through our decisions.

Given its significance, we will explore working memory in more detail in the following chapter.

For now, working memory can be thought of as our mental bandwidth. In the same way that a computer network, by virtue of its bandwidth, is limited in the amount of data that can pass through it at any given time, so too is our capacity to think limited by our mental bandwidth. As such, it is a very important concept in respect of optimising our mind to pay attention to what matters.

To the best of our knowledge, everyone has the same working memory capacity. However, some of us are less able than others when it comes to how we manage our working memory. The net effect being that some people would appear to have inferior working memory.

Our working memory is continuously receiving inputs from our environment and ourselves. At any given time, our working memory could be devoted to processing:

- A random thought.
- Something that triggered some degree of discomfort. Cramp or a fire alarm are examples.
- Something lingering that is troubling us. For example, an earlier dispute with a colleague.
- Our game plan in respect of getting our credit cards under control.

Our thoughts are thus not always under our control. The extent to which we can get them under our control, or at least manage carefully those that are (seemingly) imposed on us, is a measure of the degree to which we are have the potential to live a purposeful life.

But keep in mind that even if we have managed to free up our mind, we still need to choose whether to work through another boxset or get up off the sofa and change the world.

There is growing cadre in the scientific community who believe that reality only exists because of our consciousness. The decisions we make have a bearing on how our particular 'reality' unfolds. Without going into detail, (primarily because I can't), their perspectives are derived from the principles of quantum mechanics. So, in theory at least, your decisions shape your reality. If that is true, then, again, we had better take great care in respect of the decisions we make.

Unconscious

Our unconscious mind plays a very significant role in our lives, though we don't fully understand how it works. Think of the unconscious mind as the autopilot in our lives. Our unconscious mind does not suffer the constraints of the conscious mind. It records everything. Smart people make good use of their unconscious.

Later we will introduce the concept of the Mental Worktop. At this point, it is worth noting that, used smartly, our unconscious has the power to clear space on our Mental Worktop, which increases the likelihood that we can devote our limited attention to where it is most needed.

Again, our unconscious records everything that we have ever been exposed to. It contains a repository of all the data that has come in through our senses. It has also structured that data so that our associated feelings and experiences are also captured.

Some of these experiences will have been captured before our conscious mind had fully developed, as infants, thus giving rise to neuroses or complexes. Such experiences can go on to negatively impact our lives, unless we receive professional help. Given they were captured outside of our conscious mind, whilst we may be consciously aware of the symptoms, we may not be aware of the cause. Or even consider that there might be a cause.

Our unconscious mind will, from time to time, bring something to our attention. This may happen in the form of an idle thought, a gut feeling, a cold sweat or through a dream. It may prove costly if we are not alert to our unconscious mind's endeavours to communicate with us.

Again, early traumatic experiences may well cause these communications to be inappropriate, for example, your inner voice reminding you that you are unworthy, incapable, or just plain bad.

It could be argued that our conscious and unconscious minds are not two separate elements of our mind, but are both part of one spectrum. Our consciousness being that part of our unconsciousness where the signals generated by our mind are sufficiently strong to be picked up by our attention.

Improving our attention, may, at least in theory, give us greater access to the deep recesses / insights stored in our unconsciousness. Think personal 'big data'. If that makes no sense, ask any IT professional for clarification.

It is within our unconscious that our so-called reptile brain operates. It is a pure instinct device. No reflection, no contemplation. It receives a stimulus and it simply responds. Our reptile brain triggers our primal emotions. Fight it, run from it, eat it, or mate with it.

Back in the day, any time spent contemplating our next move, might have had fatal consequences. Our reptile brain took care of emptying our digestive tract and getting our legs in motion, as the threat moved in for the kill.

As we became social animals, we evolved our responses to ensure we were not drummed out of the pack. Thus, we have learnt to consider our response, and the social implications, before acting. This can be very challenging. Unfortunately, the predators / threats have become more nuanced too. Lecherous bosses come to mind.

The reptile brain also handles activities such as heart beat and breathing. We would have little capacity for thought if we had to consciously breathe in and out.

Habits are also part of our unconscious armoury. Like instincts, we don't give them any thought, we just unconsciously invoke the habit associated with a given stimulus. Habits do not necessitate thinking. This is good because they get things done without causing any cognitive burden. I should say that it is 'good', if the habits we have embraced are constructive.

Our unconscious is quite naïve. It doesn't seem to recognise the difference between the truth and fiction. That is why hypnotism, autosuggestion and subliminal programming work. The unconscious does not evaluate what it receives. It just takes it to be true. This is one of the main reasons that we should be very careful about what we think, say, or even hear.

Negative thoughts, or simply thoughts we have based on flawed logic, eventually become true as far as we are concerned. Thinking that the world is fundamentally a bad place, will eventually colour every aspect of your world view and the quality of your engagement with the world.

By the same token, thinking that you are a confident, wealthy and an attractive individual will have the same effect. I believe the psychoanalysts refer to this phenomenon as 'fake it till you make it'. New Age adherents similarly refer to the Cosmic Ordering Service.

As I have mentioned earlier, our conscious decision making shapes our reality. There might possibly be the unconscious equivalent. This raises some interesting philosophical issues in respect of how our minds interact with the world.

Possibly there is some energy transfer taking place? Nobody knows. But the most practical point is to recognise that what we allow into our minds, consciously or unconsciously, along with the associated decisions we make, has a profound impact on the quality of our lives.

We also know that our unconscious is a great problem solver. If you have an issue that has been niggling you all day, just pop it in the 'unconscious hopper' before you go to sleep, and there is a good chance the solution will be apparent in the morning.

Given the distractions that we face in the digital age, it is now becoming fashionable to explore ways of quietening our conscious minds. Meditation being an example. The beauty of quietening our conscious mind is that we are more likely to hear what our unconscious mind is trying to tell us.

Our unconscious mind is thus a powerful resource that can be harnessed to:

- Automate the more procedural aspects of our lives.
- Give us insights that are based on a very large repository of sensory data.
- 'Watch our backs', through our instinctual defence mechanism.

The following diagram brings all the elements together:

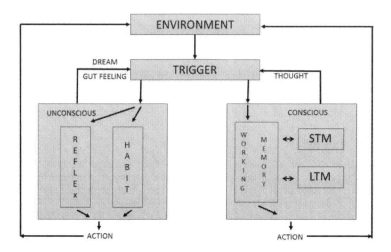

Figure 3 - The interrelationship between the environment, triggers, the conscious and unconscious.

STM = Short-term memory. LTM = Long-term memory.

Note how our unconscious mind can stimulate our conscious mind into action. Perhaps our unconscious has thrown up the answer to a problem we have been wrestling with. Perhaps it has flagged a suspicious person staring at us from across the road. Our unconscious mind may also cause us to reflexively swat a fly that has temporarily parked on our nose. No need to burden our conscious mind.

Notice how our conscious mind can have thoughts that lead to a change of activity for our working memory. If this happens too often we never advance anything far enough to act. Perhaps this reflects how an easily-distracted and undisciplined mind causes us to never succeed in life, because we never get around to acting on our goals (presuming we had some in the first place). But in fairness, it could be a random thought that gives rise to a brilliant idea that in turn leads to a high impact outcome.

Note how the actions that result from both our conscious and unconscious minds may well cause an interaction with the environment, which in turn may respond and trigger further interaction.

We may have inherited our reflexes. But no doubt, good health will help them to work more effectively. Our parents will have played a part in our habit formation, for better or worse. In any case, habits are the best way to free up our mind to deal with more rewarding matters. Best of all, habits are something that we can self-engineer.

Summary

Our mind is a fascinating place. We can either have it work for us or let it dictate our life. It is not fully clear where our mind resides. Could a surgeon dissect a brain and present her students with two handfuls of brain tissue, one being the conscious, and one being the unconscious? Based on our knowledge to date, it could be that our brain is one big supercomputer and our thoughts, memories and sensory data stores are distributed around our brain.

Some philosophers and scientists believe that there is a collective consciousness, of which our mind is a part. Possibly all our minds are simply part of one 'super mind'? This might explain phenomena such as telepathy and extra sensory perception (ESP). It is not clear whether the scientific community's inability to prove that such phenomena exist, is evidence that they do not exist, or that the experiments are flawed.

But again, it is fairly safe to say that the mind is fascinating. Many of us are not truly aware that we walk around with this supercomputer in our head. Perhaps we should treat it like a high-performance sports car? Even though we are not yet Formula One drivers, we know we should be careful with what we put in the car, and we should ensure it is well maintained. As we become familiar with our supercar, we can start to move up the gears and see what it's capable of.

If we treat our mind like a high-performance car, who knows where it could take us? The aim of this book is to give you a chance to find out.

We will expand on this car analogy in a subsequent chapter.

In respect of the mind, this chapter has provided a schematic description. In the next chapter, we will explore working memory and discover, amongst other things, the role our emotions play in determining the quality of our life.

6   Your Mental Worktop

Overview

In this chapter, we dig deeper into working memory. This can be considered the most important part of our mind in terms of its impact on our life, as this is where thoughts emerge and decisions get made.

This expanded section of the model introduced in the previous chapter will demonstrate how our thoughts are directly correlated to our quality of life.

Working memory

Working memory can be thought of as:

- Mental bandwidth.
- Cognitive capacity.
- A mental worktop.

These terms allude to the fact that our working memory is of limited capacity. Consequently, we are constrained by the number of things we can consciously attend to at any given time.

Cognitive capacity is the most scientific expression of the three. It is analogous to the number of balls a juggler can handle at any given time. Increased cognitive capacity enables us to take into consideration more pieces of information. This is useful when it comes to decision making.

Mental bandwidth is growing in popularity as a term. You might hear business people saying that they cannot take on any more projects because they do not 'have the bandwidth'.

It is analogous to the size of the pipe through which we can direct our thoughts. A bigger pipe (think cross section rather than length) enables greater thought capacity. A bigger pipe clogged up with unhelpful thoughts, is equivalent to a smaller pipe in respect of handling more constructive thoughts, ie., thoughts that will lead to better decision making.

The Mental Worktop is a conceptual model I have created to help you think of your mind as a desk, which can easily become cluttered if you do not manage it carefully. Clarity of thought is correlated to worktop availability. A cluttered worktop simply leaves little room to do good work. Plus, it is a source of easily-accessible distraction.

We all broadly have the same memory allocation. Some of us are better than others at recalling long-term memories. Often, this is because of better learning strategies. From here on in, I will use the term Mental Worktop when referring to working memory, and will provide more detail shortly.

Keep in mind, our ability to make working memory work for us is partially under our control. Our circumstances play a significant role, as do our habits, and our willpower.

Before we get into the Mental Worktop model, I want to briefly cover multi-tasking, harmony and feelings, as these have a significant bearing on getting the best from our mind.

The perils of multi-tasking

Given that our Mental Worktop is of finite size, there are only so many things we can concurrently attend to. Drivers using their mobile phone whilst driving are more likely to have accidents. The likelihood of an accident increases considerably if we are driving and speaking whilst simultaneously attempting to peel off the cellophane on the packaging of a recently acquired service-station sandwich.

Another mundane example is that it is difficult to study whilst listening to loud attention-grabbing music, or whilst enduring the screams and shouts of the neighbours, as they take their argument up a few notches.

We are not designed for multitasking. Though some people pride themselves on their, seemingly, multitasking abilities. You may enjoy an evening of watching TV, whilst typing emails, whilst keeping up with your social feeds. The reality is that you are only ever doing one of these at any given time. Though, you are swapping between these tasks at a relatively high rate. Unfortunately, there is a significant overhead in context-switching between the tasks, and consequently:

- The tasks are completed sub-optimally.
  - Perhaps you didn't hear your deceased friend's subtle last cry for help on your last call together? But you did, however, clear a good chunk of your inbox, during the call.
- You expend some of your willpower allocation in simply swapping between these tasks.

But of course, there are some tasks you can do concurrently, eg:

- Brush your teeth and think about your day ahead.
- Breathe and maintain a conversation.

In the case of brushing your teeth, this is a task which you have developed into a habit, and so can execute it without any cognitive burden. No willpower is expended.

In the case of breathing, this activity is autonomous. We do not have to think, "Time to breath in.", "Time to breath out". Our nervous system takes care of this, and so we do not have to expend willpower to maintain our breathing.

Worktops are useful. They provide an environment on which you can focus your energies. But this is only so if the worktop is restricted to items related to the job in hand. The nature of your work might be such that you need to flit between different things, and so having them all on the desk makes it easier.

World class chefs geospatially arrange their tools and ingredients, so that they sit in a configuration that has the task sequence encoded. Items needed now sit closer than items needed later. And items needed tomorrow, next week or yesterday are not to be found on the worktop.

Similarly, personal productivity experts tend to lean towards only having the items they need for the current task on their desk. This way there are less distractions, and so they are more likely to give their full attention to the task at hand.

But mentally life is a little different. Unless we have the solitude and simplified life of a monk, the chances are that we will have more than one thing to think about at any given time. There are times when you will be working, where your mind drifts off to your concerns over a loved one in hospital, or what you will have for dinner this evening.

Harmony

Harmony, for the purposes of this book, is the condition where you are devoid of tension, where you are not distracted by your thoughts, or your environment. This is the perfect condition for activities such as:

- Lining up for the Olympic 100 metre finals.
- Revising for an important exam.
- Reading a bedtime story to a young child.
- Bingeing on video.

At one end of the spectrum, we are performing at the limits of our capability, in the most challenging of situations. Exams and sports finals are representative of this. Some refer to it as being in the zone, or in a state of flow. The book entitled, Finding Flow: The Psychology of Engagement With Everyday Life, by Mihaly Csikszentmihalyi, is the definitive text on the topic of flow.

At the other end of the spectrum, we are 'zoned out' in front of a screen, mindlessly devouring junk food, whilst consuming video content.

The subtle difference is that in the former case you require a state of harmony to perform well, whilst the latter might be considered a self-medicated approach to cultivating harmony (albeit of the lowest quality). That is why it is so appealing when we are mentally frazzled, and are desperate to achieve a more harmonious state.

Not all of us need to perform like a top athlete, though the increasing competition from robots in the workplace will push us in that direction. Regardless, we will need to do tasks that require our full attention, such as diffusing an escalating row, or reading a bedtime story.

Being in a state of harmony means being fully attentive to the task at hand. Disharmony, in whatever form that takes, detracts from the task at hand. As such, it diminishes our capacity to do a task well. This is important when the task is somewhat high-stakes in nature, for example, bomb disposal, or requires a high degree of creativity, for example, most jobs in the near future.

So, one might argue that the state of harmony is one to strive for in life. However, we are not emotionless creatures operating in isolation of the environment we occupy.

Feelings

Disharmony can trigger our emotions. For example, hunger might cause you to be expectant about the meal you are soon to receive at the newly opened Michelin-starred restaurant. Alternatively, hunger might make you sad that your life circumstances have you living on the streets, not knowing where the next meal is coming from.

So, sources of disharmony result in physiological feelings that are better known as emotions. These feelings might compel us to act (eg., fight or flight), or they may be a reward for action we have taken (eg., satisfaction or relief). One might consider our emotions as a mechanism that triggers us into restoring equilibrium, or harmony, in our lives. The absence of action, when our body has in effect called us to action, causes us to remain in a state of disharmony.

Most people use the term 'feelings' interchangeably with emotions. I will be a little more rigorous in terms of definition. We can consider feelings to comprise three levels:

- Instinct.
- Emotion.
- Mood.

Instincts can be considered primal responses that have been woven into our DNA. They are passed from generation to generation because they have proven to serve us well in terms of our survival.

They are not always appropriate in the digital age. For example, if you have witnessed a work colleague at an office social function make a very direct play for the CEO's attractive partner, you will be watching our instincts in action. Being social animals, our brains have evolved to regulate such socially unconstructive behaviour. Unfortunately, alcohol puts the regulator to sleep.

Emotions can be considered as learned responses. As we grow up, we witness how our parents, neighbours and work colleagues respond to certain situations. Like instincts, there is a stimulus – response relationship. However, with instincts, the response is instantaneous, whereas emotions can arise at any point after the stimulus. Winning a football tournament as a child can continue to generate intense emotions when recollected at a later stage in one's life.

Fear is certainly an instinct. But given that we can fear a forthcoming meeting with our boss, it can also be considered an emotion. This may flag a weakness in my definitions. However, my aim is to highlight that:

- Some feelings are intrinsic to our survival.
- They have a bearing on what we think about.
- They have a strong bearing on the quality of our lives.

Not all feelings demand action. Some feelings might signal that harmony has been restored. Joy comes to mind. The feeling of control is another.

Moods might be considered as less intense emotions experienced over a prolonged period, eg., for a morning or a week. They do not demand a response, but they colour our thinking. We have described joy as an emotion. But of course, we can be in a joyful mood. Our mood might have been triggered by something obvious, such as an insult, or perhaps something less obvious, possibly a combination of a poor night's sleep coupled with self-induced dehydration.

If we think of instincts, emotions and moods as a spectrum of feelings, with instincts being the most intense, and moods being the least intense, then we will appreciate that being in a fearful mood in respect of our forthcoming exams is different to the fear that comes when confronted by a salivating bear.

The Mental Worktop

Having dipped into the topics of multi-tasking, harmony and feelings, we can now dive into the Mental Worktop model. The point of this model is to help us understand how we get the best return on our mental capacity. As you will see, there are many ways in which our mental capacity can be consumed, and not all of them constructive in nature.

The Mental Worktop comprises four work zones, as shown in figure 4.

Chatter	Acute disharmony
Chronic disharmony	Discretionary

Figure 4 - The Mental Worktop

Let us now look at each of the four work zones, namely:

- Acute disharmony.
- Chronic disharmony.
- Chatter.
- Discretionary bandwidth.

Acute Disharmony work zone

We are continuously exposed to distractions that can create disharmony within us. This typically impels us to restore harmony. An itchy spot demands that we scratch it. Thirst demands that we quench it. Curiosity demands that we explore it.

The sport and thirst examples are driven by physical disharmony. But much of the disharmony in our lives is instigated within our head, for example, a negative thought about an earlier argument with a loved one.

Often it is triggered by the environment, for example, the ping of an email (curiosity) or somebody approaching with a knife (fear, or anticipation, if it is a waiter replacing your cutlery, prior to you starting what looks to be a tasty meal).

Keep in mind that the environment in which we are located is also a great source of 'emotion cultivation' and thus distraction / disharmony. We still retain the ancestral survival instincts that served us well in the savanna. Thus, we are always on guard, on the lookout for movements / 'weak signals' that might suggest a potential threat. Most of us have learnt to regulate the alert level based on our location. We treat movements in the local library quite differently to movements by our opponent in an unlicensed mixed martial arts cage fight.

Our thoughts are often driven by what is around us. The ping of an incoming email or the growl of an angry bear all have the potential to distract us.

By distract, I mean causes us to shift our soft-focus attentive state, to a more laser-like focus. As we drive to work, roadside hoardings display pictures of an idealised you, or (with) an idealised mate. Your car radio draws your attention to a tragedy on the other side of the world.

You may have initially turned on the radio to listen to the news, but in general, the radio, the hoardings, or the device ping are external stimuli that draw our attention away from more purposeful activity, sometimes imperceptibly. As the day goes on, we become more susceptible to distractions in respect of their ability to cause us to deviate from the task at hand.

Sometimes, it is wise to suppress such environmental distractions. Social media pings, when you are trying to write a book, can destroy your flow. But other times, if for example we are writing a book in a tranquil forest in the Rockies, it would be unwise to wear noise cancelling headphones. Only to see a bear going through its pre-lunch rituals when you look up from your laptop, is going to be something of a shock.

That is why we need to pay attention to our environment, but not necessarily place all our focus on it, particularly where there is a low risk of danger.

For most of us, our environment is a source of distraction. Distraction demands real estate on your Mental Worktop. As we will see, this has the effect of leaving less space for purposeful work. The more we can control our environment the better. But, of course, this is not always possible.

Sources of acute disharmony include:

- Physical – eg., hunger.
- Psychological – eg., being quizzed by an immigration officer.
- Environmental – eg., the roar of a lion in a library.

By acute, I mean that the disharmony was brought about by a specific set of conditions. Harmony can be quickly restored by taking the appropriate action.

You can see that the Acute Disharmony work zone has the potential to occupy a large part of our Mental Worktop. If we are not careful, such disharmony can impact the quality of our decision making, and consequent behaviour.

Our ability to inhibit certain urges is key to being a social animal. However, inhibition places a cognitive burden on our brains. Suppressing emotions thus acts as a drain on our willpower, and so has the potential to eventually impair our decision making. Society itself is thus a source of acute disharmony.

Conversely, acute disharmony can save our life. As nature intended, it can lead to the production of new life. But too much disharmony, acute or otherwise, can impinge on our capacity to make good decisions.

A busy schedule, or an over-ambitious to do list is another source of acute disharmony. Perhaps, you have several meetings to attend today. They may all have very positive themes, and thus will all be good experiences. However, you are concerned that you might forget to attend one of the meetings, or inadvertently let one meeting overrun into the next, and this concern 'takes residence' on your Mental Worktop.

Alarms, when you can trust the technology, or your ability to use the technology, are an effective tool for eliminating such acute disharmony. Powerful people address this by having an entourage of officials, whose job it is to handle such potential disharmony. Thus, the President, despite having many high-impact activities to work through on any given day, can remain 'in the moment' and talk with genuine cordiality to injured war veterans, because he knows that it is someone's job to lead him to the next engagement at the appropriate moment.

Self-induced acute disharmony can have significant ramifications on your life. Sitting there on the train reflecting on the characteristics of your perfect life partner, may well obscure your awareness of an equally well-qualified alternative unsuccessfully trying to catch your eye, sitting opposite you.

The growing trend towards mindfulness is a recognition that we shouldn't spend too much time in our own heads. In other words, mindfulness encourages us to 'get out' more.

We are exposed to acute disharmony in much the same way as the Earth is subjected to meteor bombardment. It's just a fact of life. Thankfully, most meteors burn up in the atmosphere with no geological or anthropological consequences. Thus, we should accept that acute disharmony is a natural part of our life, and so we must not berate ourselves for the feelings associated with our disharmonious experiences. That would simply waste even more cognitive capacity.

Through being attentive to both the environment, and our feelings, we will be better able to detect the occurrences of acute disharmony. We are thus better placed to deal with them in a manner that requires the least cognitive burden. Otherwise acute disharmony will take control of us, and thus our path through life.

To summarise, acute disharmony is essentially triggered by something, a thought or an event, but can be resolved very quickly by taking action.

Chronic Disharmony work zone

Unlike acute disharmony, chronic disharmony cannot be so easily resolved by taking action. Chronic disharmony lingers. It may be resolved temporarily, but it is usually back very soon.

Chronic disharmony colours our lives because it is there or thereabouts when we make decisions. Work might be considered as chronic disharmony. Orders from bosses, clients and team members arrive on a continuously rolling conveyor belt. Whilst each request is a source of acute disharmony, the continuous torrent of requests can be considered chronic disharmony.

There is a seemingly endless supply of people requiring your attention and action. They must be dealt with, otherwise your economic circumstances could radically change.

Similarly, social responsibilities from family, friends and the community are similarly obligations that we would be wise to honour.

Poverty cultivates chronic disharmony because of the inherent insecurity. Chronic stress brought about by long running disputes with a neighbour, or a drawn-out divorce, are also sources of chronic disharmony.

Chronic illness is of course another source of chronic disharmony. Pain management techniques help, but they are mentally demanding.

There will be times when these appear to be very acute, but in general they form a background static that impacts the quality of our thinking. Actively trying to compartmentalise them, eg., "I can't think about the divorce now, because I am about to line up for the 100 metres sprint final" places a cognitive burden on you. The mental energy expended could be used in something more constructive from a personal performance perspective, like responding to the starting pistol.

Low self-esteem is another source of chronic disharmony. It serves as a source of constant negative emotions. It affects how we engage with the world, and in turn determines the quality of our life.

Whilst a glass of water may quench our thirst, or a bullet may resolve a bear issue, chronic disharmony requires a more structural approach. Solutions might involve:

- Attending assertiveness training.
- Getting better quality sleep.
- Learning to forgive.
- Winning the lottery.

Poverty

Dwelling briefly on poverty. Poverty is destructive, because not only might it curtail our lives through poor nutrition and inadequate shelter, but it typically results in being trapped in an unsettling environment.

Concerns over finances all add to increased stress. Thus, more of your Mental Worktop is commandeered by thoughts that are disempowering. And worse still, these thoughts result in less space for purposeful thinking. Limited capacity for purposeful thinking results in poor people not capitalising on decision opportunities, eg., access to free education, or consuming healthy food, that might lead them out of poverty.

Poverty is indeed a trap. Poor people may well be less educated than rich people, but they do not have less mental bandwidth / smaller mental worktops. The rich simply make better use of their bandwidth, because less of it is consumed on survival matters. The book entitled Scarcity is a worthwhile read in this respect.

One would expect the Internet to have a democratising effect on the ability to succeed. If everyone has access to the global encyclopaedia, and the 'how to' videos, surely the poor, what with their burning desire to get out of poverty, will soak this up, and possibly accelerate economically past their more affluent neighbours. Unfortunately, research has shown that the poor typically use this powerful life changing tool to play online games. The cage door is open, but the bird does not have the wherewithal to fly away. Role models, coupled with more proactive education is needed.

As an aside, whilst poverty reduces one's ability to think constructively, wealth and power reduces one's ability to be empathic. This finding has a scientific basis, and is detailed in the book entitled, The Power Paradox, by Professor Dacher Keltner. This is a major issue when wealthy politicians are responsible for social issues. It is an issue for us, if we have never known poverty, and thus see the poor almost as another species, rather than simply an unfortunate (or even potentially future) version of ourselves.

When it comes to world poverty, our economic good fortune has, to some degree, desensitised us to the plight of billions of our fellow humans. If global poverty is not a source of chronic disharmony for those of us with significantly more than $2.50 to live on per day, then, at a global level, we might be considered sociopaths.

Sermon over. The bottom line is that chronic disharmony has much deeper roots than acute disharmony, and thus is much more difficult to resolve. It is thus a pernicious form of distraction that, more often than not, has the power to significantly impact the quality of our lives.

Chatter work zone

Thoughts that arise in this zone appear to come out of nowhere, and often distract us from the job at hand. You may be progressing an important piece of work, and seemingly out of nowhere:

- "What is the difference between a cult and a team?"
- "Am I a good person?"
- "What is so irrational about surds?"
- "Where have I seen that actor before?"
- "What are the benefits of the paleo diet?"

You may or not be able to explain to yourself why these thoughts have arisen, but they have not been triggered by what you are doing, your surroundings, or an emotional urge.

It is likely that your unconscious mind has lobbed this 'distraction hand grenade' into your consciousness. Maybe it is trying to tell you something that is very significant and requires urgent action?

Maybe the 'nocturnal librarian' has misfiled some of your thoughts, because of poor sleep, and thus you are in 'filing mode', which, as we have already mentioned, is causing you to daydream.

So, this background chatter might well have a significance unbeknownst to us. In any case, it has the effect of distracting us from the task at hand.

As we will see below, unregulated chatter can escalate into a full blown emotional response. 'Am I a good person', might, depending on your mood, lead to a full scale internal inquiry. You trawl your memories looking for supporting evidence.

Eventually this idle thought has escalated into an all-consuming neurologically-live and physically debilitating self-loathing fest.

Depending on the nature of the work you should be currently doing, such a foul condition might still be considered a cognitively softer option, and so the self-flagellation continues. Unfortunately, the associated scars will remain.

Do this often enough and you will inadvertently create a habit that will significantly undermine the quality of your life. In this case, you are teaching yourself that unconstructive thoughts are an effective way of sidestepping difficult work.

The natural conclusion is that mental chatter is the enemy of a good life. But ongoing research is telling us that this chatter might represent important messages from our unconscious. Being mindful of the chatter is important.

Being able to assess whether it is primarily conveying a profound revelation, or is simply a mechanism for avoiding the more cognitively demanding task at hand, is a personal judgment call.

Discretionary work zone

Here we can think about whatever we like. You might say it is what remains after the preceding attentional demands (chatter, acute and chronic disharmony thoughts) have taken their share. For some of us, it might turn out that we have no space left for discretionary thought.

If this is the case, you are at the complete mercy of others, your environment and / or your emotions.

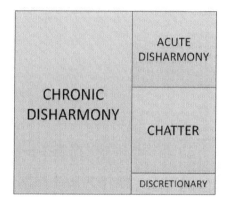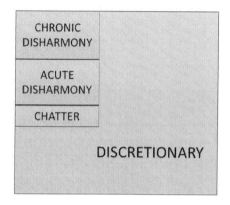

Figure 5 - Enslaved v mastered life

Assuming there is some space left on our Mental Worktop, we can use it to make decisions that will empower us. These might include:

- Exploring the job market.
- Cultivating better health habits.
- Enjoying life.

We might better call this part of our Mental Worktop the Purposeful work zone. Though it is entirely up to us as to whether we:

- Watch another video or learn more vocabulary.
- Go to the gym or re-enact dinner 'Henry the Eighth style'.

This is a part of our Mental Worktop where we have the capacity to take control of our own destiny. More fundamentally, the smaller our Discretionary work zone, the less cognitive capacity we have to pay attention to what is going on in the world.

With little discretionary thought capacity, we are more likely to:

- Be caught off guard.
  - o You didn't hear that electric car reversing in your direction.
  - o You didn't anticipate your boss making an offer of marriage to you. And in keeping with your 'please the boss' philosophy, you impetuously accept.
- Miss life-enhancing opportunities, by, eg.,
  - o Not spotting the overtures of a potential life partner.
  - o Failing to identify a market trend.

The quality of one's life is highly correlated to the size of the Discretionary work zone on your Mental Worktop. It is thus job number one to declutter our Mental Worktop, as much as our life circumstances allow, to maximise the size of the Discretionary work zone.

As we reclaim our Discretionary work zone, it provides the conditions to make further decisions that lead to further reclamation. A virtuous cycle.

Summary

So, our conscious mind (aka Mental Worktop) can be divided into four work zones:

- Chatter.
- Acute Disharmony.
- Chronic Disharmony.
- Discretionary.

Much of our mental capacity is not under our full control. Poor habits in respect of what we think about, and how we respond to events, can play a part. As can the cards we are dealt in life. Being aware of what we can and cannot control will enable us to take steps to rebalance our thoughts in order to have greater capacity for discretionary thinking. The extent to which we can enlarge our Discretionary work zone will determine the extent to which we gravitate towards self-mastery.

Given that some people have their life cards stacked against them, perhaps once we get our mental act together, we can play an active role in helping others less fortunate. Perhaps this is the essence of spirituality?

Keep in mind, the feelings that drive our thoughts are endeavouring to tell us something. That chocolate muffin marathon you have just engaged in wasn't just an exercise in addressing hunger. I am also sure it wasn't driven by a curiosity to explore the far reaches of hyperglycaemia.

Encouraging the positive feelings and minimising the negative feelings gives us the best chance of living a fulfilling life. Again, keep in mind that negative feelings are telling us something. Sometimes this can be constructive, as in - don't trust this charming person. Sometimes it is mis-wiring, as in - now that I have had one biscuit, it makes sense to finish the whole (industrial-sized) packet.

Our Mental Worktop is driven by emotions. These emotions may be stimulated by the environment, or by an internal thought. Emotions that are not handled by our habits require cognitive attention. This is mentally burdensome, so we need to automate our responses where we can through the acquisition of good habits.

Good habits are thus the basis for self-mastery.

The Problem

7   Inattention

Overview

This chapter explains the factors that lead to poor attention, and consequently to a 'poor' life.

Think of this as a 'how NOT to' chapter for those seeking a path to mastery.

Inattention defined

There are a variety of definitions including:

- Lack of attention.
- Distraction.
- Failure to attend to one's responsibilities.
- Negligence.

This list is almost in ascending order of consequence. A lack of attention might involve watching the TV, but not really taking in what is happening. To some extent you are paying attention in that you are concentrating on a source of stimulation, but you are not interpreting it.

This is a common scene in care homes for people suffering from dementia. Perhaps worryingly, it is also increasingly common in 'non-care' homes, as people's attention bounces like a pin ball between the bleeps and scene/screen changes of the various devices in their vicinity.

Distraction has the consequence of drawing us away from something we were paying attention to, and thus impairs the task to which we were attending.

A work colleague asking you if you have a 'minute'. An audience member drawing their forefinger across their throat during your stand-up comedy routine. A former school friend you meet after work who introduces you to crystal meth. Distraction knocks us off the path we have chosen to take.

Failure to attend to one's responsibilities has consequences for you and possibly others. Turning up late to collect your child from school is an example.

Negligence suggests that your inattention has in some way harmed, or potentially harmed, others. Poor banking controls would be an example. Failure to apply the braking system to your articulated lorry, parked at the top end of a busy shopping precinct, whilst you pop out to buy a sandwich, could have dire consequences.

Driving off with your security detail, having left your children alone and exposed in a den of iniquity (ie., a public house in England's idyllic countryside) is another example of inattention. This in fact happened to a UK Prime Minister. In this situation, it might be concluded that his thoughts were consumed by his ministerial responsibilities, thus leaving no mental capacity for parenting. Fortunately, the primary risk to his children was extreme boredom. English country pubs rank relatively low in terms of excitement and risk.

So, inattention can have consequences that impact both ourselves and others. The digital age is like Disney World in terms of the enticing distractions within our reach. Never has it been easier to live an inattentive life.

ADHD

Inattention is so significant today that it has become recognised as a medical condition – Attention Deficit Hyperactivity Disorder.

These are some of the questions asked (in The Diagnostic and Statistical Manual of Mental Disorders, published by the American Psychiatric Association) to establish if someone has attention issues:

- Fails to give close attention to details or makes careless mistakes.
- Has difficulty sustaining attention.
- Does not appear to listen.
- Struggles to follow through on instructions.
- Has difficulty with organization.
- Avoids or dislikes tasks requiring sustained mental effort.
- Loses things.
- Is easily distracted.
- Is forgetful in daily activities.

Many of us recognise our own behaviour in this list. Some of us will be conscious of how we increasingly meet the criteria as the day goes on. It might seem that I am implying that ADHD is a fictitious condition. Well yes and no.

The problem is that there appears to be a number of conditions that can give rise to the symptoms described. For example:

- Substance abuse.
- Dyslexia.
- Iron deficiency.
- Allergies.
- Genetic inheritance.
- Neurotransmitter 'malfunction'.
- Boredom.

Thus it would appear that ADHD is a neat catch all that both doctors and the pharmaceutical industry can use to dish out addictive drugs. (ref. 'Doctor: ADHD Does Not Exist'). Whilst some of the cases warrant medical intervention, I contest that others simply need to develop their attention management skills.

It is no wonder that most people struggle with their attention when advertisers and other experts in neural manipulation are toying with our minds.

Demographically, according to the American Psychiatric Association there has been a dramatic increase in ADHD in US children.

- 2003: 7.8%.
- 2007: 9.5%.
- 2011: 11 %.

ADHD might well be society's attempt to marginalise a set of serious conditions that are in part of our own making. Rather than drugs, with their significant side effects, being the choice of first resort, we might consider other less invasive approaches. Cognitive Behaviour Therapy is sometimes used when the drugs don't seem to do the job. Perhaps the treatment sequence needs to be reversed?

I appear to have veered onto a rant about ADHD. That revealed, I want you to be aware that it has all the signs of a societal sticking plaster. It is more likely a collection of various conditions ranging from the serious through to the medically trivial.

In any case, we have a serious attention problem, and the simple 'one size fits all' solution is to throw drugs at it. At what point does polling three devices, almost simultaneously, move from simply being a social norm in the digital age to an illness requiring addictive drugs?

I am of course, for the purposes of this book, dwelling on the attentional aspect of ADHD. Witnessing hyperactivity is distressing for those responsible for those close to the person affected. Hyperactivity seems to have its roots in genuine medical conditions, including hormone, neural and psychological disorders. One consequence of hyperactivity is the inability to pay attention.

So, chronic inattention can stem from many sources. But is it actually an issue?

Meet your ancestors

Let's first look at dyslexia. For quite some time, people with dyslexia were considered to be of low intelligence. In particular, their inability to read being proof of this. Society has tried to fix them because, particularly in later years, this was an issue in respect of industrial era work.

However, we are moving into the digital era, where creativity is sought after. Where the linear constraints of thinking through words are less attractive than the unconstrained model of thinking in pictures.

Our hunter gatherer ancestors were unlikely to have libraries in their homes, or to peruse user manuals when considering their approach to securing their next meal. The oral tradition of storytelling, along with the communication tool of paintings (strictly speaking graffiti) is something that we were doing only twelve thousand years ago. Our brains are still wired today to operate in this way.

In many respects, the industrial era was an anthropological detour (away from our true nature). However, it is one that has stigmatised and impacted the confidence of those who have not readily transitioned to this written, and probably from an anthropological perspective, temporary, form of communication.

Evidence of this misdiagnosis can be seen in the number of very impressive 'dyslexics', who include:

- Leonardo da Vinci.
- Pablo Picasso.
- Andy Warhol.
- Albert Einstein.
- Thomas Edison.
- Muhammad Ali.
- George Washington
- Richard Branson.
- Henry Ford.

It is my view, this list makes dyslexia, a sought-after gift, rather than a socially-devastating illness.

Returning to ADHD, particularly the hyperactivity element of it. It's of course embarrassing if your children are running around the restaurant, unbalancing waiters and causing fights with other children. You, and no doubt the other diners, wonder why they cannot sit still like well-behaved adults.

But if we go back a brief (from an anthropological adaption perspective) twelve thousand years, the kids would have been running wild, having fun and simulating life (aka playing). Being nomadic in existence, they would also have covered many miles every day, and so they adapted to efficiently turning energy, in the form of food, into movement, of varying speeds and duration. Back then (as today), our bodies were designed for activity. Thanks to processed food and a sedentary lifestyle, our energy levels are generally very low. Some of us have 'learned' how to adapt to the inactivity associated with schooling, work and home life. Some of us haven't quite adapted, and so we simulate being a hunter gatherer by going for, say, a run. Our ancestors would no doubt rib us mercilessly when we returned home empty handed.

Again, I would suggest that hyperactivity is not a physical condition, but a social labelling for those who have not, for whatever reason, managed to suppress their urge to behave naturally.

I am speculating, and I have no evidence for this. But I suspect we will learn more in this respect as we settle into the post-industrial economy. Returning to the main theme of attention. You are reading this book because your ancestors paid attention. Thankfully this was of sufficient duration for them to mature and procreate. There was always a chance back then, that the prey you were pursuing might turn around and eat you. The notion of being eaten by your lunch has long since passed.

We all come from a very long line of people who knew how to pay attention when it mattered. It may well be that in the age of industrialised agriculture, food science and pharmaceuticals, we are becoming neurologically damaged to varying degrees.

We may not notice it so much, because we have the military and police forces, at least in theory, watching our backs. So perhaps the original function of attention as a life-critical, survival tool is steadily becoming functionally redundant? Certainly, advertisers would have no issue with us being less hung up on managing our attention.

Inattention in action

Some people have no choice in the matter of attention. Circumstances find them living rough on the streets, so their attention is fully devoted to survival. Or, as mentioned, their attention capability is impaired at a neurological level.

For the rest of us, we have the capability to choose how we direct our attention. It is just that some of us are not using our attention in a smart way.

Physically

Working too hard, spending unnatural periods of time glued to a screen, will result in physical issues. The chair being 'the new smoking'. Paying little attention to what you eat and drink will have you hypnotically following the agenda of the industrial food giants. Sugar, fat and salt being the three attention grabbing ingredients that we seek out when willpower is not engaged, or is running on empty.

Often the initially subtle signs of a physical disease are ignored. Dry skin, spots, tiredness, aching joints and so on. Falling asleep at the wheel might be a more blatant signal that all is not well physically.

It is difficult to maintain a decent quality of life, if you are physically not 'firing on all cylinders'. In the extreme, it can result in diabetes, heart failure and cancer. Or even being trapped in a compressed vehicle that has veered into the central reservation.

Psychologically

Poor decision making, ranging from what to eat at lunch through to whether to jump the lights when rushing a loved one to hospital, has consequences. Sometimes those consequences will be immediate. More often, they will slowly, and eventually exponentially, veer you off your path to a purposeful life.

The longer you take to realise that you have wired yourself for poor decision making, the harder it will be to reprogram yourself.

Sometimes our decision-making capability is sound, it is just that we are working on the wrong assumptions. Poor assumptions often come from poor perceptions, such as:

- Not seeing the articulated lorry.
- Misinterpreting your partner's good intentions.
- Misinterpreting the nuanced career advice woven into the Fast and Furious film franchise.

Perception, our ability to detect significance in a sea of sensory data, is an indicator of the quality of our attention. The degree to which we can zoom in and out as required is critical. Dwelling on a recent romantic encounter when negotiating the flags in the Winter Olympics slalom final, or what you will have for dinner after the event, could significantly reduce your chances of gold, and significantly increase your chances of ending up in a heap.

Similarly, day dreaming when performing an organ transplant could well result in a fatality.

Having a mind like a hoarder's wardrobe, it is likely that a simple question, such as, "How are you today?", may well cause a breakdown, as you simply have no mental bandwidth left to prepare a considered response. Hence the occurrences of such responses as:

- Why are you asking?
- Mind your own business.
- Help me!

Your mind is the venue in which your decisions are made. Often you are choosing whether to pursue immediate pleasure or longer term gain. Poor life outcomes can be traced back to poor decision making.

Emotionally

We have covered emotions in some detail already. Again, your emotions are your body's interpretation of what it is receiving from your senses. Emotions might be seen as the glue that binds the body to the mind. Physical inputs give rise to mental feelings (and often physical responses too). And of course, inattentive thought can give rise to disempowering emotions.

This mind-body link is managed by nerve proteins (neuropeptides), which regulate the way cells communicate with each other. These chemicals are produced throughout the body and give rise to our emotions. Euphoria, fear, jealousy, love and contentment are just some examples.

Emotions were built into us for survival purposes. Unfortunately, our inattention coupled with the emotional manipulation skills of the attention grabbers often result in us maintaining emotional states that are not in the best interests of our health.

Fear is useful when walking through a dimly lit shopping precinct at night, particularly when you hear accelerating footsteps from behind. It is not useful when it is a tool applied by advertisers or governments to maintain control over you. Broadly speaking, living a life that primarily comprises negative emotions, such as: jealousy, shame, guilt, hate, apathy, fear, or anger will at the very least lead to a suboptimal life.

Negative emotions are often contagious. Jealous people try to induce jealousy towards their target in others. A lack of attention throughout your day might result in you lying in bed at night wondering why you feel so 'out of sorts'. Chronically negative people are bad for your health. And if you are chronically negative, smart people will give you a wide berth. Look around. How smart are those around you?

Some people fear their emotions, seeing sadness, in particular crying, as a sign of weakness. Suppressed emotions, over time, will have negative health implications.

Again, there are those that capitalise on our emotions. The media is expert at creating content that stimulates our emotions in such a way that we keep coming back for more. 'Box set gorging' being similar to working your way through an industrial packet of double choc chip biscuits.

Casinos similarly architect our emotions to keep us engaged until our pockets are empty. Alcoholic beverage providers and drug suppliers also deal in emotional architecture. Inattention to your own emotional management in the wrong environment, which is increasingly every environment, will lead to addiction.

Your local supermarket has no real interest in your emotional health. In fact, an increasing number of vendors endeavor to architect emotional imbalance in order to position their offerings as the remedy. Perhaps 'emotion architect' is a more appropriate term for 'attention grabber' in the digital age.

If we were to experience our own emotions through engaging primarily with the physical world, rather than having them pre-processed for us via a digital medium, we might become less susceptible to those that are in the business of architecting emotional responses.

Some people cannot interpret the emotions of others. In the extreme, this can be the result of a neurological disorder, such as autism. More generally it is referred to as low emotional intelligence.

DO NOT TRY THIS AT HOME – In attempting to separate a bone from a dog, you can either make the discovery that it is unhappy with your decision making, when its teeth penetrate your hand. Or you can pick up on the signals of teeth display, low pitched growling and tail inactivity, and get your own bone from somewhere else.

An inability to interpret other's emotions can lead to a life of confusion, interspersed with acute physical pain.

Habits

Habits are driven by the reward centres of our nervous system. Our reward centres both drive our emotions and are driven by our emotions. Poor emotional management will lead to poor habits. And poor habits will have a corrosive impact on the quality of our life.

Successful people are those who have developed habits that support their goal. For writers, this might include the production of X thousand words per day before breakfast. For athletes, this might include sleeping at least nine hours per day.

But, of course, success in one aspect of your life does not guarantee a meaningful life. If, prior to embarking on your daily writing habit, you invoke an LSD habit, then, your initial creative writing success will be curtailed as your drug habit sends your life into a tailspin.

A meaningful life requires a habit framework that covers every aspect of your life. The problem is that for many people, their habit framework is broken. Negative habits, often acquired through inattention, take root quickly. They may be deeply burrowed before they are identified as the source of negative behaviour, making their removal a challenge.

Socially

We are social animals and so an inability to get on with others is going to be a fundamental issue for us. As mentioned, some societies have lured us into the view that we can do just fine on our own. In fact, the implication is that others are there simply to be used in helping us achieve our objectives. Or, if they are not of use, they had better get out of the way. Visit any urban metro system during rush hour to witness this in action.

Social relationships are generally categorised such that we can apply the rules and guidelines of our society with both consistency and appropriateness for any given relationship. Nibbling the ear of your boss during an appraisal, or shaking hands with your partner on waking up, are thus generally quite rare events.

The pressures exerted on our limited mental bandwidth can often lead to poor decision making in respect of our social activity. We might take our parents for granted, and make little effort to keep them informed about our lives. Until one day they are not there to hear your exciting news.

We perhaps gravitate towards people that are valuable to us, rather than our friends, because we are fully locked on to our career progression. Eventually we realise that our lives solely comprise professional contacts and acquaintances. And none of these people truly know us, so the associated interactions are somewhat superficial.

Our social health is important to us. Not long ago, we lived and hunted with our social group. Socialising with the group, after a kill, or a berry-rich dinner, helped to bond the group together and resolve any lingering issues.

Many of us today don't appear to have any affinity to a pack. Mentally this feels like being an exile. Some cultures do not keep strong familial bonds, even though with the Internet there is now no real excuse. Some address their social needs through their religion or work. The latter approach is particularly painful when you are standing in the company car park with your belongings in a box.

Some will even gather around corporate brands such as Apple or Harley Davidson. Product ownership is the entry condition. A tattooed logo will most likely move you up the social pecking order, if only within the associated group.

Keep in mind that the digital economy is also called the social economy. Those of us that cannot integrate our social and professional branding will be at an economic disadvantage.

There was a time when a lack of social attention beyond using others, could make us rich and famous, although very lonely. Today being genuinely social is table stakes for being rich and famous. And, more importantly, for having a good life.

Financially

It has never been easier to part with our money. At one time, we were constrained by the opening hours of the retail store, and often by the inertia that had to be overcome in order for us to actually get up and visit the store. Today, big ticket purchases can be made whilst heading home in a taxi after a few drinks, in just a couple of clicks.

The use of credit and debit cards dissociate us from the reality of how much we have available to spend. In fact, credit cards dissociate us from the reality that our income cannot sustain certain purchases. It was a lot easier when we used cash. The absence of cash in our wallet was a clear indicator that our capacity for further spending was zero.

Being young is another source of financial issues. Having yet to find a mate, we are more susceptible to advertisers who are happy to cultivate a lack of confidence and self-esteem that only their products and services will repair.

Poor attention to future scenarios, such as possible unemployment, raising a family, and retirement, can seem unnecessarily sensible to someone who is only just discovering the empowerment that goes with not relying on parental largesse.

Your financial inattention makes others rich. Poor planning may result in the need to borrow, as will a lifestyle where outgoings exceed incomings. The financial services industry chides us for poor financial management, but privately rejoices in the interest they receive because of our financial mismanagement.

Money is an agreed upon proxy for value. If you don't have any when you need it, very soon you will face fundamental issues in relation to food and shelter.

Financial worries corrode mental bandwidth, which in turn leads to inattention, and further poor life decisions. Whether you are born poor or acquire poorness, the odds for getting out of the financial pit are stacked against you, given our inbuilt cognitive limitations.

Once the handbrake is off in terms of your financial attention, your downhill descent, if not addressed quickly, will have severe consequences.

Career-wise

Career is a loose concept in the digital economy. What started out as one career with one employer is now gravitating towards many careers with multiple clients / employers. A career for life is becoming a life of careers. In any case, we can think of a career as a path to mastery, where, depending on your chosen variables, progress can be measured by:

- Income.
- Discretionary time.
- Size of office.
- Staff headcount.
- Social capital.

An inattention to our career can turn what might have been forty years of increasingly rewarding experiences into one year of experience repeated forty times.

Often we forget that our employer is one of many. We become obsessed with rising through the ranks, despite the reality that the boardroom comprises family members only, or is restricted by some other, undocumented, condition of entry.

Some people become institutionalised. They have become part of the 'factory machinery', and thus would be unable to adjust to life elsewhere. The thought of having to start again, to re-establish themselves, overrides the opportunity for personal development and gaining an enhanced worldview.

The increasing market volatility is turning career planning from a one-time chat with the school career office to a daily reassessment of one's value proposition.

In my experience, some people are so tied up in their career that they have little attentional capacity available for career monitoring. Until, that is, they find themselves in what might be termed a career cul de sac.

Another more acutely attentional issue is that the digital economy is killing the need for process workers. That is to say, those jobs that involve little thought, and are typically repetitive. Such roles are technology placeholders. When the hardware, software or robot technology matures sufficiently, such people will be surplus to requirements.

A way to stay in play is to be able to carry out tasks that the market values and that cannot be substituted with technology. Today creativity gives us the upper hand on our technology rivals. And increasingly our humanity has market value.

But creativity is demanding in respect of mental bandwidth. So, if your head is filled with financial and health worries, your capacity to be creative will be somewhat limited.

Poor career decisions lead to unfulfilled potential at one extreme, and being worried sick about our ability to make ends meet at the other.

Lifestyle

Everyone has a lifestyle. More often, that lifestyle is acquired by default. Some people live a life of ill-health, begging, moving from bin to bin for scraps of food, whilst contemplating where they will sleep that evening. There is little time to peruse Trip Advisor in respect of their next vacation. Or where best to buy a new mat for their forthcoming Pilates course.

As our income exceeds our essential outgoings, we start to develop economic options in terms of where we live and how we live. The industrial era model of working means that many who do have such discretionary income do not have the time to enjoy it.

Lifestyle is often fuelled by our emotions. Some people are compelled to impress their neighbours. So, like a game of consumer chess, they make their move - buy the latest shiny 4 x 4 sports utility vehicle. The neighbour's counter move involves a property extension. And on it goes.

I do not envy those high earners, such as film stars, who are always in the public eye. Each day must seem like the final of the Affluence Olympics. Despite the obvious associated stress, many of us dedicate our lives to becoming an 'affluence Olympian', even though our financial constraints / limited talent consigns us to never achieving the required entry conditions.

Our desire to socially climb, has us mimicking those we aspire to emulate. This might involve membership of a certain country club, at least one holiday home, and a strong (unfounded) distaste for the values of others outside the set.

The cooker makers, automobile players and the estate agents, amongst others, will leap upon your emotional imbalance, and endeavour to turn it into cash. Once you tick all the boxes, you get to join your chosen set; not least by being on the same mailing list.

I am not anti-materialist, I am simply endeavouring to encourage you to build a lifestyle that you want, as opposed to what your family, friends, employer or the lifestyle vendors want.

Poor lifestyle decisions can lead to what might be called well-appointed misery. Trying to keep up with the social pack you aspire to be part of will leave you chronically overwhelmed. Such is the nature of trying to compete with those who have more money, time and discretionary mental bandwidth than you. Imagine the coroner's report, 'Death by social misadventure'. Pathetic and needy come to mind. Not much there for your eulogist to work with.

As mentioned, some unfortunate people are trapped in a lifestyle that they have not created, or have very little chance of escaping. Poverty, as mentioned, places great demands on your mental bandwidth.

Some people do have the opportunity to architect a lifestyle. Whether you create one that enables you to live as the best version of you, or a 'struggling to keep up' version of your neighbour, boils down to the extent to which you examine, ie., pay attention, and manage your own lifestyle and its underlying drivers.

Spiritually

The acts of maintaining your physical, psychological and emotional health might be considered an act of kindness to yourself. Maintaining good social ties invariably involves a degree of kindness to others.

The extent to which we act with kindness towards ourselves and to others might be considered a measure of spirituality. Though this is, of course, at one level self-serving.

How we behave to those we don't know or who we will never know is taking us into the serious end of the spirituality spectrum. In a world where, without extraordinary attention, we will be largely running at 'near empty' from a mental bandwidth perspective, it is almost impossible to think about issues impacting mankind.

Choosing a career or lifestyle that embraces the greater good is a smart way to keep spirituality centre stage. Voluntary work comes to mind.

Our collective inattention to those less 'well off' than ourselves, locally and globally, has significant humanitarian consequences. Lazily consuming natural resources and discarding goods that remain functional but are out of fashion has serious ecological consequences.

My definition of spirituality implies that being kind and considerate to yourself and others is enough. Though, I would suggest it is not a bad start. At a deeper level, the distinction between ourselves and others dissolves.

At possibly the highest level, the distinction between ourselves and the universe dissolves. Such a level of spirituality has been associated with feelings of joy and bliss. And even happiness.

This exalted state, these days, would seem to be the sole preserve of professional spiritualists such as monks and the clergy. At a basic level, a lack of spirituality makes for a lonely miserable life. At the highest level, your anxieties about the future, including death, disappear. Thus, enabling you to devote more mental bandwidth to living a more engaged life.

Inattention to your spiritual life won't kill you, but it will feel like you are not quite firing on all cylinders. Whilst you may not be aware of it, you will likely have the charisma of a pre-enlightened Ebenezer Scrooge.

Purpose

I am treating purpose in isolation of the other elements of our life because it impacts every element. If you are a beggar your purpose is to find food and shelter.

If your finances are out of control, and you risk having your credit cards cancelled, hopefully, your primary focus would be to invoke an action plan in respect of your spending.

If you are a high performing athlete, your purpose may be to win an Olympic gold.

If you anticipate your high paying job coming to an end, your purpose might focus on retaining the lifestyle that you and your family currently enjoy.

Purpose at the spiritual level is what will determine the overall quality of our lives. It will act as rocket fuel in terms of giving our life meaning. It will cause us to leap out of bed and get things done.

Spiritual purpose, as mentioned, generally involves how we treat ourselves and others. Some strive to transcend the limitations of their physical body and become one with the cosmos. Such a blissful state can be found through meditation and prayer.

Some practitioners can even arouse this state in their day to day activities. Imagine waking up to start a day where, despite what happens, good, bad or marvellous, you perceive everything as perfect, and so can enjoy / experience each moment as it arrives. The emotions you feel are genuine and not manufactured via a games console.

When we don't pay attention to our spiritual purpose, we are likely, mental bandwidth permitting, to dwell on the pointlessness of life. Is it really just arrive-reproduce-die, with some eating and defecating thrown in? Is our sole purpose to both 'man the factories' of our overlords, and to then consume the outputs; much like bar workers who spend their free time on the other side of the counter?

Perhaps we self-medicate emotionally to ensure our mental bandwidth is always in full use, to ensure such existential questions do not trouble us?

We admire Olympians and people who have achieved success in their field, but they too are faced with the same questions. The purpose void that follows their success can be very painful and lead to a self-destructive spiral.

In contrast, even the very poor can live deeply spiritual lives. Living within their means, whilst being a contributory member within a strong social support network can deliver a much richer life than one that is spent relentlessly pursuing, for example, money or social elevation.

In summary

As we have seen, an inattentive life is easy to fall into. The consequences of inattention can be significant.

Mind you, waking up each day fearful of slipping up in respect of physical, psychological, emotional, social, financial, career, lifestyle and spiritual matters, might well result in you staying in bed and pulling the blankets over your head. Such considerations taken in parallel will 'max out' your mental bandwidth, for sure, leaving little spare capacity in which to engage with the world.

So now, before we move towards a solution, we will 'call out' the culprits, who, unless we are paying attention, will steal our attention, thus rendering it unusable for mastery building.

8 Attention Thieves

Overview

Maintaining attention is a fulltime job. It is made more difficult by those that purposefully, or inadvertently, take control of our attention.

Let us look at some of the main culprits.

The commercial attention seekers

We have already identified that the commercial world is becoming increasingly expert at capturing our attention for cash flow purposes.

Gaining our attention has been the focus of the vendors from the dawn of commerce. Latterly industries have emerged to manage this task on behalf of the vendors. Advertising and public relations come to mind. Industries where your attention is the service to the vendors are already well established; sports and entertainment come to mind. Next generation players such as Twitter and Facebook don't even require any bait as such. We are both the bait and the catch.

The arrival of sophisticated data analysis tools, often collectively referred to as big data, can pick up on trends in your behaviour that you might not even be aware of. Thus, the commercial players are able to cater for the tendencies you do not even know you have.

As a parent, you may not appreciate the targeted marketing literature sent to your daughter, mistakenly assuming she is pregnant. Until you subsequently discover this is not a mistake. Loyalty cards are like behavioural tracking devices. Your credit card spending patterns might result in divorce lawyer adverts appearing in the websites you visit.

Your off-trend behaviour of staying in hotels for one night at a time, coupled with purchasing flowers and chocolate, might indicate that all is not well in the family home, and so such services will be needed in due course.

As big data matures, we will see increased intrusion into our lives. Some of the calls on our attention will be welcomed because they relate to what we need at that point in time. Most will be what we 'should' want, given the assumption that without a car or a watch like that of James Bond, we are unlikely to find a mate. Or without this perfume you will forever be an unloved ugly duckling. Emotional architecting is a highly context-sensitive, behaviourally aligned, and real-time practice.

Societal attention seekers

There was a time when you said cheerio to your school friends after school and that was it until the next school day. Today school friends are sitting right there next to you on your phone or tablet. Fail to respond and the word gets around school that you went to bed early, or perhaps even did some homework.

We are all, to some extent, at the mercy of our social networks. Our increasing inability to power down our social media activities for a bit of quiet time means that we simply cannot blame others for interrupting our lives.

Of course, part of being a social animal is being social. But social media has the capacity to make us hyper-social, which at some point impinges on applying our cognitive resources to other important activities.

Having a sense of social hierarchy can help with attention management. In the extreme, your children get the platinum service, ie., an instant or near instant response. As do parents and partners. Close friends and wider family get the gold service. And so on. You are encouraged to avoid getting into service level agreements with your children, given the penalty clauses they are likely to push for.

Recently, when listening to a millennial talk about millennials, she gave an example of her mother trying to make contact by phone. This was seen as very irritating. She explained to her mother that she is just generally too busy to talk. Consequently, she taught her mother how to text. The perceived problem now was that the mother would write letter-length texts, causing this millennial to revert to telephone calls as the primary channel. Is this an indicator of a growing narcissism, or a reminder of how young people throughout the ages take their parents' attention for granted?

My point being that some people are more important than others. If you live your life like an accident and emergency doctor, specifically one with no triaging methodology, you are going to get your life priorities all wrong.

Governments can also be a source of distraction. Poorly thought through legislation can result in citizens having to wade through bureaucratic red tape. At best, this is incompetence, and at worst it is deliberately obfuscating for reasons that might best serve the government concerned. The rich can outsource the associated red tape 'cognitive drain' to an accountant or lawyer. The poor are not so fortunate, and thus their discretionary mental work zone is further encroached upon. Poorly designed government services create, or at least contribute to, a barrier that obstructs the poor from rising out of poverty. Surely that is not by design?

Even the proliferation of road signs is a form of attention pollution. Possibly the signs are legally required, or a general response to a specific incident. Nonetheless, governments are encouraged to factor in that citizens need to retain a certain amount of their attention for the purposes of driving.

Perhaps we need a Ministry of Attention? Though thinking about it, this could quite easily become the Ministry of Propaganda, given how much easier it is to rule, if the citizen's attention is directed in a manner that suits the state. The Roman leadership talked of 'bread and circuses' as ways of distracting the populace. Today, perhaps, it is drugs and the internet.

Your environment

Noise can be very attention grabbing. However, the steady cacophony of motorway traffic can blend into the background and thus eventually make no demands of our attention.

As many of us know, an office co-worker speaking too loudly can be very irritating. As can a neighbourhood dispute taking place outside of your apartment. In the former case, your insensitive co-worker is upsetting your concentration and therefore your ability to do your work. In the latter case, the consequence could be significantly higher. Might blood be spilled, or might your prized garden gnomes be commandeered as dispute resolution weapons?

Trying to sleep the night before an important exam, whilst an impromptu party gets underway across the road, could well impact your performance, and thus your life. Having to negotiate the underpass, which happens to be the headquarters of your local teenage gang, each evening on your way home from work, again might impact your life. You thus need to direct all your attentional resources to anticipating an altercation and being ready to take evasive action. Your cortisol levels thus spike every evening.

In both cases, your mind becomes preoccupied with the disturbance. The associated irritation / fear makes even further demands on your attention. Living in a state of fear puts every other aspect of your life on hold. This emotional havoc will play out in different ways, including comfort eating and other unhealthy emotional management habits.

Your work

We have mentioned the insensitive worker. But work pressures, often brought on by out of date business models, lead to workers being overloaded in terms of their tasks. Struggling to get all your work done, you have little time for civility. Late delivery on inputs required to complete your current task may well cause you to overreact and destroy any social capital you had with the perceived offender.

Every email in your inbox is a call on your attention. In fact, practically every email is there to divert your attention towards helping the senders with their agendas. Though generally it makes good career sense to do what you can in respect of the agenda of your boss.

Call centre staff often have to deal with customers who are not in the mood for pleasantries, "So your child has gone missing. Firstly, can I ask what is your name? ..... Can I call you Mary?". They have an issue and they want it fixed. Maintaining a professional disposition in the face of a continuous torrent of 'emotional heat' will take its toll on your willpower reserves.

For those on the frontline of social services, where the predicament of the 'customer' is often a travesty, the emotional toll on the social worker will be very high. It is unlikely that after a day on the front line, an evening of solving maths problems, or an activity that requires fine motor control, will be the first choice in respect of relaxation therapy. But if you happen to be a mother too, then helping your son with his homework that evening, or patching up his torn blazer, might well cause you to suffer mental meltdown. Leaving your son perplexed, and slightly less trusting of you; and you feeling remorseful.

Your friends

We have mentioned how social media has, in effect, given your 'friends' 24-hour direct access to you. A way of de-cluttering your Mental Worktop would be to announce to all your friends that to lead a more purposeful life, you intend to discontinue the friendship. Or as the young girl mentioned in Karate Kid 5 (2010), "We can no longer be friends. You are bad for my life."

Such a radical move is usually associated with a profound change in spiritual direction, and usually involves a monastery, or some sort of 'live in' religious enclosure.

For those of us looking to travel a less solitary path, friends constitute important cast members in the story of our lives. As we do in theirs.

So, from time to time, we need to apportion part of our Mental Worktop to addressing their issues, or simply being there as a solution-free sounding board. In the latter case, holding back from communicating the obvious solution is where the real cognitive burden lies.

Friendships are typically not commercial relationships, so there is no formal agreement in terms of ensuring that both parties are obliged to burden each other equally over a set period. However, if your limited mental capacity is regularly spent extricating your friend from alcohol-fuelled altercations they have managed to initiate, then you might consider some sort of disciplinary process, where, after two verbal and one written warning, they are defriended.

In any case, we need to make mental space for our friends, but not so much that to the casual observer you are simply an expendable resource that your so-called friends use when it suits them.

Your family

Unlike your friends, you did not choose your family. Maybe, as mentioned earlier, friends are nature's way of apologising?

If you are of aristocratic, or warrior stock, then your family is more likely to be run as a business, where marriages are more akin to corporate mergers than an expression of love. In such families, there is a high expectation that you will do what is required to protect the dynasty. The TV series Game of Thrones, or even Downton Abbey, provide related insights. Your choice of viewing will depend on your predilection towards soft porn and violence.

The rest of us have a varying sense of familial obligation. Some cultures revere their elderly and so the young must commit to looking after the previous generation in their latter years. More individualistic cultures tend to take their parents for granted. When old enough to flee the nest, they do so with minimal financial rebalancing of the emotional and financial input they received prior to departure.

For some reason, many of us have high expectations in respect of how our families behave. The discovery that parents are human and not perfect can come as a shock, particularly when you are young and reliant on them for food, shelter and emotional support. Your perception of what families should be like may well be coloured by the media. This serves to create disharmony between your familial reality and the glossy ideal.

You may be very resource conscious and keep a tight tally on the attention your parents are giving to you and your siblings. You might consequently feel short-changed. You may start to resent the fact that your parents talk glowingly about your sister's academic record, or your brother's sporting prowess. You may even resent the fact that your siblings just happen to play the resource allocation game better than you.

There is no shortage of ways we can identify injustice in our families and thus, absolve us from taking responsibility for our behaviour, life path or attitude.

In any case, families can be an attentional drain. Simmering resentments surface almost randomly. How could she put our mother through that? Or we gave him everything, so why does he treat us like that? Even whilst brushing your teeth, or during some other routine that can be conducted mindlessly, your background mental chatter focuses on some previous familial injustice. Before you know it, you are brushing your teeth like a lunatic seething with pathological rage.

This will in some way colour your day. And possibly the day of those around you. Because you have other matters to think about, it never quite gets enough attention for you to resolve the underlying family issue / your unrealistic expectations. And anyway, given it's (of course) not your fault, shouldn't the guilty party be doing the resolving?

The family model exists to ensure that the next generation survive long enough to be able to create the subsequent generation. If you have made it to adulthood, then broadly that is a result. Of course, physical and mental neglect and abuse, where it happens, is an extremely serious matter.

My point is to highlight that families can be a substantial attention consumer. If that attention consumption is based on dysfunctionality then it requires resolution, or mental compartmentalisation, if only to free your mind to focus on where you want to go in life.

You (The chimp)

As I have alluded to already, you are often the source of your own distraction. In fact, you are always the source of your own distraction, on the basis that your interpretation of reality is just that, an interpretation. Your senses deliver raw data, but your brain filters it, interprets it and encodes it in such a way that it becomes your version of reality.

Through poor habits, lazy thinking or neuroses, your interpretation of reality may diverge somewhat from actual reality. So, unthreatening things may appear threatening. Innocent remarks may be interpreted as character attacks.

As evolved animals, we are wired to behave like any other animal. Sometimes this can work well for us, for example when the smell of burning invokes fear. Less so when we are sexually aroused by the invigilator during a life-impacting exam.

Emotions drive our behaviour. In modern society, we have generally learnt how to moderate the associated behaviour. Nonetheless, emotions can distract us in a manner that, whilst not socially reprehensible, are still counterproductive to our best interests.

Dr Steve Peters created a mind model, which is detailed in his book, 'The Chimp Paradox'. He labels our emotionally distracting thoughts 'the chimp'. He sees the chimp, as an anthropological inheritance that we need to manage. His model is used by top athletes to ensure their minds are an asset rather than a performance liability.

The labelling and management of this distracting chatter applies to those of us with less lofty goals. To some extent I have drawn on his work.

For all of us, as mentioned, random inconsequential thoughts can hijack our attention. The chatter can emerge from such random thoughts as, "Do microbes have instincts?" or "Could I teach myself carpentry?"

You, or your 'chimp', if you are not careful, can have you so distracted that your reality becomes distorted. When your reality diverges from actual reality you will, at some point, run into problems. More often than not, it is not so much that we have a warped sense of reality, but that our thoughts cloud our view of reality. Or, if we are too engrossed in our thoughts, you might say we bring the shutters down on our window to reality. Whilst this is not necessarily neurotic behaviour, closed shutters at the wrong time, in the extreme, can have fatal consequences.

Time

Time is an interesting concept. Not least because there are those in the scientific community who do not believe it exists. However, it is still a useful concept in respect of exploring attention.

Deadlines impact the way in which we act. Below a certain threshold, ie., too soon, and they have the effect of causing us to be anxious about delivering on time. This consumes mental bandwidth, thus leaving less for getting the job done. Beyond a certain point this unconstructive bandwidth consumption degrades the quality of our work, as silly mistakes increase in frequency.

Above a certain threshold, when the deadline is still far off, we devote too little attention to the task. Our diluted attention similarly produces substandard work. There is a temptation to delay the start. Before we know it, the deadline is looming and we regret our poor time management.

Similarly, this time issue occurs in respect of our 'life project'. When we are young, we believe we have all the time in the world, and so we put off activities believing we will have plenty of time when we are older.

On the basis that some of us won't go the 'full distance', we should not delay in progressing the life goals we have set for ourselves. For example, a working life of toil focused on retiring to a post-work life of pleasure and adventure, might never happen. So best to ensure that pleasure and adventure are a feature throughout your life.

In our latter years, fretting about our misspent youth serves no other purpose than to dilute the quality of what remains of our life. Similarly, being envious of younger people delivers very little in terms of life quality.

Planning is generally a smart move. Your goals are unlikely to materialise without thoughtful forward planning. However, planning can become obsessional to the point where the balance between planning your life and living your life is lost. It is true that our lives are not a dress rehearsal. Living requires getting out there and engaging with the world.

It is sad to hear of people who in their latter years regret that, despite having acquired all the material symbols of success, they spent too much time in the office, and not enough with family and friends. Such regret is a heavy consumer of mental bandwidth. Cognitive investment now, in terms of how you spend your life today, will pay cognitive dividends in your latter years. I think young people generally get this. Their parents, in many cases, serving less as role models, and more as cautionary tales / case studies, in this respect.

Poverty

Poverty, as discussed, is a pernicious form of attention erosion. In many respects, that is why previous generations have been so seemingly obsessed with the economic value of work. Wars, recent and not so recent, have left their economic scars. Work was perceived as a means to keep out of poverty, and to ideally banish it from one's life forever. The people we see today with their conspicuous symbols of success, were, in at least some sense, at one time driven by the abject fear of poverty.

We have some way to go before poverty is banished globally. Even developed countries appear to have an ever-widening gulf between the rich and the poor.

Being poor means that a large part of your cognitive capacity is spent in a state of anxiety, worrying about your family, food and shelter. This leaves less capacity for the clear thinking needed to bootstrap oneself out of poverty. It also makes one more susceptible to the black economy, where acquiring stolen goods, and succumbing to payday loan sharks, is the only viable way forward.

Being in a desperate situation can be unbearable, so self-medication through drugs and alcohol is common. This again consumes mental bandwidth as the consequences of drug-fuelled behaviour on yourself and others emerges.

As mentioned, poor people do not have less cognitive capacity than rich people. It's just that they have a diminished discretionary work zone, given how poverty makes high demands on both acute and chronic disharmony work zones.

Again, as mentioned, rich people can outsource their issues and administration, thus maximising the size of their discretionary work zone. Consequently, the rich get richer through better decision making, and the poor get poorer through poor decision making.

Those who have descended into poverty at least understand what non-poverty looks like, and so have a sense of direction in terms of their escape route. Those born into poverty, who know nothing else, are less likely to recognise the escape route, unless it is strongly signposted, and they are sufficiently undistracted to read it.

Giving poor people money is a solution. Creating employment is another. However, creating the living conditions for people to think clearly is the best solution. Failing to address housing issues, local crime and drug availability are collectively tantamount to keeping the poor in an economic prison.

Pre-suasion

Pre-suasion is both a tool and a weapon. As a tool, it can be used to redirect your attention. As a weapon, it can be used to manage the attention of others. Robert Cialdoni's book, Pre-Suasion, elaborates on the concept and how it can be applied. Given that we are focused here on attention thieves, we will focus on it being used as a way of influencing the way we think. Thus, making it useful for those who need to steer our attention towards a perspective that suits their purposes.

One might think of pre-suasion as the art of hacking 'weaknesses' in our brain. Such weaknesses include:

- Our sexual inclination.
- Our sense of fear.
- Our inability to discern the difference between what is causal, and what is in focus.
    - The man standing still and staring blankly, holding a knife over a dead body is not necessarily the murderer.
- Our tendency to be drawn in to mysteries.
- Our discomfort with unfinished business.

A boxer's jab, is not designed to knock out her opponent. It is merely to set the opponent up to receive the 'lights out' cross punch. It's just with pre-suasion, you are unaware that you have been jabbed. Pre-suasion is all about others 'tenderising' your head in advance, such that you will be amenable to the 'offer', when it is presented to you. In the digital age, manipulating your attention is now essentially a science.

Summary

Your attention is a valuable resource. That is why others want a piece of it. Attention has no past or future. Like hotel rooms, or seats on a plane, if they were not used at a given time, that opportunity is lost forever. The attention we waste today can never be retrieved. Squandered attention is a wasted resource.

Worse still, the associated attention vacuum could lead to poor decision making that will, over time, set you off on a downward spiral in terms of life quality.

However you define a fulfilling life, your chances of living it will be driven by the extent to which you carefully manage your attention.

The path to mastery requires management of your environment and your mind.

In this chapter, we have focused on the problems associated with being inattentive. We will look at the implications of this on our lives in the next chapter. Stick with it. Once covered, we will take a more solution-oriented perspective on attention, and thus mastery.

9 An Inattentive Life

Overview

An inattentive life might be considered the equivalent of owning a high-performance sports car, but never taking it out of first gear. There you are, crawling along in your fantasy sports car, whilst onlookers lament at the wasted potential of your gift.

Before we explore how best to optimise our attention, and thus our life, we will look at the various forms an inattentive life can take.

Poor physical health

Very few people are born physically perfect. Some imperfections, such as problems with vision, can be largely addressed, thanks to advances in science and technology. Even missing limbs can be replaced with prosthetic augmentations that surpass the functionality of traditional limbs.

Allergies seem to be a growing impairment. Possibly our increased use of chemicals in everyday life, coupled with an increasingly toxic atmosphere, are to blame.

Our physical wellbeing is not just determined at birth, but is in a continuous state of flux throughout our lives. Not so long ago, we were hunter gatherers, so our bodies are adapted for an active life. As you read this, how agile do you feel? If a sabre tooth tiger walked into your living room, how nimbly could you spring up from the settee? If a loved one became severely ill, how capable are you of running to a medical centre 5 miles away to pick up the necessary medication?

You may believe you have these scenarios covered, thanks to your policy of keeping the front door locked, and having an Uber account. In some countries, obesity is growing like an epidemic. Possibly this is a disguised form of allergy? Or might the environment be the culprit, triggering neurological mis-wiring during the gestation period? So, it would thus be unfair to lecture people on something that they have little control over.

Physical ill-health has a cognitive overhead. Concerns over our health shape / limit our discretionary thinking. It can impact our self-esteem, and thus how we engage with the world. A general lack of vitality makes us less inclined to actively engage with the world. Consequently, we revert to passive forms of entertainment. Thus, we end up living a sad pre-digested existence. The existential equivalent of a ready-meal.

Poor mental health

Again, poor wiring during the gestation period can result in us emerging into society with mental issues. An inability to grasp concepts and symbols limits our ability to engage with others, as does poor memory. Impaired decision making skills will have an exponentially detrimental impact on your life, as cumulative poor low-impact decision making leads to poor high-impact outcomes.

It is this aspect of our wellbeing where we manage, or mismanage, the emotions that our senses trigger. Here, willpower is brought to bear, as are our meta-habits. These meta-habits are the mental processes we employ when seeking to create a new habit. The more effectively we can build a new habit, the less reliant we become on our very limited pool of willpower.

Poor decision making also manifests itself when our daily plan of activities (aka to do list) is largely based on fantasy. Thus, we spend all day in a race we are destined to lose. Despondency and a sense of being overwhelmed becomes our natural state. Sometimes, this is driven by our work, or other obligations. Sometimes it is driven by our impatience / greediness, or just an inability to plan realistically (temporal dyspraxia?).

Every time we decide to do something, we have at that time ruled out every other option available to us. In a world where we have an abundance of options, choice anxiety becomes a modern-day form of mental illness. Counter movements such as the minimalists, along with books such as Affluenza and Stuffocation, highlight the cognitive stress modern living can impose on us, if we are not careful.

You will notice that very upmarket boutiques are characterised by a very limited selection of offerings on display. The rich appreciate services that proactively eliminate choice anxiety, for reasons I hope you now appreciate. Even a book like this has the potential to induce frustration, if the gap between where you are and where you want to be is too vast. As an aside, if you think of yourself as your client, then this becomes an exercise in expectation management.

In general, it is better to set small achievable goals that over time accumulate into achieving your big audacious goal. More on this later. Inattention to our mental health has a direct impact on the quality of our lives. With better attention, we can make our mental faculties drive us towards a purposeful life.

Low emotional intelligence

A limited emotional vocabulary will limit the quality of your life. Much like a poor sense of taste will undermine the experience you have when fine dining.

It will also get you into trouble, as you fail to understand why others behave as they do, and thus cause you to assume their intentions are malevolent. There is really no need to 'pop a cap' into a stranger who inadvertently steps on your shoe in a nightclub. Your inability to manage your feelings, particularly primal emotions such as rage, sexual arousal and fear, will result in you living the life of a pinball; each interaction with the world propels you into the next seemingly random encounter. Each encounter characteristically causing your life to take a downward trajectory.

Maintaining relationships and holding down a job becomes an issue when you have low so-called emotional intelligence. But even where this is the consequence of a neurological defect, there is still techniques one can employ to dampen the negative impact.

Social isolation

As mentioned, poor emotional management can have a disastrous impact on our social lives. In the extreme, it can result in us being taken out of society for extended periods.

But many of us do not lack emotional intelligence, we just don't see the need for using it, other than to garner cooperation in others in respect of our goals. Some individualistic societies see this as an admirable skill. You are either a hustler or the hustled.

The supportive infrastructure built into many modern societies can cause some people to feel as if they can achieve their goals without any concern for others. But we are social animals, and asocial, or even antisocial, behaviour will create internal dissonance to some degree. At one extreme, it can be a sense of sadness from having exploited an innocent party. At the other end, it will be the burden of having to 'watch your back', knowing that you have grown many enemies who are actively planning a payback opportunity.

Social trauma brought about by bullying and divorce has a cognitive overhead that may last a lifetime. Resolving lifelong family feuds, or disagreements at the deathbed of the person to which your ire was directed, is pathetic in more ways than one. It is a high price to pay for the maintenance of your ego.

Being hurt by someone is never welcome. But when you let that hurt linger beyond the event, then they have really scored a home run. From time to time, we hear of parents who forgive their child's murderers. This is often attributed to their religious faith – 'turn the other cheek'. It is also a self-preserving mechanism to avoid a second murder, ie., having their life destroyed by anger and a desire for retribution.

Financial worries

A culture of 'buy now, pay later' has resulted in high levels of debt. People are mentally decoupling value from cost, and decoupling cost from income. Thus, many people with well-paying employment are struggling financially.

Given that modern society is built on financial foundations, it is very difficult to partake in society unless you 'pay your way'. Some societies provide a financial safety net for those who cannot work.

Financial worries are a great source of disharmony, and thus mental bandwidth consumption. Resolution options include:

- Earn more.
- Spend less.

A life spent thinking about making 'ends meet' is one where survival overrides living a purposeful life. I have already mentioned how pernicious poverty is.

However, there are those of us who, by global standards, are doing very well financially. Nonetheless, we feel it is not enough. Thus, our life often becomes a failed quest to achieve our fantasy financial goal. So, like those who are poor, we are unable to think about, and make decisions in relation to, living a purposeful life.

Career cul de sac

The notion of a career implies a journey. This journey may be driven by money, a desire for the corner office, or something deeper. Sometimes, the journey comes to an abrupt halt. This may be because:

- You have been made redundant.
- You have a new and less supportive boss.

Sometimes it is less abrupt. Possibly you are distracted by other aspects of your life? Possibly you have become comfortable, and are simply operating in cruise-control mode?

Perhaps a fear of the unknown keeps you where you are? Joining a new organisation has a cognitive cost in integrating into a new culture.

There is no harm in 'parking' your career progression, if doing so frees up more mental bandwidth that can be applied to living a more purposeful life, particularly if your financial needs are met.

The problem is that in a volatile market, if you are not moving forward career-wise, you are in danger of being automated out of the building. We must develop ourselves daily to ensure we remain economically relevant.

So, if your career has become stale, take action. If your career has become comfortable, act. In the digital economy, if you aren't swimming, you are sinking.

No life

Working flat out in a stimulating career that pays extremely well might seem like you are living the dream. But it is a dream with a theme of living to work, rather than working to live.

No friends and a neglected family reflects poorly on you as a person. Even apes have a life beyond work. As some of us get into the latter phases of our life, we start to think about our 'bucket list'. That is, those things we want to experience before we 'kick the bucket'.

Some people wake up in a cold sweat wondering why they have dedicated a large chunk of their lives to, for example, indirectly promoting child obesity by working for a confectionary company. Suddenly realising that you have dedicated a large chunk of your life to killing the next generation is no doubt profoundly upsetting.

But there is also our non-working life. It would be a terrible shame to only discover that you have a talent for playing a musical instrument in your final years. You missed out on living a rock god. Of course, there are an infinite set of experiences we could sample, so one might make such a discovery even after having lived a full life. My point is that the more you sample life's smorgasbord, the more likely you will be exposed to life-enhancing options. And the earlier you do it, the bigger the impact on your life of the choices you make.

Being human allows us to experience life in fine detail. Eating, for example, is much more than energy replenishment. For many, it is much more than experiencing the taste of sugar, salt and fat. Our choice of entertainment can be driven by primal urges associated with sex, fear and horror. Or it can be less smash, bang, wallop and more nuanced, presenting you with pallet of emotions you have never ever experienced.

Similarly, we can stay within our own communities and only engage with people like us. Or perhaps we go abroad, but only to places where people like us congregate. Wouldn't it be more life-enriching to engage with other cultures? Seeing the world through the eyes of others and to learn something of their culture and practices, helps us to better understand who we are.

A life lived in an office cubicle, or one lived via a screen, is an unlived life.

Spiritual void

As mentioned, spirituality is a broad term. It would be wrong to imply that if you haven't signed up to an organised religion, you are banished to a spiritual abyss.

But living a life where you are indifferent to the condition of your fellow man, must be the equivalent of living in an open prison. You see those around you as either a threat or a target for exploitation. This indifference is isolating.

How can you meaningfully engage with people, if fundamentally you do not trust them? Every encounter is a source of cognitive disharmony.

You may not even trust yourself, or more specifically your potential. Rather than knowing you are a miracle of nature with a supercomputer for a brain, you view yourself as an inadequate mutation of your idealised self.

Spirituality, in many respects, means being in harmony with yourself and others. But it also means being in harmony with the wider universe(s). The notion of a God, or Gods, helps make this easier for many to conceptualise. The rest of us can either block out any celestial concerns we might have, or just see the universe through the eyes of the cosmologists, who have their own hypotheses on how the universe was created.

I think you can only be truly happy if your worldview and universe-view are both coherent and underpinned by kindness. This requires great diligence, as nature has programmed us with destructive tendencies. Lower down the food chain, these tendencies, particularly when resources are rare, serve to ensure that the strongest genes prevail. Kindness, in general, serves to levitate us spiritually from the primal depths, where fear and violence consume the bulk of our limited bandwidth.

But, whilst humans have set new biological standards in terms of how a given species can inflict largescale destruction on its own kind, we have also developed smarter, less destructive, ways of resolving potential conflict.

Keeping a lid on our 'dark side' has a cognitive overhead, unless we have subscribed to, or created, our own spiritual framework.

An absence of spirituality in our lives is not an issue, if our thoughts and actions are entangled in the other aspects of our lives. But as we age, the realisation that we have lived out life as if the universe was created purely for our benefit can fill us with shame.

Spirituality is of course more than just an insurance policy for our mental wellbeing in the latter stages of our life. But if that is what it takes to initiate your spiritual journey, then it will serve as a suitable starting point.

Your attainments and eulogy

I mentioned earlier in this book, your attainments and your eulogy offer two lenses through which to review your life. Attainments are of course a marque of your ability to achieve, and even a measure of your cognitive dexterity.

But your eulogy, which typically references your character, and thus how you made others feel, will be the greater indicator of how you played the game of being human.

Again, whilst attainments are impressive, without a track record of being a decent human being, you, and others, are likely to feel that your life was hollow. Though if you can maintain self-centred until your death bed, then there is no issue. You can 'rest assured' that on the day, your eulogy, when read to the congregation, is unlikely to cause you any embarrassment or shame.

In contrast, that the world perceived you as a 'good egg' might be considered a pretty good life mastery result. However, in carefully managing your 'life brand', you might have neglected yourself. So, eyebrows will be raised, if you died 'before your time' because of fizzy-drinks-induced liver cirrhosis. Or with large debts to pass onto your next of kin.

Life mastery is not about ostentatious displays of how 'together' you are, or how agreeable you appear to be. It is about how you feel about your life, and the extent to which you can develop yourself in whichever direction you choose, without the cognitive, and even physical, drag caused by an unattended Life Stack.

Summary

It is easy to live an inattentive life. I have provided some examples of the associated consequences. Recognising the symptoms, and recognising that the underlying condition might be one of inattention, goes someway to resolving the problem.

So enough of the problem. In the next section, we will explore a framework that will enable us to better allocate our mental resources. Step by step, we can become increasingly attentive. We can then direct our newfound attention capability to where it is most needed in our life. In turn, we will increasingly become the architects of a life well-lived.

A Solution

10 The Unified Attention Model

Overview

In this chapter, I will pull together the concepts and models, we have covered so far in this book. The purpose being to help you a cohesive and coherent framework for understanding the 'buttons and levers' that determine your life journey.

I am also going to weave in some anthropological considerations, so that we can make Nature our partner in striving for a more purposeful life.

We will use a car as an analogy for how you optimise your path to mastery. And by looking at some of the associated journey scenarios, we can better prepare ourselves for our preferred journey.

Health, wealth and happiness

It is a fairly common to hear people wishing others 'health, wealth and happiness'. It is a succinct way of encapsulating the things that most people value. If I had to devise a questionnaire to establish whether you had reached life mastery status, it would comprise three tick-box questions associated with these timeless conditions. Three ticks, and you are one of life's winners.

As you can see from figure 6, the Life Stack, covered in an earlier chapter, maps on quite neatly.

I cannot be sure that these three outcomes are listed in the order they are because our wise ancestors realised their interrelationship, or whether it just runs off the tongue better than, say, wealth, happiness and health.

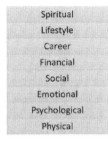

Figure 6 - Health, wealth and happiness mapping

I am proposing, using American psychologist Abraham Maslow as backup, that these are, in reality, a hierarchy of needs. It is unlikely that you will achieve happiness, unless you have health, and some degree of wealth. Wealth in this case being a state where your incomings exceed your outgoings, rather than being in possession of a fleet of Maseratis.

But by way of short digression, famed life coach Anthony Robbins has a very uplifting interpretation of wealth. He highlights that there are many things we take for granted. These include:

- The building of the infrastructure that keeps our towns and cities functioning.
- The production of food that arrives neatly packed in our local store.
- The hard labour associated with the mining of materials needed for the goods we enjoy.
- The parental investment involved in the upbringing of our loved one / mate / 'other half'.
- The joy of connecting with friends and family.

Admittedly, some of these have an economic cost, but it is a small price to pay relative to the time we would take if we had to do it ourselves. Robbins makes a strong connection to the consequent need to have an 'attitude of gratitude'.

When we compare our predicament with those of our ancestors, or those in less developed countries, or those who produced the goods we perhaps take for granted, we are indeed wealthy.

This mindset is conducive to growth. It engenders curiosity, which in turn suppresses the fear response that keeps people trapped in their own personal prison. This goes a little deeper than 'turn that frown upside down', though the intended outcome is no different. But let's return to Maslow.

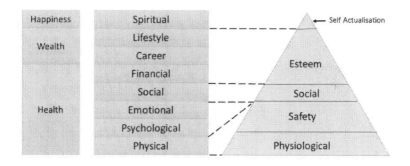

Figure 7 - Mapping to Maslow's Hierarchy of Needs

Maslow's model is very well known. There are plenty of references to it on the web. Very briefly:

- Physiological – The need for air, food, water, shelter and clothing. Sexual instinct is included here.
- Safety – The need to feel safe and to know that this safety will be ongoing. In modern society, this includes economic safety.
- Love/belonging – The need for belonging, as part of a family or a society. As well as intimacy.
- Esteem – The need to be valued by others. This can come through our professional standing or through some other pursuits beyond work.
- Self-actualisation – This is where happiness happens. At this level, we have discovered our true purpose and are now taking action to pursue it.

It is not a crime to dream of happiness when one is struggling to find shelter, but finding shelter must take priority. Maslow lays out a set of steps we need to take in our quest for fulfilment, along with the order in which we take them. His model is well regarded, hence my reference to it.

Maslow doesn't distinguish between how his model maps onto societies that differ in terms of their degree of individualism. My aim is to embrace both an individualistic and collectivistic approach. In other words, I want to show that we can wire our self-interest such that it serves our fellow man as well.

In any case, you can see how the Life Stack maps neatly onto Maslow's Hierarchy of Needs model. Maslow does not appear to explicitly consider the psychological and emotional aspects of our lives, though he is not ignoring them. How you go about addressing your needs and what propels you to do so is implicit in his model.

One might strongly argue that my Financial layer would be better mapped to Maslow's Safety layer. And it would certainly make the mapping neater if I flipped my Social and Financial layers. But I believe that if you do not have the social skills needed to interact with people, you will find it difficult to find / maintain employment, or sell your skills for money. Plus, money is a relatively new concept in mankind's existence, whereas the need to be social is not.

By mapping my Financial layer onto Maslow's Esteem layer, I am highlighting that the ability to 'pay your way' contributes significantly to your self-esteem.

In any case, the Life Stack proposes an order of business in respect of building a purposeful life that broadly aligns with Maslow's model. As I have already mentioned, it would be considered a lack of focus to be ruminating over Pilates versus yoga, if you had no idea where your next meal was coming from.

Survive and thrive

Another way of looking at our hierarchy is as shown in figure 8.

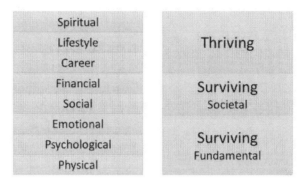

Figure 8 - Surviving and thriving

If you do not have your act together in respect of your physical, psychological and emotional wellbeing, you are in survival mode in its most fundamental sense. No food or shelter, a warped perception of reality, and an inability to manage one's emotions is a cocktail for self-destruction. Moving out of, and staying out of, this zone is a priority.

When your issues reside in this zone, and consequently so does your attention, it can be said that you are in what might be called Fundamental Survival mode.

But even if you have control over these three lowest layers, if you have issues relating to the Social and Financial layers, you are still in what could be termed Societal Survival mode. You might be able to live on scraps, and shelter in disused buildings. And so, you are, from a societal perspective, living 'off the grid'. Even the ascetic Spartans would find it tough to live this way. We are social animals, and even though a death certificate would never have 'death by loneliness' as the reason, even though it could be the underlying cause.

Even if our circumstances were shared by friends and family, without a source of income, we would again be constrained to begging, and perhaps employing more forceful approaches to making ends meet. There may well be a healthy supply of weak and distracted victims-in-waiting, but unless you are a genuine sociopath, preying on others will cause extreme mental disharmony. The cognitive cost of which is to increase the likelihood that you will be sentenced to a life of survival. Or consequently, at some point, sentenced to a life in and out of prison.

Some of us are fortunate enough to have careers. Thus, we can think beyond making ends meet. We can think about buying goods and experiences to add some colour to our existence. We can even buy discretionary time. At this level, we are thriving. We have transcended our existence as an animal, whose day is mainly focused around matters of survival. We can stop to smell the roses, knowing that we do not have to concern ourselves as to whether there will be food on the table, or a roof over our head. Careers, at least traditionally, had an upward trajectory, so it would be fair to say in such circumstances that we are thriving.

The notion of a career in the industrial era sense is disappearing. Increasingly people are pursuing multiple careers, often in parallel. Similarly, we are seeing a shift away from permanent employment. So, the word 'client' will increasingly replace the word 'employer' in matters relating to work. Nonetheless, this will not detract from our upward trajectory. Though this will be less about clambering up management ladders, and more about improving one's ability to create value. The notion of a career may be changing, but our sense of thriving will likely continue.

Careers, at some point, start to create cash surpluses, ie., your incomings exceed your survival outgoings. It is not solely a question of how much you make, but how much you keep. This, of course, is determined by your spending behavior.

Again, we can buy material goods, for example, our own home, or a piece of art. We can buy time, by outsourcing those aspects of our life that are important but difficult / dangerous / mundane / tedious.

We can use our cash surplus to acquire further skills, which in turn bootstraps us further along the path to even greater discretionary financial wealth and time.

For some people, this is living the dream. At one end of the spectrum, you can simply enjoy a life of increasingly nuanced sensations (hedonism). At the other end, you can explore how far you can raise the bar in respect of your human capacity (artist / athlete).

The next level of transcendence, perhaps, is when we reach a point, where our surplus resources are more than just a means to heighten our existence, but as a way in which we can make the world a better place. This might be considered spirituality.

Thus, we are thriving at the highest level, when we are spiritually active. Being kind to others is a common theme. Buying a sandwich and a coffee for a homeless person is good. Curing malaria is even better. Those operating at this level recognise that whilst they are a miracle of nature, the universe was not created solely with them in mind.

Anthropological considerations

Much of what I do involves considering how the digital economy is returning us to our true nature. Whilst the industrial era brought about great advances and economic benefits, it suppressed key critical natural characteristics that, at least in part, define our humanity. These include:

- Mobility.
- Sociality.
- Decision making.
- Creativity.
- Work life integration.
- Productivity.
- Spirituality.

To clarify:

Mobility – From walking around 10 kilometres per day as hunter gatherers, we find ourselves confined to office cubicles of just a few square metres.

Sociality – Because we are now generally paid for our time, we are strongly discouraged from being social in the workplace, 'no talking on the factory line'.

Decision making – As technology placeholders in the 'factory machine', our role is to follow instructions rather than think for ourselves.

Creativity – As per decision making, creativity is frowned upon.

Work life integration – Our private lives are to be kept out of the factory / office. In turn we endeavour to keep work out of our private lives. Prior to the industrial era, work and life were highly integrated.

Productivity – The transition from the agricultural era to the industrial era saw a shift from being judged on our outputs to being judged on the time spent at work. We typically have employment contracts that define our hourly commitments per week, rather than actual deliverables.

Spirituality – As industrial society evolved, we became more confident about our survival, independence, and self-determination. In the latter stages, it has led to a degree of self-centredness that might be considered the antithesis of spirituality.

The factory model has driven these departures from our true nature. Today, the factories are furnished, and referred to as offices. In fairness, this is changing for the better, albeit very slowly.

A meaningful life is thus one where we eschew the repressive practices of the industrial era. As you can see in figure 9, there is a reasonably good mapping of these anthropological drivers to the Life Stack.

Figure 9 - Anthropological drivers mapping

Some comments:

- I have mapped work-life integration onto Career, but one might argue that it is a Lifestyle matter. On the basis that most of us have an issue with work pushing into our lives, rather than the reverse, I have made it a Career layer matter.

- Interestingly there is no mapping onto the Financial layer. Possibly this is because money is a recent concept in respect of mankind's evolution.

- Lifestyle is an industrial era invention. Whilst agricultural era farmers might have developed a cash surplus through smarter farming, and thus been well placed to spend in a discretionary manner, they nonetheless still generally adhered to living the life of a farmer.

- The mapping of creativity to the Emotional layer might seem odd. However, there is a strong correlation between our emotional state and creativity.

The mapping I have portrayed in figure 9, may seem a little arbitrary, or even self-serving, as if I am trying to fabricate a mapping.

My point is less about which anthropological factors impact which Life Stack layers, and more about the reality that if we ignore our natural tendencies, we would be living a suboptimal life, because we would be, in essence, fighting nature. And nature doesn't generally lose.   A life of self-mastery is a life that embraces our anthropological drivers.

The Unified Attention Model

With the Life Stack, we now have a framework to guide us on the prioritisation of the self-improvement tasks / activities we need to undertake in order to reach a point where we are:

- Self-actualised.
- Following our destiny.
- Leading a purposeful life.

In other words, living life like a master.

Now I am going to show you how the elements of this framework are integrated with concepts we have covered, such as willpower, habits, motivation, goals and so on, so that you develop a sense of their contribution to your life journey. I have given it the somewhat grandiose name of the Unified Attention Model. It is my intention to bring together all the key elements that impact the quality of our journey through life.

Imagine that a car represents your mind. The extent to which you can control it will determine where you go in life, and where you will end up. A poorly functioning car will impact the journey, as will overbearing passengers. Let's look at the relevant elements.

The driver

You are the driver of your car. As such you have access to all the controls needed to take you on your desired path.

Any deviations from the path you intend to take, regardless of their source, ultimately require you to make this deviation happen.

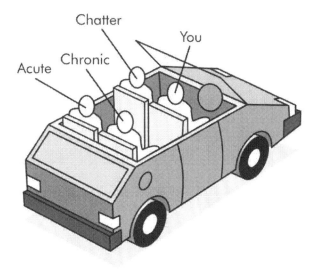

Figure 10 - The Unified Attention Model: Passengers

The passengers

You have three passengers. Sitting next to you is Chatter. She represents the Chatter work zone from the Mental Worktop model I introduced in an earlier chapter. From Chatter, random comments emerge such as:

- "What's down this road?"
- "Are you sure the boot is closed?"
- "Mind that cyclist".

Sometimes her comments and questions are of great significance. However, they are usually hidden within a torrent of distracting commentary. So, Chatter must be managed. When you are driving up a one-track mountain road, negotiating a hairpin with a bottomless ravine to one side, you need to concentrate.

In the backseat, you have the disharmony twins – Chronic and Acute. Acute spends a lot of his time looking out the window. Roadside hoardings seem to trigger impulsive yells from the backseat. For example:

- "I want to buy that."
- "I want to go there."
- "I want to be like that."
- "Chronic hit me!"
- "I am hungry."
- "Squirrel!"

Chronic, on the other hand, is less of a 'live wire'. More jaded, with the weight of the world on her shoulders.

- "Why do our neighbours have a nicer home than us?"
- "My teacher hates me."
- "Why do I have to share my toys with Acute?"
- "I have got so much homework to do, and I haven't even started."
- "Am I really going to die, when I am older?"

The disharmony twins are potentially a large source of distraction. It takes great serenity to negotiate a swaying articulated lorry on the outside edge of the Devil's bypass, whilst the passengers are attacking your attention across all wavelengths.

Passengers have the effect of weighing down the car, thus they increase your rate of fuel consumption. If they are sufficiently large they will start to bear down on the wheels in such a manner that it distorts the steering mechanism.

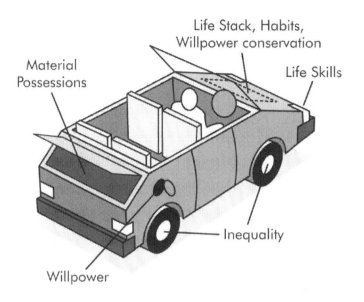

Figure 11 - The Unified Attention Model: The car

The boot

Your material possessions are kept in the boot. The more you have, the fuller it is. The fuller it is, the greater the fuel consumption. Each possession has an ongoing mental 'cost of ownership' charge. This manifests itself in thoughts such as:

- "I wonder if my holiday home in the south of France has been maintained properly by the summer lettings management firm."
- "I had to leave my Ferrari at my parents' home in a not so salubrious neighbourhood. I hope it doesn't get damaged. Or that my parents become a target for burglars."
- "I am not sure that the CFO of my latest start-up is one hundred percent trustworthy."
- "I must remember to take off my Rolex, if we stop at a roadside diner, just in case the cook and the waiter conspire to have a bit of anti-affluence fun."
- Which outfit shall I wear today?

Some will say, what nice problems to have. The key point being that possessions come with an attention tax. And the more you own, the more you are taxed.

The fuel tank

The fuel tank represents your willpower. You get a fresh tank every day. When it runs out, your progress on your life journey stops. Though as we will see next, under certain conditions, it is possible to continue driving without willpower.

The engine

The engine determines the rate of progress you make on your life journey. Fortunately, this is a hybrid engine. The traditional petrol engine is accompanied by an electric battery. If the engine runs smoothly, it will charge the battery as it converts the fuel into motion. Thus, should your fuel / willpower run out, you can still make progress.

This engine comprises eight cylinders. Each cylinder represents each layer of the Life Stack, ie.:

- Physical.
- Psychological.
- Emotional.
- Social
- Financial.
- Career.
- Lifestyle.
- Spiritual.

More specifically these cylinders represent the habits associated with these life concepts. Poor habits in any area impair the engine's functioning, and thus its ability to both make the best use of the fuel and charge the battery.

An absence of any positive habits will require you to be totally reliant on willpower to maintain your path to a purposeful life, because under these circumstances the battery will never charge.

Smart people don't have bigger engines. They simply have better habits, and are thus not as reliant on willpower as those seemingly 'not so smart' people. The same may be said in respect of poor and rich people. And happy and sad people.

The turbo charger

The turbo charger enables us to gain greater fuel economy. The turbo charger comprises the following elements:

- Motivation.
- Energy.
- Positivity.
- Habits of mind.
- Goals.
- Kindness.
- Values.

Our willpower consumption is significantly reduced if we can capitalise on these elements. They keep us mentally strong throughout the day because they enable us to stretch our willpower such that it is still available to us late in the day, every day.

The wheels

I am bundling the car wheel and the steering wheel together. They are of course critical to the journey. Unfortunately, not everyone is equipped with the same set of wheels. Those who have grown up in affluent / loving environments will have a power-assisted steering wheel, along with top of the range new tyres. Others, despite being equal in every other respect, must work harder to steer their car. Their wheels will be less inflated and more worn.

This will result in greater fuel consumption, and less margin for error, if the car gets into difficulty, on say an icy patch. Some people, simply need to work harder than others to reach their goals. Fair or unfair, that is the way it currently is. Determined individuals will turn this inequality into positive energy, rather than give up before even trying. The steering wheel can also be considered as representing our intention. With clear intention, we will steer purposely.

The Lights

See 'Air Conditioning, lights and wipers' section, below.

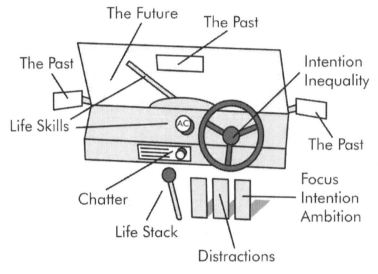

Figure 12 - The Unified Attention Model: Driver interface

Windscreen

The windscreen shows us what lies ahead. As such, it represents our future, particularly our near future. Whilst it is important to have a destination in mind, it is what happens next that has the biggest impact on your life.

In the digital age, given the ever-increasing volatility and uncertainty, it makes sense to devote the bulk of your attention to what is happening now, because the future is likely to play out in ways we could never have anticipated.

The mirrors

The mirrors are important in respect of detecting potential hazards, eg., an upcoming motorcyclist, as you are about to take a corner. But if you spend too much time looking backwards, you will not see what lies ahead. This could lead to an accident, but it might also blind you to the opportunities and threats in front of you. Too much focus on where you have been, will negatively impact your attention in respect of where you need to go, and how you are going to get there.

Air conditioning, lights and wipers

Through the windscreen, we can see the road ahead, along with the directional signage. Life being life, not every part of the journey is coated with sunshine. The dark, the elements, including fog, all impair our vision. Thus, we need to call upon our wipers and lights. But they draw upon our battery reserves. As does the need to use the heater / climate control. Using these appliances has an energy cost. We need to ensure that our engine is as efficient as it can be to ensure that their usage does not ultimately cause us to stall. As such, these car elements can be thought of as energy-consuming life skills / tools. For example, interpersonal skills will enable us to deal with people who might otherwise try to lead us away from our path.

Steering Wheel

See 'The wheels' section, above.

The radio

As far as your attention is concerned, the radio is another passenger drawing your attention away from the road. But every now and again, like Chatter, it serves up valuable insight. Usually in the form of a traffic alert. Chatter and the radio might both be considered as conduits to the wisdom contained in our unconscious. In the perfect scenario, we would tune both our radio and Chatter to serve up our unconscious wisdom 'straight' rather than on a bed of distracting irrelevance.

The gears

This is a manual / stick - drive car. It has eight gears. The gears represent the life concepts, with first gear representing the Physical layer and eighth gear representing the Spiritual layer.

If you are currently at a stage in life where your focus is on resolving physiological issues, you will need to drive in first gear. If these have been resolved and you have good associated habits in place, you can step up to second gear. And so on. The higher the gear, the faster you can travel.

If you attempt to drive in a higher gear than is appropriate for the conditions, ie., your current life status, then the car will consume fuel inefficiently, or may even stall. Those of us struggling with, say, emotional issues (layer three), will be overtaken by those who have systematically worked through, say, the first six lifestyle layers and are now working on enhancing their lifestyle.

The accelerator

The extent to which you are focused will determine the confidence you have in pursuing a particular path. Your ambition, and thus your intention, will compel you to speed up the journey. Thus focus, ambition and intention all have a bearing on the extent to which you try to accelerate your journey. The accelerator thus represents these three very positive characteristics.

But too much acceleration, particularly when you are stuck in the lower gears, will simply burn fuel inefficiently. Focus, ambition and intention, again, are important to your life path. But there is a risk in that by travelling too fast, you:

- Miss out on what life has to offer beyond your blinkered focus.
- Miss the turn that will lead you to your preferred destiny.

The brakes

Car brakes have evolved to enable us to go faster, rather than to simply bring us to a halt. Their increased sensitivity enables us to travel at very high speeds with the knowledge that we can slow down in a graceful manner, when required.

Smart drivers tend to minimise their use of the brakes, because it squanders fuel. Smart drivers never travel so fast that they will need to apply their brakes unnecessarily.

The digital economy with its myriad of distractions causes us to brake unnecessarily, as we:

- 'Rubber neck' at the misfortune of others (eg., reality TV).
- Get entranced by the billboards (eg., commercial attention grabbers) that seem to (and will eventually) tailor their message to trigger our primal urges.

ooOOoo

I appreciate that the notion of a car with a driver is fast becoming an outmoded model, given the imminent arrival of driverless cars. Such next generation cars may be an indicator of us slipping into a new 'anthropological low' in respect of surrendering our attention.

Or it could be that we are fast approaching a new 'humanity high'. Driverless cars will eliminate stress, accidents and wasted time. Thus, freeing us up to use our reclaimed cognitive capacity for better things. Or maybe such gains will just dissipate through 'policing' the twins and keeping up with your partner's random comment generation.

Time will tell.

Here is a summary of the elements of my Unified Attention Model framework:

Element	Symbolising
Accelerator	Focus, ambition, intention
Air conditioning	Life skills
Boot / Trunk	Material possessions
Brakes	Distractions
Cylinders	The Life Stack
Driver	You!
Engine	Habits
Fuel tank	Willpower
Gears	The Life Stack
Lights	Life skills
Mirrors	The past
Passengers	Chatter. Acute and Chronic disharmony
Radio	Chatter
Steering wheel	Intention and inequality
Turbocharger	Willpower conservation
Wheels	Inequality
Windscreen	The future
Wipers	Life skills

Figure 13 - The Unified Attention Model elements

Car scenarios

To provide some clarity on the car analogy, let's look at some scenarios.

Perfect

In an ideal world, we would have no distractions, enabling us to focus our attention on living a purposeful life. Every action we took strengthened our resolve and reinforced our excellent habits.

In the real world, we do have distractions, some of which we are the source. In the digital world, the availability and accessibility of these distractions has never been easier.

So, in this perfect scenario:

The twins, Acute and Chronic, are no longer in the car. If it helps, you can imagine abandoning them at a service station. But I appreciate this may cause alarm, particularly for bookshop visitors who happen to open the book on this page.

Your partner, Chatter, has turned into a philosopher. Her utterances are condensed wisdom. She is sensitive to your need to concentrate when the conditions are difficult. She also acts as an extra set of senses in terms of looking out for threats and opportunities on your journey.

The car engine purrs like a cat, because the cylinders are working at maximum efficiency thanks to the carefully cultivated habits you have ingrained across all aspects of your life. Should a disaster strike, for example, the passing away of a loved one, your car battery is fully charged. It is unlikely that even under the worst circumstances, you will be tempted to revert to your former unconstructive behaviour.

Your boot is empty. Why have a holiday home that obliges you to go to the same place every year, and to worry about it for the rest of the year? Belongings are now utility services.

You acquire / hire them when you desire them, and stop paying when you have had your fill. You are no longer locked into debt, or last year's model. Your cash flow is like the surface of a tranquil pond, rather than a metaphor for the perfect storm.

You are flying along in eighth gear, because you are largely able to focus on spiritual matters such as addressing global poverty.

You have a zest for living, and that is reflected in your positivity, energy, motivation and socially-focused goals. Your kindness leaves a comet's tail of goodwill, wherever you go. Bar room brawls stop and the piano player resumes when you enter the saloon. Not because you have a reputation as a competent assassin, but simply by your benevolent presence. You barely need to call on your willpower, and so you do not lose sight of your goals as the day progresses.

Using your mirrors, evokes emotions, sadness associated with long deceased friends, and joyfulness as you recall your times together. These emotions are given their due attention, before your eyes are back on the road ahead.

You barely need to touch the brakes, because you are fully aware of the road conditions. You capitalise on the natural geography of the road to apply the accelerator only when it is needed. Your journey feels like a pleasant trip down a nursery slope at a ski resort. The incline is just about enough to entrust gravity to take care of momentum.

In this, state you would find it very difficult to move off track to what might be considered a wasted life.

Worst case

Your mind is a jalopy. Any second, your car could fall apart. The twins are primarily systems for turning food into fat and noise. Their erratic and occasionally 'off the scale' emotional behaviour provides the serenity you might associate with dodging sniper fire whilst making your way hurriedly across a freshly-cultivated mine field.

Your physically and emotionally overbearing partner considers herself the captain of the ship, and is spewing edicts as to where you should head. The term 'sat nag' comes to mind. But, of course, you wouldn't say that to her face, and so must simmer in a pool of your own resentment.

Your attempts to move out of first gear cause the engine to overheat, and occasionally stall. You look at the fuel gauge. In shock, you assume that there must be a fuel leak. The turbo function does not kick in on low gears, so it is not contributing to your journey.

From time to time you crash, mainly because you spend disproportionately large periods of time gazing into the mirrors. "If only I could go back in time and make better decisions". Or worse, some previous, never to be resolved, trauma still looms large in your everyday thoughts.

Being in a constant state of distraction, your journey comprises endless detours with excessive use of the accelerator and brakes. Your journey feels like a surreal maze, where every junction is free of signs, and every junction offers you a choice of ever steeper paths.

It's getting dark and it's raining full pelt. Your battery appears to be flat, so the lights and wipers are only working intermittently. You dare not stop for a break, because you fear you will not be able to restart the car.

Your boot is full of acquisitions. Many of which are depreciating in value. And some of which you are still paying for. Locked into buyer-unfriendly contracts, you cannot unburden yourself of these draining financial commitments without taking an even bigger financial hit. You reflect on what made you buy this 'stuff'.

There appears to be no way out of this nightmare. It is no wonder people contemplate crashing the car, so to speak, and being done with it.

Most likely

It is more likely that you sit somewhere in between these two scenarios. Each of these have their own 'event horizon'. If you were to cross the associated event horizon you have very little chance of escape. For the worst-case scenario, this might be considered the poverty line. For the best-case scenario, this is the abundance line. These lines are not just defined in financial terms. These lines represent the overall status of our lives.

However, financial is as good a proxy as any. As financial poverty is more recognisable in others than say career or psychological poverty.

Those below the poverty line are truly trapped. Even where ladders of escape do exist, they do not have the mental wherewithal to act, or even associate the ladder with an escape route. Sometimes their environment discourages their use of the ladders. In some cases, it might even be the state, preferring to corral the economically-negative, for ease of 'management'.

In the best-case scenario, you cross the event horizon line, when you have created the conditions where it would require great effort to screw up your life. For example, you have built a financial base comprising low risk instruments that throw off enough interest for you to enjoy financial freedom without having to work. And to top it all, this financial base requires no management.

Living life between the two event horizons manifests itself in different ways. For example:

- You wade through life, on a day to day basis, looking forward to that drink in the evening, before you get some sleep and hop back on the hamster wheel the next day. You are so caught up in pursuing your job, or raising children, that there is no time to reflect on your broader goals and personal development.

- You are very much interested in self-development. However, whilst you have the energy to read the literature and visit the websites, you do not have the energy to absorb your findings into your life. You become a person who can talk a good life-game.
- You are seemingly doing well at work, but your mental and physical health is crumbling, because you do not have good habit foundations in respect of the 'lower layers' of your life. You are heading for some form of burnout.
- You spend a lot of your time planning and setting goals. You act, but lack the will to achieve your goals when either your resolve is tested or another shinier goal presents itself to you.
- You are generally happy to follow the path of least resistance. Sometimes you agree to things that make you feel uncomfortable, or even, on reflection, violate your principles.
- Success, in whatever arena, seems to come more easily to others. You feel you are missing a key part of the puzzle. In your determination to find out what is missing, you become hyper-suggestive to even the most superficial and unfounded advice.

The good news, if you operate in this zone, is that fundamental survival is not an issue for you. The bad news is that you have this niggling sense that you are not playing the game of life very well. Mainly because it is true.

But that is only an issue if you seek to live a purposeful life.

Greater discretionary thinking

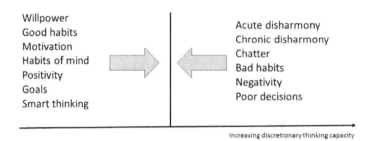

Willpower	Acute disharmony
Good habits	Chronic disharmony
Motivation	Chatter
Habits of mind	Bad habits
Positivity	Negativity
Goals	Poor decisions
Smart thinking	

Increasing discretionary thinking capacity

Figure 14 - The forces acting on discretionary thinking

In my view, your chances of living a purposeful life, which can be seasoned with, for example, financial, sporting, and career success, is greatly increased if you have more discretionary mental capacity. Think back to the earlier chapter, where I introduced the Mental Worktop conceptual model.

With greater discretionary mental capacity comes better decisions in respect of your life journey. Most of us make bad decisions in respect of the food we eat, the career choices we make, and so on, because emotional or environmental disharmony has driven / conditioned our behaviour.

There is a constant battle raging between the attention thieves and our willpower. At some point during each day, the thieves win and your brain becomes occupied by enemy forces. These enemy forces set up bad habits to increase the need to utilise your willpower, and so make their occupation easier, when the battle resumes tomorrow.

We in turn must cultivate good habits to enable our willpower to go further. Desire, energy, positivity and habits of mind, ie., the way we cultivate good habits, work with our good habits to fight back the attention grabbers.

Keep in mind that not everything that diverts our attention is bad in respect of being a 'mental pollutant'. I want to be startled by the scorpion sitting inside my shoe, before I put it on. Your baby's cry for a nappy change is to be heeded. As does the cry of your boss at work. But missing a potentially life-enhancing job interview, because you missed the bus, because your private online pornography fest overran is a serious, and life degrading, problem.

When your ability to think smartly is impaired, you are no longer in full ownership of your mind. Improving your discretionary thinking capacity can be considered a personal movement to reclaim your mind, and, in turn, your life.

Summary

In this chapter, we have brought together the Life Stack, the Mental Worktop and the Unified Attention Model. We have used Maslow's Hierarchy of Needs, as a further 'life' reference point.

The Unified Attention Model framework helps us understand the factors involved in our life journey and their contribution, or otherwise, to our progress. Many of us place too much emphasis on willpower. Failures of willpower are seen as failures of character, whereas they are really failure of habits in what might be a very unsupportive environment.

Good habits are critical to life mastery. My aim in writing this book is to help you understand that habits cannot be considered in isolation of the wider factors that determine the quality of our lives. But by understanding these wider factors, you will be better placed to acquire good habits. And to maintain them through a positive attitude and a strong desire. Understanding the dynamics of attention is thus important to getting the best from your time on Earth.

11 Planning An Attentive Life

Overview

It is now time to take what we have covered so far and turn it into action. Planning your life is not a trivial exercise. Creating a template that is applicable to everyone is even less so.

Having just covered the issues of living an inattentive life, it should come as no surprise that attention is the key ingredient to harnessing the models presented in this book.

Simplicity is a key principle in respect of attention management, and the pursuit of mastery. It would be ironic if your plan for a more attentive life, through its complexity, led to it being the largest daily consumer of your cognitive capacity.

Before we start the planning process, we need to establish where best we focus our planning efforts. This requires self-calibration.

Calibration

The following calibration exercise will help you decide on where your life needs attention. Again, if you have improvement opportunities at more than one level, you are advised to build your corrective plan around the lowest layer. Once addressed, you can move to the next level up, and so on.

Each lifestyle layer has three statements. Score each question as follows:

Response	Score
Very true.	5
Some truth in this	3
Untrue	0

Physical

1. You worry about having a roof over your head.
2. You live in an unsafe environment.
3. You feel unhealthy.

Psychological

1. You have difficulty making decisions.
2. You spend most of your time in your head, rather than engaging with the world.
3. Your thoughts often spiral into negativity directed at either yourself or others.

Emotional

1. You often respond inappropriately to mild environmental triggers.
2. You have one or more destructive habits.
3. You require high stimulation to feel anything.

Social

1. You rarely concern yourself with how others might see a situation.
2. You do not rely on anyone for anything.
3. You try to avoid situations where you may have to engage with people you have never met.

Financial

1. You worry about your finances.
2. You are unable to think beyond the next pay check in terms of financial matters.
3. Your outgoings exceed your incomings.

Career

1. You have a job rather than a career.
2. Your progression has stalled.
3. Your career is about to be disrupted by, for example, new technology, or people who are at least as productive as you, but significantly cheaper.

Lifestyle

1. You have no discretionary time to pursue interests beyond your professional life.
2. Your lifestyle is more 'cautionary tale' than inspirational.
3. There is little in your lifestyle that defines your preferred identity.

Spiritual

1. You don't particularly like yourself.
2. You are indifferent to the plight of humanity.
3. You rarely reflect on your relationship with the cosmos.

Evaluation

For each Life Stack layer, add together the scores from each question. For each layer, your resultant score should lie between zero and fifteen. So, a score of zero would suggest there is no work to be done. Conversely, a score of 15 would suggest the opposite is true.

A score above zero suggests that some work is required. Even if you score three for Physical and fifteen for each of the remaining seven layers, you must reduce your Physical score to zero as a priority. It might appear that there are some easy wins in the higher layers, but you are best served by devoting your limited resources to addressing the lowest non-zero scoring layer.

You might feel that despite scoring well in each Life Stack layer, you have a sense that there is more you need to do. That's fine. This is a very rough and ready calibration tool. If you score 15 for the Physical layer, but feel that there is more work to be done, in say sexual health, then address that issue, before moving up the stack. Of course, if reading this book has highlighted that certain aspects of your life can be changed with approximately zero effort, then by all means make the changes. However, you only have so much willpower, so I want that to be applied as deeply into your life's foundations as is possible.

Congratulations, if the sum total of all your scores across the eight layers is zero. You can focus on living life to the full. Nonetheless, you need to be vigilant to ensure you don't slip. Or more positively, you can continue to take opportunities to strengthen the great habits that are serving you so well. Much like a master craftsman, martial artist or chess player, the journey never stops.

If all layers score fifteen then, again, you must focus your attention on the lowest layer. Aspiring to a grand total score of zero will seem impossible at this stage. However, by taking a bottom up approach to getting your life in order, you will start to see positive changes automatically occurring further up the stack. Basically, your progress will be exponential rather than linear. But only if you address the lowest layer first.

Many of us choose to ignore our physical, psychological, emotional and social health to focus on the layers that society has perhaps deemed more important. Therefore, from time to time, we see people who appear to have it all have some sort of breakdown. For one reason or another, they have not developed mature habits in these lower layers, and so their life was built on very shaky foundations.

The plan

Firstly, we need to define what living a purposeful life means. Only once we have clarity on this, can we then decide on the actions that will take us towards this goal.

It is likely that your definition of a purposeful life may vary in its grandness, depending on your Life Stack profile. If finding food and shelter are a priority for you, then these represent your purpose. If, on top of that, you have a family to look after, then your purpose will likely extend to embracing their needs. Having surmounted such a dire predicament, you might reset your purpose to ensuring that, globally, no other human need suffer the way you have. So, our purpose can evolve as we evolve.

At the other extreme, you may have no financial worries, and you are doing great things to help others locally, nationally and globally. However, you are undermining your capability through unresolved emotional issues that are leading to poor dietary behaviours, which in turn leave you feeling disinclined to look after yourself physically. Consequently, the foundations on which your impressive life rests are crumbling. Once the foundations fail, your life will implode. So, whilst in this case, by anyone's measure, you already have a lofty purpose, your primary purpose must be to get your emotional issues resolved.

So, even though we have eight Life Stack layers to address, at any given time, there will be one that delivers the best return on attention invested / action taken. Having completed the Calibration exercise earlier on in this chapter, if you have improvement opportunities at multiple layers, then, again, you are advised to focus on the lowest of those layers. Having identified the layer requiring critical attention in respect of your life, you are advised to do the following:

Define a goal such that its attainment enables us to consider the layer in question to be in full repair. In fact, the goal might simply be eg., Physical life repaired. At first, this might seem vague. But if we break it down into milestones, it becomes more actionable.

In the case of the Physical layer, these might include:

- Permanent and suitably secure shelter found.
- Healthy dietary habits in place.
- Healthy sleeping habit in place.
- Moderate exercise regime in place.

Associated with each milestone, there will be a set of sub goals. For example:

- Eliminate biscuits, cakes and confectionary from my diet.
- Get seven and a half hours sleep every night.
- Walk at least 5 miles per day.

Each of these may involve a further set of actions. For example:

- Stop buying biscuits.
- Go to bed before 11pm.
- Take the dog for two extended walks per day.

Some of these actions are 'one off' in nature, whilst some may be 'habits in the making'.

The milestones, sub goals and actions are for you to decide. The examples above may not apply to your situation. It is generally best to seek professional advice in respect to all aspects of your life. Doctors, financial advisers and career coaches are examples of professionals who will be able to help you tailor your actions to your circumstances. Not all of us will be able to pay for such services, therefore it is imperative that societies provide appropriate support. Sometimes, our assumptions underpinning what needs to be done may be 'off the mark'. Without realising it, we may find that we are fixing a symptom rather than the underlying problem. So again, professional advice should be sought, particularly if the issues you need to address are extreme. But it may be that you know what needs to be done, but simply lack motivation.

Motivation

There are two ways to improve motivation. The first is to lay out the vision of what your life will be like, if you were to take the best course of action; no more worries about making ends meet, or feeling more attractive would be examples.

Alternatively, you can imagine what life would be like if you took the worst course of action; your children get taken from you, or you are housebound and unable to dress yourself.

I have presented these examples like a shopping list, factual and devoid of emotion. To really marshal your emotions to propel you in your preferred direction, you need to imagine these outcomes as if they were real. Invoke all your emotions. Imagine what failure or success look like, smell like, feel like, sound like, and taste like. Your ability to create a repulsive negative image, or a compelling positive one, will determine the extent to which you will turbo charge your commitment to change.

You can use both positive and negative approaches. Keep in mind that it has been shown that we are more motivated by avoiding pain than by acquiring pleasure.

I recommend you run the scenarios in your head at least daily until you get to a point where the desired behaviour does not require willpower to induce action. If the plan is to lose weight, but you are still struggling to decide whether to go for a jog or slump on the settee with an industrial-sized bag of nachos, then you need to deepen the intensity of the visualisations and continue with this exercise.

If change is required in respect of your weight, then perhaps imagine yourself in a coffin that looks more like a fragile freight container. One that falls apart at a critical point during your funeral.

Developing a sense of purpose in respect of addressing your target issue is important. 'I am acting because I do not want to die early', or 'I do not want to hand back the keys of my Porsche', will provide some degree of motivation.

We can ramp up the intensity of our scenarios by involving others in our sense of purpose. Both in terms of the implications for them, and by making them aware of your improvement plan.

In respect of those closest to us, we can spice up our visualisations by including, for example the humiliation they will endure because of your 'coffin failure'. Or how those around you will likely act because they were inspired by your action.

By making those around us aware of our intentions, we are in effect entering a social contract. The fear of having to tell others we have 'given up' impacts us deeply, given we are social animals. So, this will certainly help with our motivation.

Mentally playing out scenarios will help motivation. Writing out the scenarios, perhaps nightly, as well as recording and repeatedly listening to the scenarios will deepen the impact. Meeting people who are living your potential futures (a successful business woman, or a dying patient in an emphysema ward) will have a galvanising effect.

If money is no object, hire one or more large billboards / display spaces you typically encounter on a daily basis, and work with a world class creative agency to produce some hard-hitting content designed to keep you on track. Include your name in the creative output to give your goal some social oomph. But do be clear with the agency in respect of what constitutes a successful campaign.

Summary

To progress towards a meaningful life, we need to prioritise where our attention is directed. The calibration exercise in this chapter should help. Knowing that we have a framework for the bigger picture, we can direct our energies to addressing the most critical layer in the Life Stack, knowing that we will address the wider issues in due course.

It might be a good idea to run the calibration exercise on a periodic basis. Perhaps at year-end, when you are contemplating your goals, and resolutions, for the year ahead. It will help you to see whether you are steering towards or away from life mastery.

Next up, we will look at some implementable approaches we can take to accelerate our progress towards self-mastery.

12 Life Tools – Physical

Overview

You now have a greater sense of where you need to place your attention. Again, you need to focus on the lowest layer first. This and the following seven chapters, one for each Life Stack layer, will provide you with some simple techniques to help you live a more attentive life.

Even where you have one or more layers under control, you might still find the associated chapters beneficial in refining your maintenance approach.

Invariably the tools / advice that I present for a given layer are also directly / indirectly valuable in respect of the higher layers of the Life Stack. In this respect, the lower layer tools will deliver the greatest returns on your investment in their usage.

Physical tools

The Physical layer is the foundation of everything in your life. You may be living the dream as a Silicon Valley billionaire, but if you are disregarding the Physical layer, then the enjoyment of your success might literally be short lived.

Safety

Our environment has changed drastically over the last few thousand years, even though we are still physically wired to be hunter gatherers. The threats have changed, but there are still threats, particularly if you are homeless. Prevention is always better than cure. So being attentive to your environment is important.

I practise a variety of martial arts. Over the years, I have studied seven disciplines, and currently 'focus' on three. I also enjoy running, and it's also my primary form of self-defence. I have been known to boast that 'brave men run in my family'. But the reality is that martial arts cultivate an unwarranted sense of confidence when it comes to real-world street situations. More often than not, they do not prepare you for the abject fear, and associated digestive system 'fall-out'. Violence is very difficult to simulate in a well-lit club environment furnished with a cushioned-floor. Even where the club has a large membership, you need to avoid hospitalising your fellow practitioners, if only to preserve membership fee cashflow.

Attentiveness means, for example, that you can anticipate trouble ahead. You have detected the agitated bunch of youths shouting from a distance. Or should you find yourself in a dimly lit street, you need to have an expectancy mindset that a threat may be imminent.

A way of managing your attention is to label your environment according to the threat level. The British Government uses the following:

- Normal – An attack is unlikely.
- Heightened – An attack is possible.
- Exceptional – An attack is likely.

From a personal safety point of view, Normal means that we can relax, but we still need to be vigilant. Heightened means 'wear your running shoes'. Exceptional means 'start running'.

Of course, running is not always an option, particularly if you are infirm or are with infirm friends or family members. It's always fascinating to observe humanity's inbuilt preservation system at work, particularly when you see your friends and family sprint off into the horizon, as you reflect on your sprained ankle, and imminent beating. Do keep in mind that it is likely that you have come from a long line of 'cowards'. Brave people are those that decided to eat that bitter tasting plant, or 'square up' to that sabre tooth tiger. Those of us whose ancestors sidestepped, or reversed rapidly, from conflict went on to live long enough to procreate. Being smart trumps being brave.

Whilst it is good to know that you can look after your loved ones financially, it is also good to know you can look after them in physical threat situations too, where running is not an option.

Military personnel are generally known to be able to look after themselves. An anti-aircraft launcher, or even a fighter aircraft, is a confidence booster, for sure. But even in hand to hand combat, they can generally take care of business.

But military personnel are generally not trained as martial artists. They are trained in a small number of bare hand and weapons techniques (eg., Knife or bottle). These techniques are simple, do not require fine motor control, nor an extensive warm-up before they can be executed. They are short, sharp and effective.

I encourage you to seek out self-defence classes (not martial arts classes), and to attend a course in respect of your physical safety. Better that you have ten effective techniques built into your muscle memory, than know hundreds which you can produce if your memory doesn't play up, and you are not expected to get them right first time, keeping in mind that attackers are not generally as patient in this respect as a fellow club member. Also, courses that teach you how to improvise in terms of weaponry are valuable. Car keys, coins, pens and perfume applicators can be used to great effect.

Remember that street fighters do not stop applying their technique when you 'tap'. They do not understand the concept of 'illegal moves'. And whilst it may not initially seem like it, they often operate in packs.

Look for self-defence training that regards defence techniques as a subset of the skills you need to possess. The ability to detect the attacker's motive, deescalate the situation, and overcome the natural freeze that can occur when surprised in a life-threatening manner need to be part of the programme. I found that the book, Meditations on Violence, by Rory Miller, to be quite sobering in this respect.

Keep in mind that poor safety management can also have career consequences. Being unable to type for several months because the mugger broke your arm is an acute example.

But a 'low level' chronic concern in respect of safety will have a pernicious impact on your health. If you live in an unsafe neighbourhood, you will be constantly on 'high alert', primed for a response to an attack. This has a corrosive impact on your cognitive capacity; in effect, making you less bright than you actually are.

As we transition into the digital age, our ability to be creative is one of the key capabilities that give us an edge on technology (for now at least). Being creative requires a soft (panoramic) attentiveness rather than a laser (where is the predator) focus. Thus, if we feel unsafe we are less likely to be able to deliver creativity-fuelled value.

Workplace design needs to embrace this reality too.

Sleep

Beyond safety, sleep ranks highly in respect of our physical wellbeing. Whilst everyone, without exception, is a practitioner, there are many of us who do so inefficiently.

The truth is, we don't really understand sleep. We are not even sure that the idea of getting, say, seven hours sleep per night is the optimal approach. Our current sleep patterns have been designed by the industrial era factory owners, for their convenience.

In any case, it is a sign that you are doing it wrong, if you wake up feeling anything other than alert. I would rate sleep as more important than nutrition and hydration, on the basis that in the absence of all three, it would be the absence of sleep that results in your death.

We have a sense that sleep plays a key role in our physical maintenance and our mental health. So, in the absence of being under attack, quality sleep becomes our top priority.

A few suggestions in respect of maximising the quality of your sleep:

- Reduce the ambient lighting in your environment in the hour before you go to bed.
- Desist in engaging with electronic devices, including TV, in that hour.
- Avoid eating in the two to three hours prior to going to bed.
  - Though there is evidence that eating a small amount prior to going to bed, aids quality sleep.
- Stimulate a drop in body temperature by keeping the bedroom cool and / or by having a warm shower or bath before going to bed. The idea is not to freeze in bed, but to trigger your body's sleep mechanisms by cultivating the temperature decline.

As with all the recommendations in this book, you are advised to seek professional advice in respect of your own circumstances.

Nutrition

Nutrition, including hydration, is critical to our physical wellbeing. Malnutrition kills millions of people each year. Over 3 million children per year aged under five die this way.

Most of us in the developed world do not run the risk of death by malnutrition. But we do run the risk of living a fuzzy-thinking, slightly arthritic sub-optimal life because we are failing to manage our nutrition.

Much of this is tied into emotional issues that trigger self-medication in the form of food engineered to be highly addictive (ie., high in fat, sugar and salt).

In respect of our physical wellbeing, my advice would be to focus less on sticking to a diet, or beating yourself up when your willpower caves into the come-hither allure of a double choc chip muffin. Better to focus on ensuring that in the course of the day you have eaten a significant percentage of food that is recognisable as food. By that I mean that the food you are about to consume is recognisable, rather than embedded in some form of industrial food science flat-pack meal.

The underlying philosophy being that if you start to eat more good food than bad food, your inclination for the good food will increase, and vice versa for the bad food. Set yourself up to succeed, by for example, not putting a muffin on each corner of your desk every morning.

I suggest that you simply monitor the number of items you eat that are either raw or are still recognisable after being cooked. You might impress others by counting the number of peas you have eaten, but portions would be a better measure. You decide what constitutes a portion. Simply aim to grow the number of natural portions over time.

My approach may sound vegetarian, or even vegan. This is not the intention. Consult with a medical specialist, or your spiritual guide, for what you can and cannot eat.

You should be aware that at least one generation of people living today have been brainwashed into believing that fat is bad and carbohydrates are good. Whilst there are bad fats, fat is an essential element of our diet. And whilst we need carbs for energy, we can acquire them from non-starch sources. The current thinking is not on eliminating potatoes, bananas, pasta and cereals from our diets, but on demoting their nutritional importance, and thus the volume consumed.

Exercise

I have lived most of my life under the smug assumption that just because I exercise, approximately every day, that I have bought myself a ticket for the extended life tour. Mankind was not designed for one intense bout of activity, where the rest of the day involved being glued to a chair, leaning over an electronic device. Our hunter gatherer ancestors, physiologically us, walked between ten to fifteen kilometres every day. In contrast, as mentioned, many people in the modern world spend the bulk of their time in a cubicle of a few square metres.

Sitting is the new smoking. So, my regime of intensive exercise topped and tailed by a sedentary life, is not the way forward. Thus, we need to incorporate more activity throughout our working day.

I suggest that after every meal you go for a short brisk walk of ten to twenty minutes. It will help digestion, and will spread physical activity more evenly across the day. Certainly, getting off the train / bus earlier and walking more of your commute helps as well, though not if you attempt to do this when the vehicle is moving, or if the train only stops at major cities. Using stairs, rather than lifts and elevators, clocks up the mileage. Pedometers and their digital successors, wearable health bands, are very helpful in keeping track of your progress.

I endeavour to not sit at my desk for more than an hour. So periodically, I get up and walk purposefully, in no particular direction, around the house. This is quite confusing for my dog, who believes a walk is imminent, as I accelerate towards the door. Instead of opening the door, I seem to push off it like a competitive indoor pool swimmer, and accelerate in the opposite direction. The reactions are equally bemusing when my behaviour draws the attention of other Starbucks' customers.

The perfect scenario would be that you and your family chase down some wild beast over a period of a few hours. But it is unlikely that the zoo authorities would condone this behaviour, despite your anthropological reasoning.

Health and fitness specialists also recommend that we work on our:

- Flexibility.
- Mobility.
- Strength.
- Power.
- Endurance.

There is a great focus on developing our core muscles. These in effect stop our top-half flapping about when we use our lower half when, for example, running.

This is all good stuff. And particularly important if you are pursuing physical goals, for example, in respect of sport. My focus here is to encourage everybody to have a base level of fitness brought about by regular movement that does not necessarily require any apparel transitions.

When you develop a sense of vitality in your day to day life, you will know that you have your Physical layer under control. If you want to take up ultra-distance running or power lifting, that is a lifestyle decision, rather than one based on your physical needs.

Though keep in mind that we are wired to be hunter gatherers, so we need to incorporate both speed and resistance work into our lifestyle, whether we are an Olympian, or a call centre operator.

On reflection

It would be easy to forget that we are physical beings. Modern conveniences have relieved many of us of physical toil. In some countries, there are no pavements, the expectation being that you will travel everywhere by car. The Internet is causing some of us to spend more time in our virtual life than in our physical life.

For most of humanity's existence, we have relied on our physicality. This 'recent' de-physicalisation of our existence is not in accord with our true nature.

Job number one for all of us is to ensure we have good physical health.

13 Life Tools – Psychological

Overview

Psychological wellness runs a close second to physical wellness. Poor decisions at critical life junctures will lead to a poor life. Similarly, a view of the world that is decoupled from reality leads, at the very least, to a bemused existence.

In this chapter, I provide some guidelines for better psychological health. The presumption is that you are already in reasonable psychological health, but need some fine-tuning for life optimisation purposes. As always, you are advised to seek professional help as a priority, if your psychological health, or any other aspect of your wellbeing, requires it.

Psychological tools

Poor outcomes are an indicator that your decision making is flawed. Poor processes and poor habits also yield poor outcomes. Arriving at the airport without your passport, is not so much an act of poor decision making, but that your travel preparation methodology is flawed. Similarly, if you miss opportunities because you are decoupled from reality, eg., dwelling on the past, then you again have some work to do in respect of taming your own mind such that it works for you.

Irrational negative thoughts directed against you and others, similarly come from a poorly managed mind. Poor physical health will also lead to an 'under-performing' mind. However, every other aspect of your life, including your physical health will be determined by the extent to which you have addressed this layer of the Life Stack.

Getting this wrong will lead to stress and 'overwhelm'. These in turn will cloud your perception of reality. A psychological tailspin will follow.

Willpower and habits

Firstly, take every opportunity to protect your willpower. You have a limited supply, and will drain it if you squander it on trivial decision making. Once drained, it is likely that all subsequent decision making for the rest of the day will be counterproductive to living a meaningful life. That's why impulsive online shopping behaviour happens in the evening and not in the morning.

Consider making a list of all the decisions you make each day, and establish whether some of them can be eliminated. Former President Obama circumvents 'clothing decision anxiety' by wearing the same combination of clothes every day. As did Steve Jobs.

Better to plan your day the night before. That way, you don't squander prime time thinking capacity each morning on what is an administrative task. Make this a habit, ie., hand it over to your unconscious to manage. You have probably done this already in respect of brushing your teeth.

What is considered an unnecessary decision can be subjective. Some may regard deciding what to wear as a joyful consequence of having a refined lifestyle. It's your call.

Having eliminated your willpower-draining decisions, ie., one's that inhibit your path to a meaningful life, you then need to look at the decisions that you have no choice but to make, for example:

- Your boss wants you to work late, even though you have a one-off opportunity that evening to meet a childhood friend.
- You don't feel great, but you have a Pilates class this afternoon.
- Your mother calls in the middle of a business meeting.
- A distressed stranger pleads to use your mobile phone.

These situations require a set of policies to be in place. Once established, there is no dilemma. You simply follow the policy you have for this situation. Some scenarios will be resolved by your belief system, for example, I will not be eating this, regardless of how offended the host might be.

Some decisions are procedural. For example:

- I will not take phone calls or meetings in my first hour at work.
- I do not eat carbohydrates after 6pm.
- I reply to every email.
- I keep a diary.
  - And if I live an interesting life and have it published, the diary will 'keep me'.

There are plenty of good books on habit formation. But to give you a condensed primer in respect of forming good habits:

1. Decide on the habit you want to acquire.
2. Emotionally connect to why you want to acquire it.
3. Vividly (and regularly) visualise what your life will be like if you do not acquire this habit.
4. Identify triggers that will invoke the habit.
5. Consciously practise the habit, until it requires no conscious effort.

How long does it take to acquire a habit? Nobody knows in terms of exact number of days, or exact number of conscious positive responses to the trigger. You will know when you do not have to apply any conscious effort to invoke the desired behaviour.

If you choose to give up alcohol, then if when you walk into a bar with friends, and your brain actively starts to explore why you might be able to justify having a beer, you still have work to do. Even though such thoughts might include:

- But it's St Patrick's Day.
- I won't see these friends for another year.
- I can't bear reality.

This is not a sign of weakness. It just implies that your habit formation is still a 'work in progress'. Don't beat yourself up when you fail. It is an indicator that your desire for change is less than your desire for your old behaviour. Simply up the frequency and intensity of your visualisations.

It is generally better to think of habits as practices that you acquire rather than eliminate. So rather than trying to give up biscuits, reposition it as your intention to eat more fruit, nuts and seeds (this applies to humans, as well as rodents).

Your 'biscuit habit' may be triggered by the end of a meal, or simply when you are peckish in between meals. Ensure you have the substitute nutrition to hand when the triggers occur.

Heroin addicts use methadone to wean them off the drug. Chocoholics use 'eighty percent plus' cocoa concentration chocolate to achieve the same outcome. Find your methadone equivalent.

I suggest you start with habits that are well within your reach. You may even contrive to acquire a new habit that is not really on your habit radar. This is only to 'programme' you with the self-confidence to believe that you indeed have the capability to acquire a habit. An example might be that you resolve to cheerily greet the security guard in your work's reception, regardless of their demeanour or lack of response.

Once you have proven to yourself that you can acquire a habit, up the stakes in terms of adopting habits that are aligned with your plan.

Once you get good at this, you can move into the advanced class and start the process of habit stacking. In essence, the aim here is to use the execution of one habit to be the trigger for the next habit. Get this right and your life becomes a series of positive habit cascades, where little or no willpower is consumed.

But won't that turn me into a robot? Putting aside the general philosophical uncertainty around whether we are already robotic in our decision making, it makes sense to run the mundane and procedural aspects of our life on autopilot. Thus, when we are involved in something that involves creative thinking, or deeper engagement of the senses, we can fully commit ourselves to the activity. So, whilst the subject here is habit formation, there are some aspects of our life that if we surrender them to habit, we miss out on the experience.

Gulping down food, rather than savouring it is an example. When was the last time you genuinely tasted the food you consumed? Reaching for the camera when something dramatic comes into eyeshot, rather than savouring it is another example. If your willpower is on empty, or you are feeling overwhelmed, even the most beautiful, or traumatic, of events will not register with you. For all intents and purposes, from a reality engagement perspective, you are in a comatosed state.

The problem for many of us is that we are already advanced habit stackers. Unfortunately, the stack comprises self-destructive habits.

1. I've had a rubbish day at work.
2. Consequently, I reach for the alcohol when I get home.
3. I am now hungry, so I overeat because my attention is on my terrible day.
4. My increasingly sore stomach seems to be telling me that a very sweet dessert is the cure.
5. I am feeling pretty awful now, and unfit for anything other than falling into bed with a 'cannon ball' resting in my stomach.
6. Inevitably, I wake up feeling groggy.
7. Unsurprisingly, I consequently underperform at work. Plus, I am snappy at colleagues.
8. Return to step 1. Continue ad infinitum.

Getting our habit act together is critical. Small changes lead to big gains, when you consider how your new habits will take you on quite a different journey, when compared to your old habits. Much like compound interest rewards those that invest early in their lives, the earlier you can start a good habit, the greater its impact on your life.

Mindfulness

Not so long ago, the term mindfulness would be strongly associated with saffron-dyed robes and sandals, and a shorn head. Today mindfulness has the blessing of western science, and as such it has entered the mainstream in western cultures, perhaps to the point of becoming an industry (McMindfulness).

I see mindfulness as a consciously directed effort to be aware of both yourself and your environment. It requires you to simply accept the information you receive, rather than cast judgment on it, or even to become 'locked' on it to the exclusion of everything else that is happening, both externally and internally. Not everyone would agree with this definition, but it helps me to decouple my opinions (often fictional) from reality (always fact-based).

At one end of the mindfulness practice spectrum is meditation. You find an environment where there is little external distraction and you sit and listen to the thoughts that come into your head. You consider them as clouds, and so let them drift out of your mind without trying to interfere with them.

The other end of the mindfulness spectrum is where you are attacked by multiple people at an open-air rock concert, where it is raining and the ground is muddy. Despite the chaos, you are able to deal with your assailants in an effective, but kindly manner. No broken bones, but the floundering attackers, having picked themselves up out of the mud depart with their tails between their legs. You on the other hand, have been emotionally unmoved by the attack. In fact, at one point you were humming along to the classic anthem blasting out from the main stage.

Tai chi and qi gong are practices that sit along the mindfulness spectrum.

As mentioned, savouring your food is an act of mindfulness. As is listening attentively to a colleague, and so resisting the urge to butt-in with a rebuke, or a set of solutions.

Even walking up the stairs can be done mindfully. Sensing how your muscles and joints interplay, along with your posture, provides you with great insights into yourself. Some might even regard this as a pre-digital era form of self-analytics. Though the aim is to not turn this into a self-absorbed experiment, but to develop a sense of your relationship with the environment. This is an exercise in awareness rather than concentration. Should a fellow passenger come tumbling down the escalators towards you, then your ability to sense this unexpected event and respond accordingly will have a significant impact on your wellbeing.

My suggestion is that you aim to be mindful for at least a minute each day. Then increase this in increments of a minute, as you see fit. If you prefer to take the meditation path, then aim for at least ten minutes in one sitting. If you insist on taking the samurai warrior path, possibly start with one assailant in a controlled environment, such as a boxing ring, or dojo. In any case, everything you do can be turned into mindfulness practice. Other examples include:

- Making the bed.
- Washing the dishes.
- Reading a bedtime story.
- Sitting in traffic.
- Taking an exam.

Some things will create strong emotional responses. This is natural. But like the clouds, acknowledge they are there, and do not fixate on them. Just let them run their course.

In many respects, mindfulness might seem like a contrivance to find yet another thing that requires thought, and thus acts as a drain on our willpower. Those starting out on their mindfulness journey might see it as an exercise in concentration, and this can make it very tiring. But over time, mindfulness adherents learn to not so much direct their focus, which has a cognitive cost, but simply to be aware of what they are thinking, what they are sensing and how they are engaging with their environment.

The greater our sensitivity to ourselves and our environment, the less likely we will be caught off guard and be the subject of a potentially life-threatening event. Or at the other extreme, miss a life-enhancing opportunity through our inattentiveness. More mundanely, being mindful, we are more engaged with the world, and ourselves. A mindful bull would be less likely to smash up a china shop. And most likely it wouldn't enter the shop in the first place.

Mindfulness enables us to see it as it is without applying our prejudicial filters to the world. From an internal perspective, mindfulness teaches us to recognise vital internal signals that might indicate we are no longer in good health.

Consequently, mindfulness helps us make better decisions. This is very important when it comes to our psychological health.

If this all sounds like too much effort, then that is a true indicator that you have much work to do in terms of your psychological wellbeing.

Decision triage

The digital age is the age of infinite choice, and thus infinite decisions. One of the few perks of being poor is that you are spared a whole range of lifestyle and luxury-related decisions, for example which yacht to acquire, or where to buy one's next holiday villa.

For most of us, what with being continuously connected via the Internet, we are faced with:

- Whose comment we should 'like'.
- Whose WhatsApp message should we reply to.
- Which video we should watch.
- How much we should bid for that eBay item.

And these are on top of the important daily decisions you need to make. The traditional approach of creating a daily 'to do' lists is going much the same way as strategy in the digital age. This can be summed up by the saying, 'When man plans, God laughs'.

Imagine the doctors and nurses at a city centre accident and emergency unit starting each day with a meeting to list what they are going to do, and when they are going to do it. As the philosopher and former professional boxer Mike Tyson once noted, "Everyone has a plan, until they get punched in the mouth". The decision making becomes even cruder for the medical staff in the event of a disaster. Those who are likely to live will take priority over those who are likely to die.

In the digital age, it is easy for our lives to resemble an accident and emergency wing.

If we are not careful, we could find ourselves just responding to an endless stream of stimuli, such as an edict from our boss, the ping of our email, or the attractive courier who has just arrived at reception. Each new stimulus has the potential to disturb us.

Back to A&E. Given that we are not designed to truly multitask, we need to make some difficult decisions when more than one patient / issue / opportunity appears.

I suggest that we use the Life Stack model to help with our decision making. If you are faced with the option to choose between an all-expenses paid holiday to Ibiza, or guaranteed shelter for the next six months, your choice will depend on which Life Stack layer you are currently focusing on. You may already have a roof over your head, but if you are in desperate need of money, then finding income needs to take precedent over two weeks of drug-fuelled hedonism.

What if your boss insists it is your responsibility to drink yourself senseless, whilst entertaining overseas clients on Friday night? Knowing you will feel awful handing over your daughter at her wedding the next day, you may have to make a decision that could result in you needing to find yourself a new job, which may in turn result in your inability to pay for the wedding. But if you are serious about living a meaningful life, you would not subject yourself to such physical abuse, and so, in any case, might be better working elsewhere.

This scenario does raise the question as to where your family sits in the Life Stack. Given your family, in theory at least, act as a unit, it can be said that family has a bearing on all layers of your Life Stack. A daughter's wedding can be said to impact the layers as follows:

- Physical – We need to ensure there is enough food and 'water' for the guests.
- Psychological – How much do we spend? Where will it take place? Should we scupper the relationship?
- Emotional – Are we losing a daughter, or gaining a son?
- Social – Who should we invite?
- Financial – How much?!
- Career – See above.

- Lifestyle – Bentley or unicorn-drawn carriage?
- Spiritual – His church or her mosque?

If your issues are at the financial level, then this might well drive your decision making in respect of the earlier work-wedding scenario. But what may be a wise financial decision, might well be a poor physiological decision. And hopefully you now have a sense of which is more important. Whilst the Life Stack was not primarily designed to address matters beyond the individual, we see here that it can be used for broader matters.

In the industrial era, with its factory timings and work-life balance model, it was quite straightforward. Work stuff got done during working hours, and private life matters were handled outside 'office hours'. But with the arrival of the digital era, work started to creep into our private time, most often via our electronic devices. To varying degrees, our private lives are creeping into our working life. The trend is (returning) towards work-life integration. This makes decision making more complex. As an aside, whilst I am seeing a lot of home working, there is little by way of 'work homing'.

Do I rearrange the shareholder meeting because it clashes with my son's school swimming gala? Do I dip out of the family holiday for a few days to meet a new prospect on the other side of the world?

Maybe as a family you have decided that you love the lifestyle that your high paying job provides, and so missing the odd school event is an acceptable loss.

You may decide to put a policy in place such as:

- Family trumps work.
- Work trumps family.

Such policies may be at odds with the Life Stack model, particularly if, for example, you opt for the Ibiza trip when you are without income and about to be turfed out of your present sheltered accommodation.

One might conclude that a path to a more contented life is one where you adhere to the priorities implied by the Life Stack. So, you arrange your life such that your decision-making policies do not clash with the Life Stack.

Engineering your life can help in this respect. Having a very high income and a high degree of autonomy is one approach. Reducing your outgoings and lifestyle luxury goods consumption is another.

Decision triage requires consideration of the short-term benefits against the long-term. Keeping the long-term in mind at each decision point will generally guide us along the best path.

On reflection

Life can be a constant fight between what we desire and what we need to do to live the best version of our life. Not living up to our chosen standard is painful, and over time soul-destroying.

By aligning our needs and desires through good habit formation, and a better sense of what is driving us, we can work through this tension to a state where living a purposeful life seems relatively effortless.

That stated, in this digital age of distraction, we do need to maintain vigilance in order not to slip back into our old ways.

14 Life Tools – Emotional

Overview

Life would be easier perhaps, if we were rational beings, unhindered by emotions. If this were the case, our focus would perhaps be on efficient living, whereby you could reduce life down to a set of rules, which if followed would lead to greater wealth, health and happiness.

Unfortunately, or fortunately, that is not the case. Whilst the rules might exist, our emotions drive behaviours that to the outsider might seem quite irrational. Thus, we must factor emotions into how we live our life. We must keep in mind that it is our emotions that provide the texture of our lives, and in that respect, we are fortunate that they are part of our makeup.

Nonetheless, our emotions need some degree of management, if we are to make the best of our stay on the planet. This is the focus of this chapter.

Emotional tools

We have already explored the role of habits in respect of the Psychological layer. This makes sense, as it is our mind that makes the decisions. Sometimes those decisions are based on weighing up the facts, for example, "shall I take the train or the bus, given the time of day?" More often how we feel determines the way we make decisions. "I would be more readily accepted by the wives of the other directors, if only I had a Louis Vuitton handbag" or "Wednesday is never a great day to start a diet".

Thus, our emotions are a significant driver of our decision making. If we are not careful, our life may become underpinned by hedonistic paranoia. This is not to say that we should consider our emotions as some sort of weakness to be suppressed.

But given how our environment has evolved relative to our hunter gatherer wiring, we need to ensure that our decision making is an astute balance of logical and emotional thinking (heart and mind).

One proposed method is to make your decisions using all the facts available, and to then factor in your gut feeling to see if your logical decision feels like the correct one. Our emotions can get us into trouble, but they are also a conduit for our unconscious to advise us. Given the wealth of data it has 'to hand', built up over many millennia, we should not ignore it.

Sometimes our cognitive faculties incorrectly assign emotions to certain triggers, causing us to react inappropriately if, say, your partner makes a simple request. Or a person approaching you, dressed in a particular way, causes you to become fearful, even though they are just about to hand you the glove that fell out of your pocket.

You may be unhappy at home, and conclude that it is totally your partner's fault, and so the very sound of their voice is a reminder of your unhappiness. The reality is that it might well be that you are part of, if not the entire cause of the problem, and, either way, rather than address it, you let it simmer and fester, thus causing your partner to suffer unnecessarily.

It may be that even a knock on the front door, if you live on a crime-ridden estate, sends you into fight or flight mode. Such a response has a cognitive cost. Mopping up the emotional mess after you have snapped at your boss, or partner, similarly weighs heavily on your cognitive capacity.

When we are fearful, our focus narrows, and our cognitive bandwidth is consumed with survival. Faced with a peckish sabre-toothed tiger, this will serve you well. But chronic fear is corrosive. It destroys creativity. When business leaders threaten job cuts, and draw out the culling process, it has a paralysing effect on the organisation. Any collective cognitive capacity that could have been applied to getting the company out of dire straits is rendered useless. Ask yourself whether you are carrying chronic fear.

Fear of losing your partner, fear that by downgrading your car, you will be the butt of jokes from your more affluent golfing 'friends', or simply fear that you are a poor decision maker.

So, to get this layer of our Life Stack in order, we need to respond appropriately to emotional triggers. Get this right and your life will become emotionally richer. You will savour your food, rather than treat it as a form of functional self-medication for your general sense of emotional malaise. The physical beauty of others will inspire passion, but without the selfish lustful cravings.

Habit formation and mindfulness have a role to play in this respect. In respect of habits, we simply need to create more appropriate responses to the emotional triggers we face.

We identify the triggers that need fixing by being mindful of our associated responses. If your dog's behaviour induces rage then, recognising what is happening enables you to ask the question why it is happening. Spending a little bit of time considering that it is in a dog's nature to bark, you may conclude that it is neither a defiant act, nor a threat to your status as the alpha male in the family pack (so I have been assured).

A fear of flying is not without substance when you can consider what might go wrong and the consequences of how your last few seconds might be spent. But when considered against the statistics, particularly in comparison with those of more mundane activities, it can be considered an irrational fear. But whether it is rational or irrational, if it is stopping us from visiting loved ones, or experiencing the wonders of the world, then it is something we must address.

Like treating allergies, desensitisation is a technique for reducing the intensity of our inappropriate emotional responses. Exposing yourself to the trigger in a controlled manner, and upping the intensity of the trigger in small stages has proven to be effective. Applying this to a fear of flying is not always practical. Asking the pilot to fly just a few feet off the ground initially is unlikely to happen, unless you are an oligarch.

For the rest of us, exposing ourselves to information associated with flying, including crash statistics versus number of flights per year might be a better approach. Talking to other flyers about your concerns will help too.

In respect of our thoughts, once we start to identify and isolate them, we can start to dissect them by asking questions such as:

- Is my thinking based on facts, opinions, or emotions?
- What filters might I be applying that are colouring my perspective?
- What if I take no action?
- Am I being played for someone else's benefit?

As mentioned, meditation is an effective way in which to listen to your thoughts. Even though the aim of meditation is not to fixate on your thoughts, unconstructive, emotionally-fuelled, or otherwise, it does give you a 'heads up' on where you might focus your reparative attention.

Being mindful that you are strangling your irritating sibling does suggest you are developing self-awareness, and are therefore progressing along the path to mastery. But it also suggests that your behaviour is still emotionally driven, and somewhat unbridled. If strangling your siblings doesn't erode your discretionary cognitive capacity, then subsequent emotional-fuelled incidences, which might include road rage, or a dirty cutlery restaurant transaction, will. Again, you may be fully 'in the zone' / mindful during all of these events, so ten out of ten for that. But you will also likely find yourself in jail, barred from an increasing number of eateries, and/or the recipient of a 'fat lip'.

The Chinese philosopher Mencius promoted the idea of heart-mind. Our encounters with the world would be more rewarding if our responses were not just purely emotional, or purely rational. They must be used in conjunction. In short, whilst you might be inclined to strangle someone for disrespecting you, your mind will jump in and lay out alternative responses that offer better long-term outcomes.

Mindfulness is good. But it is not enough, if we are to engage with the world in a smart manner. By smart, I mean that all parties are better off because of the action you chose to take.

Breathing

Some situations give rise to intense emotions. These include:

- Taking an exam.
- Receiving an appraisal.
- Becoming aware that you are in the crosshairs of an unkindly group of individuals.
- Asking someone out on a date.

The emotional intensity is often associated with the potentially negative outcomes of such events. On deeper inspection, it might be said that the intensity comes from the associated uncertainty of the outcome. The exam might go well, as might the appraisal. But you do not know for sure, and thus anxiety creeps in.

It has been shown that breathing is strongly linked to our nervous system. At the extreme, not breathing eventually leads to neurological shut down. Breathing slowly through our nose has a calming effect on our nervous system. Thus, you are encouraged to get your breathing under control as a priority in a stressful situation, or in any situation for that matter.

Street fighters use breathing to assess the readiness of the other party. If you are breathing slowly, it will suggest that you are 'ready to rumble'. Casual and cowardly muggers subconsciously factor in your suitability as a victim based on your pattern of breathing.

Slow breathing suggests alertness, and so they will most likely seek a more distracted victim. Similarly, at high stress ballroom dancing competitions, slow breathing indicates that you are indeed 'ready to rumba'.

Deeper breathing ensures greater oxygen delivery to all parts of your body. Consequently, your brain and body are primed, should you need to take physical action. Who knows how your request for a date might turn out.

Anxiety and fear have their place as indicators that all is not right. By controlling our breathing, we are taking a significant step to ensuring they do not dominate our subsequent behaviour and decision making.

We generally do not consider the power of breathing, because we do it without thinking. Plus, it doesn't require an app, or a coach, or even technical clothing. But breathing lies at the heart of many well-established philosophies. However, it goes by a variety of monikers. Here are some examples:

- Ki (Japan).
- Chi / qi (China).
- Prana (India).
- Pneuma (Ancient Greece).
- The Force (Star Wars).

Gratefulness

Emotional states, such as feeling depressed, are less likely to happen if you maintain a feeling of gratitude. In other words, you do not live your life as if you are entitled to everything. Your life may not be rosy, but there will be elements of your life that you can be grateful for. Maybe it is the beauty of nature, or someone's smile, or your circumstances when compared to others on the planet. Spending your life envious of someone who is taller than you, more financially successful or famous than you, is a guaranteed formula for lifelong emotional self-torture.

Before you go to sleep, why not list three to five reasons for being grateful. You may call upon your major achievements of the past, or minor achievements of the day to build your list. But of course, achievements are a mere subset of the myriad of reasons for feeling grateful.

Implied in gratefulness is contentedness. Smart goal oriented individuals, whilst keeping one eye on the prize, savour the journey towards their success, rather than feeling incomplete until the goal is achieved. Having goals in the digital economy is a challenge, given the manner in which the goalposts zigzag around the pitch. As mentioned, planning in such a volatile world will increasingly lead to feelings of failure.

One option is to not have goals. Simply living in the moment, making decisions as threats and opportunities present themselves, has a lot of merit. That's how I find myself writing this book. Spending your life trying to grind your way through obstacles can lead to a weary and jaundiced existence.

That said, if you have specific goals to achieve in respect of your Life Stack, I would veer away from this approach, because it is likely to be the 'cupcake every time'. But even in respect of the Life Stack, such an approach might be the only way to 'chart' a career.

Curiosity

Curiosity is a wonderful mindset. It cultivates an open mind and a willingness to explore and learn. A colleague challenges you. You can either crush them with a withering response, because they had the temerity to challenge your authority, or you can explore their challenge. It will demonstrate your respect for their ideas, and potentially expose yourself to a better overall outcome.

In How to Have a Good Day, Caroline Webb explains how our mind is either in discovery or defend mode. The latter is very important to our survival, but it has the effect of constraining our thinking and thus limiting our potential to make good decisions. A mindset of curiosity is a natural way to put us, and keep us, in discover mode. Asking, in a curious manner, where a would-be assailant purchased his knife, could well lead to a de-escalation of the encounter. Though I wouldn't necessarily have this as your sole self-defence strategy.

It's very difficult to be depressed or unhappy if you live a life of curiosity. Imagine you are about to be attacked (a bit of a recurring theme, I know), and the attacker is baring their teeth and going through the motions of triggering your fear buttons. What if you smiled at the individual as if to say, "this could be interesting"? This was not part of their plan. You have the upper hand. They think they have mistakenly picked on an assassin. You were simply interested in whether the attack is a gang initiation ritual, or purely an economic transaction.

So, if a decision makes you uncomfortable, reposition it in terms of curiosity.

- What is the examiner really asking?
- I wonder if my boss is having a mid-life crisis?
- What are my options in respect of concluding this argument gracefully?
- Is it the red or the white wire with this type of IED?

You know you have cracked the code, when people refer to you as:

- Cheerful.
- Cool.
- Calm.
- Unflappable.
- Phlegmatic.

If words such as serene or charismatic are ever used in respect of your demeanour, you are operating at the top end of the emotional spectrum. Be careful not to spend too much time with any single group of people, as you might inadvertently start a cult.

On reflection

Emotional management is a very subjective topic. It can vary from culture to culture, and from job role to job role. Curiosity is lauded in Silicon Valley, but frowned open by totalitarian governments.

Emotions are in many respects like food. You can live your life on a diet where the primary tastes are sugar, fat and salt / fear, anger and lust, or you can develop your palate and enjoy ever more nuanced experiences.

Emotions are not a weakness, but an essential part of our make-up. Those of us who are in touch with our emotions are more likely to interpret and act appropriately when stimulated by either external (our environment), or even internal events (our thoughts).

But there is always the risk that even if we are in touch with our emotions, we might not respond appropriately to them, leading to poor outcomes. Therefore, we need to pay great attention to the Emotional layer of our Life Stack.

15 Life Tools – Social

Overview

We are social animals, and regardless of whether we are extravert or not, the quality of our life is largely determined by the extent to which we are socially integrated. This chapter provides some guidance on how we can enhance this very important Life Stack layer.

Social tools

You are not going to get far socially if you are emotionally immature, and misinterpret the signals transmitted by those you engage with. The concept of emotional intelligence (aka EQ) has been created to suggest that there is an emotional equivalent of intellectual intelligence (IQ). If you are a wallflower at networking events, it suggests that your social muscles need developing. If you gracefully hop from person to person at a pace that is of your deciding, leaving a trail of good will in your wake, you are a social intellectual.

Emotional intelligence is a useful notion, but there are factors such as personality and culture that make it difficult to determine absolute EQ in the same way as for IQ. Similarly, the further you move up the social strata, the more nuanced the social interaction becomes; at least before the alcohol kicks in. So, the lack of uniformity in respect of social mores makes developing this layer of our Life Style stack more challenging.

At the very least, having the emotional management skills to respond, rather than react to triggers, regardless of whether they have been designed to agitate you, will be necessary. Otherwise you will either become an object of amusement for others, as they press your buttons, or you will find yourself developing an increasingly intimate relationship with your local justice system.

Keep in mind that we are social animals, even though your economic strength might make you feel that you can go it alone. Again, the digital economy is the social economy. There is a correlation between social skills, on line or face to face, and economic success. Egotistical CEOs are being swapped out for more social CEOs.

One might say that level 1 social skills include the ability to communicate and get along with others. Level 2 being the ability to influence others in respect of your goals. If you ever find yourself receiving 'out of context' compliments, it might be worth considering whether you are in the company of a level 2 player. The best level 2 players will establish your drivers, and then seek to guide them towards the goal they have in mind.

Getting along with others is something most of us learn as we grow up. Engaging with brothers and sisters, school friends and work colleagues all polish our 'sharp edges' in respect of our clumsy social habits. To see boorish or self-aggrandizing behaviour in an adult suggests that they have somehow missed out on the 'University of Life' social skills programme. Or they have a neurological disorder. In either case, pity, rather than irritation, is the best response.

Teaching people how to get along with others is big business, particularly in respect of industries that have traditionally prided themselves on their IQ, and paid little attention to their EQ. My formative industry (IT) comes to mind. You will, no doubt, form your own conclusions about me through reading this book.

Harvard professor, Michael Puett, whose Chinese philosophy course is one of the most popular at the university, has written a book, entitled 'Path'. In it he repositions Confucius as a philosopher, less obsessed with social hierarchies, and more focused on self-cultivation through better social interaction. In doing so, Professor Puett, is asserting that the quality of our lives is only as good as our ability to respect others, regardless of how we feel about them. In doing so, we may discover a different side of them, and of us, in the process. As an interesting aside, he goes on to add that setting life goals is meaningless, because the world is too chaotic, and being overly focusing on what we want causes us to miss out on life itself.

You can if course buy as much or as little of that as you like. But I suspect there is more than a grain of truth in Prof Puett's interpretation. Developing your social skills is one of the greatest acts of personal development. A well-appointed social skills toolset will enable us to achieve our goals with minimal friction. In fact, the extent of our social mastery is a very good proxy for the extent to which we have mastered life. If much of your day is spent in conflict with others, this is a wakeup call.

Care

It is unlikely that your social skills will develop if you do not care about others. The exception being sociopaths, who regard social skills purely in the context of achieving their own ends, with no concerns for their victims. NB. Not all sociopaths have finely developed social skills.

Helping others flows naturally from caring for others. Helping others, of course helps us. As we have explored earlier in the book, 'givers get'. Wharton professor, Adam Grant, proves this in his book 'Give and Take'.

We tend to help others who have a caring disposition, because they represent the best of humanity. From a professional perspective, in the social economy, caring is an important brand value. However, given the increasing integration of work and life, if you care purely for professional gain, you will be found out eventually. From a personal brand perspective, this is something that is very difficult to recover from.

YouTube has plenty of examples of those further up the economic / social stack haranguing those less fortunate, or of lower social status. Regardless of the underlying justification, it comes across as cruel.

You may consider yourself skilled in this respect, if you are equally comfortable engaging with a dustman at a social function, as you are with meeting a professional peer, or head of state. We are all humans, and at some level, we all have the same concerns.

Engage

If your care level is sufficiently high, you may now feel inclined to engage. However, you may feel a little shy / inferior to the person or group you intend to approach. What if they reject you? What if everyone in the room simultaneously looks towards you, and taunts you 'à la playground'? This, of course, is the sort of doomsday thinking we engage in when we allow our thoughts to control us.

In this circumstance, sociopaths can teach us a thing or two. The first step is to focus on your intention to speak with someone, rather than think of all the reasons you might be rejected. The second is to just do it. Think: Observe. Decide. Action. Don't prevaricate. Just get on with it.

Approach slowly, and within your target's line of sight. This gives them the opportunity to 'flee' without a major scene, or 'guide you in' with positive body language, such as a smile, or a resetting of the tie knot.

A smile is the most powerful of social techniques. A directed smile tells someone that you acknowledge them, which is a large part of making others feel respected. The timing and the length of the smile are important. Too long and you may be mistaken for a Botox accident; too short and it will be missed.

Over the years, I have met many people, particularly through my public speaking and classroom seminars. I often find myself in environments where I know I have engaged with some of the people in the past, but cannot for the life of me remember the details, face, name and so on.

Thus, I have developed a kind of half smile, which is a hedge bet against appearing rude to people I should know, and acknowledge. It is much less unsettling than a full beam perma-smile. It also has the effect of making me feel good about life in general. It's difficult to feel negative when you on the verge of smiling. It's to be recommended.

So, you have arrived and have made a successful 'social docking'. You have exchanged a few pleasantries, and are now struggling to maintain the dialogue. The trick here is not to be another one-dimensional bland room-filler, but to make an impression.

Making an impression is not an invitation to dump your accreditations and accomplishments on others, but to get them seeing you as a unique individual that they will not forget (for the right reasons).

Professionally, it is my job to provoke people. In other words, to move their minds. Corporations pay me to do that on their behalf. Irritating people is one approach, but is not recommended. Helping people to see the world differently is a better approach. In a more social setting, making people feel good about themselves, or sharing a joke, or provoking them in a teasing manner, works well in respect of making a positive impression.

This of course must be tempered for polite society. Best to steer away from comments in respect of erogenous zones, particularly at trade shows or spiritual gatherings.

In my experience, the most socially skilled people I have engaged with, were more focused on me than on themselves. People who take an interest in us, trigger us to be interested in them. Your interest-loaded questions might take the form of:

- How they arrived at where they are today from a career perspective.
- What they think of the event.
- What they like to do in their spare time.
- What are they hoping to achieve by being at this event.

Share

These questions can yield shared values and interests. So, it may be that you can help the other person in some way. Sociopaths would regard this technique as the law of reciprocity. It is in our nature to return acts of kindness, and to feel a degree of disharmony until we have done so.

For those who are genuinely interested in others, sharing provides a great means of deepening the relationship. The social economy does not simply value experts, or those with significant resources.

It values those that are gateways to others who are valuable and resource-rich. One of the exponential benefits of being social, is that the more people you know, the more people you can help through the people you know.

Your online social network, in my view, will increasingly be part of your professional value proposition when you apply for work.

I find that the reverse reciprocity law works well. Rather than looking for opportunities to help others, look for opportunities to be helped. Begging takes this to the extreme. However, used sparingly, it can help others feel valued and of course helps you at the same time. Through the act of being helped, your relationship is deepened.

Maintain

It has never been easier to maintain relationships, given the proliferation of online social media. In the old days, meeting someone might result in swapping phone numbers or business cards. This might be followed by an email or a call saying how much you enjoyed meeting, and possibly even a suggestion that you meet again. More often than not, this relationship would fizzle out after one or two meetings, as real world priorities restricted your capacity to maintain a connection with such acquaintances.

Social media enables us to maintain connectivity forever, with minimum effort. Occasionally their comments, tweets, shares and so on will show up on your feed / wall / timeline. By simply liking or making a comment, you remind them of your relationship. Get the timing right and possibly this casual online engagement might trigger something more substantial, for example, a call for your expertise. Of course, this is a two-way street. The more you share on social media, the more likely you are to gain. Increased sharing leads to increased visibility amongst your friends, colleagues and acquaintances.

Importantly, you need to share things of value, which may include humorous graphics, or the sage utterances of former tech moguls.

In terms of what to share, think of whether it will reinforce your personal / professional brand, and whether your community will see it as valuable. Do you really want to come across as a foul-mouthed pervert? If not, then don't use curse words or graphics that have a lascivious tone.

These days, from a professional basis, if I meet someone, who is not on LinkedIn, it is unlikely that I will invest in maintaining that relationship, because the overhead in giving ongoing personal attention to very loose ties does not justify the investment.

As an important aside, if you have just met your future spouse, do not dismiss him because he is not on the popular social networks. Though you may want to explore why this is the case. That said, many will find my advice incongruous, now that spouse-acquisition is largely cloud-based, thanks to social dating apps. Data-driven heuristic romance is now just a click away.

Manipulation

I have used the terms skills and tools in respect of the Social layer of the Life Stack. These terms have a somewhat manipulative feel to them. We must keep in mind that 'social' is not something you do to people, but with them.

Business-social, as opposed to social-social, is usually conducted with an objective in mind, even if it is to simply widen the net of people who know of your capability. However, the pursuit of being social is very much in our nature, and so the act of being social is its own reward.

If your social encounters do not leave you with a heightened sense of connectedness and wellbeing, then you will need to address this before moving up the Stack.

On reflection

Our survival once depended on our ability to fit in and contribute to the wellbeing of the pack. Today there is societal infrastructure to enable us to live in safety, and in isolation, if we choose.

Social standing over the centuries has morphed from who was the greatest contributor to the pack, to who has played the game best. In other words, affluence has become a key marker of social status.

An interesting development, as we morph into the digital age, is the rebalancing of contribution and affluence as social standing yardsticks.

We all enjoy receiving, but there is something more rewarding in giving. The extent to which we can give, and thus the extent to which we can enjoy the associated reward, is determined by the degree to which we yield to our social nature, and our capacity to engage in a skilful manner.

We are social animals. The more we embrace this reality, the more likely our path through life will feel propelled, rather than obstructed.

16 Life Tools – Financial

Overview

In modern society, our options become somewhat limited if we do not have access to money. Borrowing can defer this, and can even create the illusion that we can enjoy a lifestyle that is decoupled from our income(s).

Financial management is therefore a fundamental life skill. It is thus odd that many education systems choose to omit this from the curriculum. Perhaps having the citizens in a parlous financial state makes for better control. Certainly, the financial services sector is keen to load us up with debt. And the retail sector, amongst others, is keen for us to use that debt to buy rapidly depreciating liabilities.

In this chapter, we look at how we can get this aspect of our life under control. Financial management is fundamentally about spending less than you earn, and as such, nothing could be more straightforward to do. But we do not always spend in a rational manner, and this leads to our finances, and our circumstances, becoming complicated. For this reason, you should always seek the help of independent professionals in respect of your own circumstances.

Financial tools

Money makes the world go around. Rich people seem to have it all. Even though many rich people claim that great wealth makes them unhappy, us poorer folk want to personally verify this observation.

Nonetheless, it has been shown that happiness only correlates with income up to a point. Beyond which, extra income leads to only a negligible happiness bump, and in some cases, it can even erode happiness. Many of us who sit below that point would benefit from a better financial situation.

Most would agree that being rich, but being of poor mental and physical health, coupled with emotional issues and no friends, makes for a very poor life. So again, we need to get our Life Stack underpinned below the Financial layer, before we can fully devote ourselves to financial stability.

Given the nature of society, we cannot live without some form of financial income, so this layer, is in many respects a priority, even if you are without friends, morbidly obese and have a tendency towards road rage. In this respect, we need to ensure that we have enough money coming in to at least survive, even if it means living in low quality accommodation, eating 'reduced to clear' items from the local supermarket.

Let's assume that either through the state, charity, friends or employment you do have income / financial reserves, so you are in a position now to start raising your financial game. For some of us, our main source of income is our career, so why doesn't the Career layer sit below the Financial layer in the Stack? Well for a start, many people do not have a career, they have a job. Jobs generally offer little by way of career development opportunity. There are more people with jobs than careers in the world, hence the ordering.

So, let's explore some basic guidelines:

Make outgoings less than incomings

As with businesses, people who spend more than they receive will eventually go bankrupt. Credit cards will provide some sort of illusory buffer from this reality, but you will be conscious that the day of reckoning, in the accountancy, rather than religious sense, lies ahead.

Knowing that you are careering to this day will be a source of stress, and thus a large consumer of your cognitive capacity. In turn, it will diminish your mental ability to steer yourself off this self-destructive path.

This is not an issue confined to the poor. Many middle-class people are living beyond their means, buying goods and maintaining lifestyles that are only possible with loans and delayed repayment plans. Job number one is to reduce your outgoings to ensure you are not 'leaking' financially. Fortunately, there is a growing interest in frugal capitalism, and minimalism. If you can't bear the opprobrium of your social set, declare your situation as a lifestyle change, as opposed to a lifestyle collapse.

Increase your income

The lower your outgoings, the more choices you have economically in respect of the work you choose to do. However, you may feel that you could benefit from more income, if only to provide you with a financial safety net should you lose your job, become infirm, or need to pay for the medical treatment of a loved one.

If you are increasing your income so that you can just about afford the purchase of a high mileage bottom of the range Porsche in order to meet your local golf club's car park entry criteria, then you ought to reset your social sights. Pretending to be affluent is the fast track to poverty.

Save first then spend

Rather than save what is left in your account at the end of the month, extract the amount you intend to save at the start of the month and live the rest of the month within the constraints of what is left.

Buy appreciating assets and rent depreciating assets

Property generally appreciates in value, but even this cannot be assumed. Cars generally depreciate in value. It makes no sense to buy a new car, whereby after the first few metres of driving you have lost a significant percentage of its original value.

It makes more sense to treat cars as if they are a service, rather than an asset. Maybe you have a three-year rental agreement with your local dealer, or you hire a car as and when you need one. 'Car as a service' ensures that you will always have a well-maintained car. Issues will be dealt with as part of the service.

The same goes for technology, books and other forms of content.

Strictly speaking an asset isn't just something that over time grows in value. Such increased value is only realised when the asset is sold. True assets generate income whilst you own them. Financial instruments such as bonds, funds and securities come to mind.

It is smarter to acquire income generating assets, than assets that just appreciate in value. Again, it is smarter to buy assets than to buy liabilities.

Income-generating assets

If you can create your own income-generating assets, all the better. Actors may not own the films they star in, but if they have negotiated not just a large appearance fee, but a percentage of all profits going forward, then they have created a continuous stream of income.

Could your expertise be woven into an online membership service? You produce the content once, and in effect 'sell many times'. In the digital economy, it has never been easier to create our own assets.

The skill is to become a value-added attention grabber. With compelling content, people will pay to access your services. Yoga teachers, for example, can earn good money providing private lessons in the comfort of their client's home. However, in this respect they are just labourers, being paid for their time.

Digital economy yoga teachers, in effect, are moving from 'live interactive theatre' to 24-7 on-demand 'film'.

Rocks stars make money from their concert tours. But the tours are simply catalysts to selling merchandise. That is where the real money is.

Be aware that this is how the wealth game is played. The trick, if financial rewards is your key driver, is to turn your time on the planet into an income generating portfolio of assets. But, of course, living a meaningful life is much more than being purely an asset creation machine.

Personal development guru, Anthony Robbins, has written a very impressive book entitled, Money Master the Game. Whilst the book is tuned for an American market, and is not free of 'product-placement', the principles Robbins espouses are universal. I recommend you read this book, if you are concerned about whether you will run out of money before you run out of life.

On reflection

Sound financial management is critical to living a worry-free life. The quality of our life in modern society is governed by our ability to pay our way. We can rely on social welfare, but that leaves us at the mercy of the current, and future governments.

Of course, many of the best things in life are free. But many of us would feel more comfortable with a financial cushion to support our journey, and that of our family's journey, through life.

Better to be a 'have' than a 'have not'. But many of us ruin our lives because we cannot distinguish between 'have' and 'have yacht'. One doesn't have to be a billionaire to live a life worth living.

17 Life Tools – Career

Overview

The notion of a career has morphed in recent years. As mentioned earlier in the book, a career for life is being replaced by a life of careers. Increasingly, these careers are playing out in parallel, rather than serially. And increasingly, we are not just in competition with other professionals, but robots and algorithms too.

The notion of a career might well become a topic consigned to history books covering the industrial era in years to come. But we are not there yet, and so, given the amount of time we spend at work, we need to ensure that our careers are managed with care.

In this chapter, I provide some advice on how to keep your career goals on an even keel.

Career tools

You should know that, I have written a book in respect of managing one's career in the digital age (Beyond Nine to Five – Your Career Guide for the Digital Age). I wrote it for my son. Unsurprisingly, I would recommend it. Though it appears my son is a little circumspect when it comes to author self-endorsements.

In keeping with the Life Stack model, your career success will be largely based on the extent to which you have your act together in respect of the lower layers.

Unhealthy, psychotic, anti-social ditherers who steal office stationery to pay off their gambling debts, tend to find it difficult to remain employed long enough to acquire the skills that will propel their career forward.

Qualifications

From my perspective, the value of tertiary-level academic qualifications is diminishing. In part, because curricula cannot keep up with the rate of market change. And in the main, front loading your career with the bulk of your educational investment makes no sense. Learning needs to be increasingly just-in-time, to ensure it is relevant to when it is needed, as we transition along our career trajectory.

That said, certain professions need their people to have a basic grounding in the subject concerned. In the case of medicine, one will not be let on to the career ladder without the requisite qualifications.

For the rest of us, it has a delaying impact on career progression, and in some countries, it can have us starting our careers with a significant burden of debt. This restricts our career options, given that our primary focus will be the elimination of that debt.

Most employers do recognise that having a degree does highlight an individual's ability to think conceptually, cope with pressure and manage their time. The extent to which these are demonstrated is largely determined by the subject studied and the academic institution where the studying took place.

I am starting to see employers place value in our broader life experiences, which in the past these experiences may not have found their way onto our curriculum vitae. Skirmishes with the law, time with the French Foreign Legion, or even your commitment to anarchy might, in some employers' eyes, be seen as valuable.

Similarly, your social network is part of your value proposition. It is a case of who you know and not what you know. Your wider network is a 'ready to use' crowdsourcing platform that can be applied to extending the brain trust of your prospective employer.

In the digital economy, you are encouraged to bring your true self to the market, not some sanitised infallible hyper-qualified cyborg. Unless of course, that sounds like the real you.

A path to mastery

Consider your career to be a path to mastery. The journey will be determined by how you surf the market. The final destination may not have been part of the original plan. What you will know is that when you get to the end of the journey, you will be a better version of yourself. The definition of better version is up to you. It could reflect:

- Financial success.
- Making a dent in the universe.
- Being a world authority.
- Elevated social standing.
- Being kind on an industrial scale.

The trick is not to plan and then review on a periodic basis, whilst slowly despairing at how your dream and reality are diverging, but to re-plan on a periodic basis, resetting your dream in the light of reality. In this respect your career is akin to a data-driven Silicon Valley start-up.

Rather than trying to impose your business model / career on the market, you tune it to the market realities. Unless you are Ford (ignoring the market demand for a faster horse) or Apple (who wants a computer without a physical keyboard?), or you have secured significant venture capital funding, the market tends to have little time for upstart challengers.

Branding

What comes to mind when you think of people you admire? Whether they are celebrities or just ordinary people, you will likely have a sense of clarity with regards to their value proposition and personality. Rarely is this clarity the result of chance. It is typically engineered with great care. Corporations work their brands to achieve their corporate goals. In the digital economy, this applies to individuals too. Visit Twitter and study those within your career space with a high number of followers. They may not be household names, but they are well known in respect of their capability. Though admittedly, some will have purchased fake followers, so beware of extreme outliers in your market.

You too need to decide what your brand is, and to then engineer (not lie about) your experience to date to reflect that branding. You then need to act in a manner that is consistent with your intended brand. We all have a brand. Like a garden, we need to tend to it on a regular basis, otherwise it might grow out of our control. If that happens then your career intentions will be considerably more difficult to achieve.

Test test test

Do you know what you are worth in the marketplace? This could be quite different to what you receive in payment from your current employer / clients. The only way to find out is to test the market. Go for interviews, even though you are not looking for a job. You may find that your stock is much higher than you were aware. Or that your skills are, more or less, obsolete, and it is only a matter of time before your paternal employer reluctantly releases you back into the economic savanna.

Skills

It is practically impossible to anticipate the skills required by the market in the next few years. Many of the jobs that will be in demand then, do not exist today. Many of the jobs existing today may well be fully automated in the next few years.

It is fairly safe to say that those skills that give you the edge over technology will be in demand. Because if a piece of software, or a robot, can do your job, it will do your job. This makes economic sense.

Technology, today, cannot compete with human creativity. So, you are encouraged to develop yours. An open mind, and a sense of curiosity, is a start.

In the social economy, those with high emotional intelligence will be in demand. As people become more time-starved and under pressure, the ability to work with customers and citizens who are sometimes at breaking point will be considered very valuable.

As permanent employment gives way to increased freelancing work, your ability to handle commercial relationships will be important. Leaving 'money on the table' because of your commercial naivety is not smart. Similarly, your ability to market your capability, of which your brand is a key element, will be very important.

Digitally declutter

Technology is interwoven into our working lives. Whilst it offers great productivity gains, it can also create unnecessary noise and distraction. This 'work static' can impair our performance and steer us off our life mastery path.

We were never designed for days laced with bleeps and pings. Or to work with filing systems that emulates a multi-layer fantasy video game each time one needs to retrieve a document.

Have you ever noticed how your inbox is totally uncorrelated to your intentions? Whilst, at the same time, the more you ignore your inbox, the more your anxiety rises?

Unless it is a professional requirement to respond to every bleep and ping, eliminate all digital distractions. Set up inbox rules so that incoming emails get filed into specific folders, for example, key clients, family, suppliers. You can then then check those at a frequency appropriate to a productive day. It is worth periodically scanning your inbox to check whether you need further additional rules/ folders.

Your organisation's filing system may not have been designed with retrievability in mind. That doesn't stop you setting up your own parallel system designed for your benefit, unless of course there are governance rules that disallow such maverick behaviour. NB. Where this is possible, ensure that your filing system is backed up on a regular basis.

If you do not digitally declutter, then the digital distractions will steadily take control of you, and your career.

Competence, demand and passion

In your career choices, ensure that all three of these are present. No competence, and you will unsurprisingly be perceived as incompetent. No demand means that you have a hobby not a career. No passion and each day will feel as if a small piece of you has died.

If you have all three, then your career will seem less like the stuff you do to fund the enjoyable part of your life. In fact, it will become a major element of that enjoyable life.

On reflection

Given we spend so much of our short time on Earth at work, it makes sense to optimise our career so that it is aligned with our values, competence and what fills us with passion.

In the digital age, the traditional career path associated with many professions is being dismantled. Traditionally, management of others was the only sign that you were making progress. Today, there is little need for managers. We are only as good as our most recent gig, so it had better be a good one, if we are to ensure the next gig. Such a dynamic does not require a 'man manager' to ensure the work is done. In the digital age, you are either a highly skilled deliverer of services, or a leader of such people.

Smart people will have data-driven careers. They will choose their next gig / role based on where there is growing demand. They will acquire new skills with at least the same vigour as they pursue a higher salary.

The increased market volatility of the digital age means that career management is becoming something of a real-time pursuit.

18 Life Tools – Lifestyle

Overview

The term lifestyle conjures up images of privilege, wealth and the developed world. As mentioned, we all have a lifestyle, it is just that for many it is imposed on us.

However, for those of us smart enough to be spending less than we earn, and who have some discretionary time after a day at the office / mill, we have the option to consider how we live our life.

The very nature of our career choice will have a bearing on our lifestyle. Perhaps work enables us to travel the world, or forces us to work nights for half of the year.

Our energy levels and discretionary cognitive capacity will also determine our lifestyle. Learning a complicated and physically challenging new skill, such as pole vaulting / dancing, after work may just be too much for some.

In this chapter, we explore some lifestyle options.

Lifestyle tools

You sometimes hear people state that they have no life. Maybe their day is consumed with work matters or running a family. Certainly, those who are working to a point where they are unable to enjoy life are missing the point. Even though they intend to work hard now in order to retire early and enjoy life to the full, there is no guarantee that they will be around to enjoy the post-work part of the plan.

Thus, we need to ensure that every day has a non-obligatory element to it, such as taking the dog for a walk in the park, or listening to your favourite music, whilst enjoying your favourite food or drink. Correction: From a mindfulness perspective, it is better to enjoy each of these in isolation, ie., music, food and drink, so that you can savour each experience, in full. Overloading the senses can be a sign that you are attempting to block out some fundamental life issues.

From my perspective, one's lifestyle can be classified as follows:

- Non-existent.
- Ordered.
- Stimulating.

Non-existent

We have touched on this. The focus here needs to be reclaiming your life. You may well have literally no time to smell the roses, or to enjoy the transactions you have with the people you meet.

Adrenaline plays a large role in maintaining the capability to operate at full tilt. But ultimately it is unsustainable. Your circumstances may well be caused by poor management of your lower Life Stack layers, or it could ultimately lead to issues with those lower layers.

If it is a lower layer issue, then address that as a priority. Otherwise you need to start reclaiming your life, even if it is on a second by second basis.

Options include:

- Taking short breaks during the day. Step away from the grind. It might involve a little bit of muscle stretching, a cup of your favourite tea, a call/ text /email to a loved one or friend.
- Engaging more deeply in what you are doing. Being mindful of the conversation you are having with the aggressive client, or the taste and smell of the food you are eating.

Ordered

People operating at this level have their lives under control. They have discretionary time and make decisions in respect of how they spend that time.

They have systems in place to minimise cognitive leakage. Their time is not wasted hunting for lost car keys or fixing malfunctioning printers. They have good processes in place and use their discretionary income to buy themselves more discretionary time by outsourcing wherever they can. So, they will have an IT guy, a house cleaner and /or a life coach. They may even have an account with a catering company that delivers fresh and healthy meals to the doorstep, thus relieving them of the need to find recipes, source ingredients and prepare their own food. Outsourcing is thus another mechanism that inadvertently creates a lifestyle gap between the 'haves' and 'have nots'.

To develop an ordered lifestyle, ie., one which maximises your discretionary time, you need to consider how you might use your discretionary wealth to buy yourself discretionary time. Look at ways in which you might benefit from outsourcing. You don't have to run a corporation to use outsourcing services. You don't even have to work for a corporation to have your own virtual personal assistant. Having someone handle your social obligations in terms of travel plans and gift buying, frees you up to enjoy the trip / event.

Identify areas of your life that are more stressful than they need be. Maybe you regularly run out of milk, or lose your car keys, or waste time trying to remember where you got to in your book, so that you can continue with the story before you drop off to sleep. Create systems (ie., habits) that ensure that you do not squander your limited cognitive capacity through inefficiency.

You might also consider jettisoning possessions that have a poor pleasure-to-anxiety (P2A) ratio. If parking your 'top of the range' sports car at the local supermarket invokes digestive issues, then you might consider opting for a less ostentatious, less likely to be vandalised, model. Though if you have such an expensive vehicle you may well have shopping matters outsourced.

Beyond the realm of dependents, there may be some people in your life who similarly have a poor P2A ratio. If their presence in your life has a draining impact on your mental resources, then you need to free yourself of their influence. No need to wait until spring to streamline your relationships.

You know that you are living an ordered life, when you never have the sense of being in a rush. You can chat happily with friends or family. At least until your virtual PA's calendar alert causes your wristband to vibrate. At which point you cheerily head off to where you are supposed to be next, knowing full well that you will get there on time.

Stimulating

An ordered life is a stress-free life. However, you recognise that stress, acute rather than chronic, can be a lot of fun. So, a stimulating life is one where there is a certain degree of uncertainty and / or new experiences.

In the extreme, such a lifestyle might include skydiving, or even urban running in war zones. But for those of us who prefer a more balanced blend of stimulation and uncertainty, we might choose to:

- Learn a new language.
- Be an entrepreneur.
- Try new cuisines.
- Say hello to strangers.
- Achieve a personal best in something that interests you.
- Learn first aid, knowing that you may save someone's life one day.
- Study art.

Life is no longer about surviving or efficiency, it becomes a journey in exploring the world and exploring your capability. It's about quality rather than quantity. And it's about what excites you, rather than what might impress others. Better to savour the book you are reading, than to rush through the classics just so that you can argue that you are very well read.

By all means hitchhike with a fridge around Ireland, or radically change career on a regular basis. These will no doubt make for great blogs and books, which is great if you are stimulated by entertaining or informing others.

Adventures are to be encouraged. If you are not quite ready to lose the odd toe in your quest to reach the South Pole, you might settle for what has been called a microadventure (the book, Microadventures, is worth reading), a term coined by British adventurer Alistair Humphries, to describe a modest overnight outdoor excursion. You might argue that a more popular term for this is camping. There is some overlap, but microadventures do not require you to sleep under canvas, and are characterised by proximity to home and low investment.

But if we just focus on the spirit of microadventuring, we do not have to concern ourselves with meeting its criteria, other than its sense of breaking our routine with something that requires some effort, is memorable, and possibly even social.

Taking microadventures to the extreme, pursuits might include:

- Leaving work on time knowing that you are going to have to decide how to use this reclaimed free time.
- Life coaching someone whose circumstances blocks them from seeing their true potential.
  - Extreme variant: Choose a one-off encounter with someone who, when first approaching you, did not have your best intentions at heart.
- Rather than planning your career, just be alert to new opportunities, and see them for what they truly are, rather than trying to shoehorn them into your game plan, thus limiting their potential.
- Never respond to emails that have been sent on a Friday.
- Practise five acts of kindness before breakfast.

In respect of lifestyle, if we are lucky enough to have one that extends beyond survival, then we should try to enjoy it. By enjoying it, we find ourselves in a better place mentally to both increase the level of personal joy and to perhaps make the world a better place. This is life mastery.

On reflection

We should be the architect of our lifestyle, rather than the victim of it. Some see their lifestyle as a form of personal branding – "guess where I was at the weekend?" We might call this an extrinsic lifestyle.

Smart people choose their lifestyle primarily to please themselves, rather than please others. It is of course their choice whether that lifestyle is primarily hedonistic at one extreme, or selfless devotion to others at the other extreme.

Our lifestyle can be considered a vehicle for expressing our values. When we are aligned with our values, we are living a harmonious life.

19 Life Tools – Spiritual

Overview

Spirituality can take many forms. Established religions offer a variety of frameworks for pursuing a spiritual life. In some cases, they have had millennia to evolve their models, so must not be dismissed as spiritual life options.

There is a sense that religion is a digital matter, you are either 'all in' or 'out'. Anything in between constitutes spiritual failure. Even so, we talk about 'practising' a religion, which must surely mean that 'all in', in respect of thought and action, is a destination, rather than the starting point.

There is no reason why you cannot take the best principles from each religion, and follow your own personalised path. Fundamentally spirituality relates to how you treat yourself, others and the wider cosmos. Each religion placing slightly different emphasis on each.

In my view, if you are acting with kindness towards all three of the aforementioned domains, then you are living a spiritual life. This might be a simplistic perspective, but it's not a bad starting point.

It would be wise to recognise that the world, and beyond, has an inbuilt degree of malevolence. Muggers tend to mug people. Comical-looking chickens will poke out your eyeballs, if given half a chance. Visitors to outer space will find it, at the very least, unwelcoming, unless they are wearing some form of protective suit. So, we must imbue our spirituality with some gritty realism.

So with this in mind, let's look at how we might strengthen our spiritual muscle.

Spiritual tools

My limited interpretation of living a spiritual life is really a continuum from the previous section on cultivating a lifestyle. If you are happy in yourself, you are more likely to make others happy, or at least not cause degradation to their current state.

If you consider the plight of man in terms of his relationship with the Earth and the wider universe, then you will be more inclined to act with more wisdom and serenity. Death, of course, is a very serious form of illness (fatal in fact). But, with rapid advances in biological sciences, if we can manage to stay alive long enough, we might well become immortal.

There are already services on offer that anticipate such a breakthrough. Cryogenic freezing comes to mind. Though jumpstarting the dead is even more of a challenge for the scientific community, and something of an ethical issue for government leaders.

That aside, those that have got their spiritual act together know what lies ahead, and rather than trying to prevent the inevitable, with its associated cognitive burden, they enjoy life as it happens, for however long it happens.

They also know that a solitary life is a suboptimal life. We are social animals. Much of our instinctive behaviour is based on our need to be part of a pack. It might be said that those who act with the interests of the pack overriding their own self interests are truly spiritual.

I think a balance must be struck. A farmer who gives all her food away to the starving, will soon have no farm, and will soon after die of starvation. Thus, to really help others, we must ensure we are physically and mentally optimised to do so.

Charity is important. I have met some very generous people, who contribute to charitable causes abroad, but would be aghast if the recipients of their kindness moved in 'next door'. Spirituality is less about compartmentalising other people, as in 'you are poor', and more about treating people as equals whose destinies are entwined with ours.

In the lower layers of the Life Stack we have explored ways in which you can give yourself the best chance in life, through better health and so on. The associated actions might be considered as acts of kindness to yourself. We have also covered how we engage with others, and so are addressing kindness to others.

But at a spiritual level it is less about 'doing' things to yourself and others that lead to positive outcomes, and more about 'being'. Specifically, being natural. Or being in a state of flow, or 'in the zone'. These latter terms are more associated with high-octane sports such as Formula One racing. But these are states that we can also enjoy in the broader aspects of our life.

Being natural means that living becomes less a series of cognitive decisions and more a daisy chain of full-immersion living. The Chinese have a concept called wu-wei (literally, non-doing). So for example, when a dog barks, it does not choose:

- Whether to bark.
- Whether it is their best bark this week.
- What others think of their bark.
- How much longer should they bark for.

They just bark, as nature intended. There is no reflection and no decision making. They have not drained down their willpower reserves. Though they might, if their owner has trained them to not bark when, for example, the postman delivers mail.

This concept might be thought of as doing without thinking. Examples might include:

- Stopping eating because we are full, rather than because our fitness app tells us we have hit our calorie limit.
- Smiling at a stranger without consideration of whether they will reciprocate.
- Catching a ball without involving your cognitive processes.

Are these simply habits? They are of sorts. Some are 'habits' that are built into our DNA, and so we have inherited them. Some need to be learned, because our society has placed too much emphasis on analysis, and so we must de-programme ourselves back to our natural state. In any case, such an existence is both less burdensome on our mind, and enables us to operate naturally.

We sometimes admire animals because of their graceful motion. I often watch squirrels in my back garden. They have excellent muscular control; both gymnastically and with an ability to freeze their motion at will. Given that their world solely revolves around mating, nuts and predators, they have developed their capabilities with these three attention filters in mind. Possibly if we reduced the number of attentional filters we have, we may become much more optimised in our actions?

With this in mind, it might be worth considering what aspects of your life are distracting, and what aspects are core to your existence. Simplifying your life will enable you to deepen your experience of life. If your life is a 'to do' list, with each item requiring a cognitive commitment, you are living a processed rather than natural life.

Similarly, if your bucket list is too long, you will spend all your time flitting from one experience to the next, and very little time enjoying the actual experience. Unless you are looking to enter the Guinness Book of Records, there is no requirement for you to prioritise quantity over quality.

I appear to be drifting off topic in respect of spirituality. To some extent that is true. But keep in mind that spirituality might be considered as acting naturally, engaging with the world as it happens, rather living in your head. The development of cognitive capacity was a significant adaptation for us as a species. However, if we spend too much time in our heads, then we will simply become organic computers. We are already on a convergence path with technology, given how portable technology (spears) are becoming wearable technology (health bands), and even embedded technology (pacemakers). So, maintaining our humanity needs to be a key spiritual theme.

Engaging with others can be challenging. Your first playground encounter with a bully who clearly fights in a heavier weight category is a wake-up call that life is not friction-free. Mindfulness and meditation are useful tools to improve our environmental awareness. They enable us to spot friction on the horizon, and consequently change course to a more friction-free path. Our choice, of course, will depend on the maturity of our heart-mind coordination.

Martial arts

In the Physical tools section I was somewhat dismissive of martial arts as a means of self-defence. Some martial arts, however provide very effective spiritual tools, because they offer useful lessons in dealing with friction. I am referring to the soft end of martial arts, rather than the kick-punch-strangle end.

Soft martial arts are less about dominating the opposition, and more about working with them to reach a conclusion that minimises damage to both parties. In essence, their role is to restore harmony in the universe. Aikido, an art that I practise, encapsulates this very well. Rather than meeting force with force, you join in with the energy of your opponent, sensing where they want to go, and with minimal conflict, redirect their energy such that their strike does not connect with you.

This principle is useful for engaging with people in general. Should you find yourself in an argument, rather than trying to 'logic them to death', with your intellectual superiority, you follow their argument and lead them gently towards the point you are trying to make. At no point, did you inflame them by the use of force. Or the word 'fool'.

The point here is not so much about winning, but in engaging in a harmonious manner with others, whether the encounter is purely social, or potentially deadly. If both parties walk away from a transaction without injury or revenge in mind, then harmony has been restored. Yielding to others is not a sign of weakness, but a smart way to engage with others. Flexible branches survive the storm, whereas stiff ones do not.

Once you understand this principle, you do not need to get dressed up in 'white pyjamas' to practice. Life provides a continuous stream of opportunities.

The idea of martial arts, no matter how soft, may not appeal to you. Possibly the very thought conjures up visions of Bruce Lee taking out bad guys to the accompaniment of snapping wood noises.

As an aside, Bruce Lee, was an accomplished actor, his choreographed scenes of uber-dominant violence are what sold tickets. Lee's personal journey into martial arts moved him beyond the intellectual, 'this defence for this attack', to a more unconscious, 'I have no idea how I will respond, but I know it will be appropriate for the attack'. Again, this is doing without thinking. Such naturalness does not come naturally. He spent many hours developing this apparent effortlessness. As an aside, Bruce Lee, with his partner, was also the Hong Kong cha-cha dancing champion.

Dancing

Dancing is a fascinating tool for developing your engagement skills, particularly 'full contact' dancing. As a dancer, I went through the following stages:

1. Clueless to the rhythm, and thus of little value to my partner.
    a. I vividly recall watching the joy drain from their face, as this became apparent.
2. A sense of rhythm, but a need to direct my partner.
    a. I felt the need to be in charge.
3. A sense of rhythm, with a sense of leading my partner.
    a. My leading considered my partner's intentions.

The subtle difference between level two and three is that at level two, my aim was to impose my moves on my partner, giving her little option but to comply. Whilst it was never my intention to restrain those I danced with, it may have appeared to an onlooker as if I was a plain clothes police officer attempting to subdue, a 'slippery' suspect.

Level three, like aikido, was more about feeling where my partner wanted to go and to work within that constraint to provide us both with direction. As I moved from level two to level three, the expression of my partners morphed from terror (think gyroscopic astronaut training) to pleasure (think surprisingly pleasant beverage).

The big transition happened when I moved from being self-centred, 'I do dancing to people', and embraced the notion of dancing 'with' my partner. This is empathy in action. It is also harmony in action. For that reason, I would consider dancing to be both a spiritual act and a tool for developing one's spirituality.

Level two dancing is cognitively exhausting. Level three is effortless, and joyful.

Paying it forward

As mentioned in an earlier chapter, paying it forward is an approach where instead of repaying the originator of an act of kindness towards you, you repay someone else.

There may be something hierarchical in this, in that the person that helped you is in no need of your help, so there isn't anything you can do, other than to help someone who is less fortunate than you; a sort of spiritual 'Ponzi scheme'. That said, helping others should be a natural act, not one that requires the pre-checking of the prospective recipient's credit or social status, or being nudged by the kind actions of a stranger.

If we all practised this, then generosity would cascade down from those with the most to give to those who are most in need. Money can be the currency in such transactions. But so can time, attention and kindness. Thus, it is possible for someone living in poverty to dedicate their time and kindness to a wealthy person in need of help.

Imagine a rich socialite who drank too much at a nightclub, who is now on the street sitting in a puddle of her own vomit looking distressed and disoriented being helped by a homeless youth living rough.

Whether you choose to pay it forward, sideways or backwards, the act of being kind is spiritually uplifting. As mentioned, five acts of kindness before breakfast, or throughout the day, is an investment in your spiritual life.

The concept of the five-minute favour comes to mind (See Appendix D). What could you do that might only take five minutes, yet will have a positive impact on the recipient? Examples include:

- Writing a personal recommendation on LinkedIn.
- Adding a thank you comment to a well written article.
- Buying a coffee for a homeless person.
- Sending a link to a new phone model review to someone you know who is considering buying one.
- Disposing of a piece of litter you did not drop.
- Complimenting a service operative on the manner in which they handled your transaction.

Acknowledgement for your gesture would be nice, but don't go looking for it. Yielding to an oncoming car to let it pass through a narrowing of the road can be frustrating, if your concession is not acknowledged by the other driver. However, there may be a whole number of reasons for their behaviour, including incivility, so do not take it as a personal affront. If there is a good reason, then their behaviour is understandable. If it is sheer incivility then, they clearly have issues, which deserves at best our pity, and certainly not our anger.

Covert acts of kindness can be very rewarding, particularly to people who you do not like or trust. Covert acts, in these circumstances, may go against your natural inclinations. At the very least, such behaviour helps to stop you from descending into a pit of all-consuming hatred.

Life is too short, and our cognitive capacity too limited to expend energy on those we feel have slighted us, don't respect us, or generally don't have our best intentions at heart.

As previously mentioned, it is incredible to hear of people who forgive the murderer of their child. Such people often have strong religious faith. They know that whilst revenge might deliver some form of relief, they would become the murderer's second victim. A life filled with hate is a ruined life. Some might call this response smart cognitive management. Others might call it spirituality in action.

So, when considering your five acts of kindness before breakfast, you might want to include some covert actions.

Grace

The concept of grace occurs in a variety of religions. In many respects, grace is a synonym for kindness, whether that be man-to-man, or deity-to-man. Some will argue that grace is advanced kindness, in that it is easy to be kind to someone likeable, but when it comes to kindness towards malevolent characters, a state of grace is required. So, we might consider kindness and grace to be just bands on the spectrum that defines how we engage with others.

A more prosaic, and perhaps more helpful, definition of grace is provided by Sarah Kaufman, in her book entitled, The Art of Grace. She posits that grace is the art of making others feel comfortable. As such it is the lubricant that ensures the smooth running of societies. She astutely points out that grace as a virtue has fallen out of fashion, and so, if not addressed, will have serious societal implications.

You can quickly establish if you are wanting on the grace front by how you would respond to the following:

- Your friend 'breaks wind' in the car.
- The youth across the carriage is watching a noisy video without the use of headphones.
- One of your parents draws attention to your lack of career focus.
    - o Advanced test: Both parents are involved.
- Your neighbour makes a tactless joke about your recently deceased pet cat.

- You overhear a stranger making a caustic remark about something important to you.

Alerting all passengers, prior to 'rolling down' the car window, or 'decking' the vituperative stranger are not graceful responses, should you need clarification on this.

But as Kaufman points out, grace goes even further. It's not just how we engage with others, but also how we engage with our environment. Walking confidently, whilst being aware of what is happening around you is an act of grace. Free runners (as in parkour) also demonstrate grace as they glide over obstacles that lie in their path, as they make their way across an urban landscape. The intersection of grace and flow is where you will find the top athletes.

For me, grace is a useful and simply proxy for defining a spiritual life. I would encourage you to periodically reflect on whether you are generally graceful in nature, or whether you might be perceived as a 'tool' that enables others to stress test their grace level. The key question is whether people enjoy your company, or whether they are simply tolerating you.

On reflection

All of us are spiritual to some extent, unless we are truly committed to self-hatred and devoid of kindness. The extent, and reach, of our kindness will determine the quality of our life. Having a general positive disposition towards others makes social interactions rewarding, rather than threatening.

Spiritual people tend to be calm, even serene, in how they conduct their lives. I am not suggesting that people who enjoy loud music, wave their hands about in conversation, or shout uncontrollably at public gatherings cannot possibly be spiritual. I am referring to how, despite what might be happening to them, or around them, they appear centred, like a Samurai warrior in the heat of battle. Or an Italian cleric at an Iron Maiden concert.

Such people are not happy one day, because they won the lottery, and sad the next, because they lost the winning ticket. Regardless of life's vicissitudes, they maintain an even keel of contentment. They know that life is short, but they are part of something much bigger then themselves, and even humanity, and they are more than okay with that.

They look to live in a state of harmony, in as much as reality allows. When challenges to their harmonious state get the better of them, they consider how they could have better responded, so that their harmonious state remains unperturbed come the next occurrence.

This process of conflict – reflect – improve lies at the heart of taking the path to life mastery. Life itself is a reality gym. The more you engage with the 'equipment', the greater the load you will be able to bear. The quality of your spiritual life, and in turn your life as a whole, will be determined by the extent you to which you can bear the load with good grace.

In summary

In this, and the previous seven chapters, we have looked at actions you can take to move yourself further towards living a meaningful life. It would be overwhelming, at any given time, to address every layer of the Life Stack with equal vigour.

Having calibrated each layer in respect of your own circumstances, you are encouraged to focus your attention towards the lowest layer that needs addressing.

That said, feel free to perform acts of kindness, even if your focus is not yet on the Spiritual layer. The world will appreciate it. But it is better that you address your pre-spiritual levels as a priority, because once they are in shape, your capacity for kindness will be so much higher. Not least because of factors such as greater energy, wealth and social connections.

In any case, addressing your own Life Stack is an act of kindness towards yourself, which in many respects is as worthy as an act of kindness to others. Self-mastery means learning to be kind to yourself as well as to others.

20 Creating A Plan

Overview

In this chapter, I provide an approach that will enable you to attend to what is important.

Please note that it is only an approach. Some of you might see this as a proof of how the first two syllables found their way into the term analysis. Your success in terms of achieving life mastery is not contingent on taking this approach. But for those that like to keep score, it offers a way to manage your progress.

Game on!

One of the buzz terms of the digital age is gamification. In other words, using the competitive/scoring nature of games in contexts not usually associated with games. Firstly, we set up the scoring mechanism for the Life Stack game. And then we monitor how we perform in practice. Here is a table of how we might monitor our progress.

Layer	Planned Score	Actual Score
Physical	8	8
Psychological	7	6
Emotional	7	5
Social	8	10
Finance	6	0
Career	5	7
Lifestyle	5	9
Spiritual	4	4
Total	50	49

Figure 15 – Keeping score

The table shows the planned scores for a given day, along with the actual scores achieved. We will come to the scoring method shortly.

What typically happens is that reality gets in the way of our plans. However, if we set our targets based on a weekly average, or even a fortnightly average, then we can iron out the spikes and troughs caused by unexpected events, for example:

- A friend shows up who you haven't seen for a while, so you decide to party hard, which has a bearing on your Physical score (negative) and your Social score (positive).
- You are unexpectedly made redundant, which has a positive impact on your Career score, as you were planning at some point to get out of that dead-end job and explore new opportunities in the meantime. You are now able to step up the search for new opportunities.

Keeping score

Initially, I would encourage you to limit your attention to between one and four key improvement areas, and then review monthly. When the associated new behaviour is embedded, ie., a habit, then we can replace it with a new area for improvement.

As mentioned throughout the book, you are encouraged to focus on improvements at the lowest layers of the Life Stack, otherwise you are building on sand. It may be that these improvements all relate to the Physical layer, for example, 'Stabilise sleep patterns' or 'Eliminate junk food'.

You can decide which improvement investments will give you the best return on your path to life mastery, and prioritise accordingly.

Here are some examples of behaviour changes for each layer of the
Life Stack.

- Physical.
  - o Get to bed earlier.
- Psychological
  - o Declutter life.
- Emotional
  - o Practise meditation.
- Social
  - o Reach out to friends and family on a regular basis.
- Financial
  - o Avoid unnecessary spending.
- Career.
  - o Enhance my brand.
- Lifestyle.
  - o Learn a foreign language.
- Spiritual.
  - o Be kind.

How you turn these general targets into a 'points system' is entirely up
to you. 'Declutter your life' or 'Learn a foreign language' are open to
interpretation (as are the others). The former could refer to material
goods, or even to people you engage with. The latter could imply the
ability to have a social conversation constrained by topics that interest
you, or the ability to make a professional presentation, and handle the
associated questions.

The scoring should thus be designed to reflect the scope of your
intention, along with where you are on the path to achieving that goal.

I suggest you create a scale for each layer that runs from zero to ten.
Or if that feels too analytical, then limit the scoring range to 1 (Low), 2
(Medium) and 3 (High).

So, the previous examples may be quantified as follows:

Physical: Getting to bed earlier

Score	Achievement
10	In bed by 9:30.
9	In bed by 9:45.
8	In bed by 10:00.
7	In bed by 10:15.
6	In bed by 10:30.
5	In bed by 10:40.
4	In bed by 10:50.
3	In bed by 11:00.
2	In bed by 11:30.
1	In bed by 12:00.
0	In bed after 12:00.

Figure 16 – Physical layer: Scoring example

Psychological: Declutter life – email management

Score	Achievement
10	Process emails once per day.
9	Process emails twice per day.
8	Process emails three times per day.
7	
6	
5	Process emails four times per day.
4	
3	Process emails five times per day.
2	
1	
0	Drop everything for anything that sounds ping-like.

Figure 17 – Psychological layer: Scoring example

Some targets do not warrant having 10 distinct outcomes. Again, in terms of the scoring system, it's your call.

Emotional: Practise meditation

Score	Achievement
10	Meditate for 30 minutes per day.
9	Meditate for 25 minutes per day.
8	Meditate for 20 minutes per day.
7	Meditate for 15 minutes per day.
6	Meditate for 10 minutes per day.
5	Meditate for 5 minutes per day.
4	
3	
2	
1	
0	

Figure 18 – Emotional layer: Scoring example

Social: Reach out to friends and family...

Score	Achievement
10	Meaningful conversation with a loved one.
9	Meaningful conversation with a friend.
8	Meaningful conversation with an acquaintance.
7	Meaningful conversation with a stranger.
6	Social conversation with a loved one.
5	Social conversation with a friend.
4	Social conversation with an acquaintance.
3	Social conversation with a stranger.
2	
1	
0	

Figure 19 – Social layer: Scoring example

Financial: Avoid unnecessary spending

Score	Achievement
10	Break a spending habit – eg. Morning Starbucks coffee.
9	Deferred a significant purchase, rather than acted impulsively.
8	Reduced my outgoings because I reengineered my day, eg. Not having to incur travel costs.
7	Adhered to my shopping list in the supermarket.
6	Evaluated potential purchase options based on need and value, rather than shininess and fashion.
5	
4	
3	
2	
1	
0	

Figure 20 – Financial layer: Scoring example

Hitting multiple targets could happen. Your score is now the sum of all scores. If you adhered to your shopping list (7) and planned your day to minimise travel spend (8), you would score yourself 15.

Career: Enhance my brand

Score	Achievement
10	20 social media actions, eg., tweets / retweets
9	15 social media actions, eg., tweets / retweets
8	
7	10 social media actions, eg., tweets / retweets
6	
5	5 social media actions, eg., tweets / retweets
4	
3	
2	

Figure 21 – Career layer: Scoring example

Lifestyle: Learn a foreign language

Score	Achievement
10	Attempt a conversation in the target language.
9	Attend a lesson.
8	Learn a new element of grammar
7	Learn 10 new words.
6	Learn 5 new words.
5	
4	Identify / acquire supportive learning tools.
3	
2	
1	
0	

Figure 22 – Lifestyle layer: Scoring example

Spiritual: Be kind

Score	Achievement
10	5 acts of kindness.
9	
8	4 acts of kindness.
7	
6	3 acts of kindness.
5	2 acts of kindness.
4	1 acts of kindness.
3	
2	
1	
0	

Figure 23 – Spiritual layer: Scoring example

Both the scoring and the choice of achievement is entirely for you to decide, based on your circumstances. In the above examples, some are a little convoluted in respect of what act warrants a given score. Others are more clear cut.

If you intend to be kinder, then, you might need to decide what represents an act of kindness, and how it should be scored. You may in general be a very kind person, but your improvement opportunity lies in how kind you are to strangers.

This may of course be overkill. Again, you might prefer a High, Medium or Low scoring model that reflects your level of endeavour in respect of the goal in question.

I would gravitate towards simplicity to make tracking easier, and as a way of preserving your cognitive capacity.

If having to consider how you score progress has no appeal, then simply play a volume /cumulative game. Here is an example of how you might monitor your Life Stack progress in respect of the above goals:

- Physical - Number of hours slept.
- Psychological – Number of social/email-triggered distractions.
- Emotional - Number of minutes of meditation.
- Social - Number of non-work conversations.
- Financial - Amount of money spent on non-essential items.
- Career - Number of tweets dispatched.
- Lifestyle - Number of new foreign language words learnt.
- Spiritual - Number of acts of kindness.

With some of these you will be aiming to increase your score, for others the opposite will be true.

Again, the way you gamify your life is up to you. You may choose to have your goal(s) focused on the Physical layer, as you feel that is where your attention needs to be as a priority. I would recommend a layer by layer approach, so that you build a strong foundation.

The example above, where there is goal for each layer, might be for someone who has worked through all their layers and is now focused on fine-tuning their life. You might say that such a person is now a high-performance player / master.

Life gamification

I understand if you find this approach too analytical. For me, at the very least it reminds me that I have perhaps not paid enough attention to an important aspect of my life. It might also highlight that I am becoming generally inattentive to my life purpose. This might well indicate that you need a more compelling life purpose.

I hope it will inspire you to raise your game. Mutating a quote from Ernest Hemingway, "Nobility is not about being better than other people, but being a better version of yourself".

It is of course up to you as to whether you keep score, or just broadly reflect on your progress at the end of each day. Keeping a diary will add a qualitative perspective to the insight this game will generate over time.

Be aware there is a growing trend in the digital age towards what is being called the 'quantified self'. This is the capturing of personal data such as heart rate, steps taken during the day. and amount of deep sleep acquired. You may already be part of this movement. If you are not, look around at all those people wearing wristbands one would normally associate with:

- A prisoner on day release.
- A 'top gun' fighter pilot.

Depending on the environment you are in, it is likely that those people are literally monitoring their every move.

There is also a growing set of apps to help you monitor your progress (eg., Myfitnesspal.com). And even apps to help you help others (eg., freerice.com).

You might conclude that this approach is a sure sign of self-obsession / narcissism. My view is that if you want to enhance / manage yourself, you need to measure yourself. Keep in mind that this activity will also benefit those with whom you come into contact.

Hopefully you will consider this exercise, or some variant of it, well worth pursuing. Monitoring what is important to you will improve:

- Your life.
- The lives of your dependents.
- The lives of your friends and acquaintances.
- Those whom you will never meet.

Gamifying your life has many benefits:

- Life becomes fun.
- Games bring out our most natural/primal behaviour. We want to win!
  - Watch how granny 'gets her financial groove on', when invited to join in a family game of monopoly.
- It presents a constructive way to get your dopamine hits.
  - Bad news for cocaine dealers.
- It accelerates your path to mastery in any area of your choosing.
- You can either choose an established model, with its own reward system, for example the belts model of Eastern martial arts, or the hearts system associated with the Duolingo language learning app. Or you can even create your own reward system, eg., candlelit bath, new ebook, or a pimped-up Learjet.

Pay attention

Less is more. Changing behaviour / learning new skills has a sapping impact on your willpower. Embarking on too many changes simultaneously will likely end in disappointment.

Excitement and adrenalin may give you the initial propulsion to 'parallel process' your behaviour modifications, but eventually this will fade. Only to be followed by some degree of self-loathing.

I am not suggesting you focus on only one behaviour / skill at a time. Just choose goals that are decoupled from each other.

Examples include:

- 'Spend less' and 'Smile at strangers'.
- 'Lose weight' and 'Study cosmology'.

Problems will ensue if you choose conflicting goals.

- 'Take up powerlifting' and 'Lose weight'.
- 'Resign from dead end job' and 'Invest in speculative stocks'.

Similarly, problems will occur if your goals are too similar in terms of their demands:

- 'Study for an MBA' and 'Learn to speak Russian'.
- 'Spend more time with friends and family' and 'Expand the business internationally'.

I suggest you list all the skills and behaviours you would like to address and order them such that:

- The ordering is based on the Life Stack model. Lower layers take priority over higher layers.
- Where there is no conflict, perhaps work on two behaviours in parallel.

Look for 'quick wins', so that you develop momentum in your behaviour changes. So initially, set your goals such that they are well within your reach. They can evolve to 'stretch' goals once you develop the habit of goal management.

You are already perfect

Many of us go through life with a sense that we are not good enough. Every good deed by the likes of Richard Branson reminds us that we are living our lives 'small' by comparison. But even 'do gooding' billionaires need to have discipline in respect of their attention.

In many respects, it is their finely attuned attention that helps them identify opportunities and act on them. As they get richer, they can even outsource the opportunity sensors (ie., employ others to find opportunities), plus they can take bigger bets. So, this is a matter of scale. There is no reason why we too cannot bootstrap ourselves into such a life, if that will help us fulfil our purpose.

The key point is that you are already exceptional. You are descended from a long line of people who were skilled enough to survive extreme discomfort and create the next generation, despite the odds. When it comes to Darwinian adaptability, you are the latest model!

Our perceived imperfections are often so because of societal standards. In fact, our imperfections make us human, and make us unique. So, our starting point is that we are literally best of breed (measured over all time).

The approach I am proposing in terms of living a meaningful life might be considered one of many games we can play to 'kill time' in between eating, sleeping and mating, for the precious little time we have on the planet. Our ancestors have had tough lives by comparison to us. They have contributed to the comforts and lifestyle we today, perhaps, take for granted. I believe we owe it to our ancestors to make something of our lives.

Of course, we need to get the balance right between monitoring our lives and living it. As we gravitate towards our preferred selves, and as our engineered practices become habits, we can taper the time we spend on monitoring.

Personally, I think it is a good game, because, played well, it should make the world a better place for all. Plus, your very existence becomes a beacon of best (life) practice / mastery, and so shortens the journey towards a meaningful life for others. Parents take note.

At the end of the day, some of us will benefit mankind on a grand scale, and be remembered for centuries to come. Most of us will perhaps have some positive bearing on those close to us.

But given the exponential / domino effects associated with our actions, particularly when measured across time, our modest impact today could lead to profound positive changes for generations into the future.

That's a nice thought to 'check out' on.

Finally

Afterword

Attention is key to mastery. But as we have seen, attention is a scarce commodity. How we allocate it is controlled by several factors including motivation, habit, willpower and the attention-grabbing capabilities of others.

The advent of the advertising industry might be considered the birth of the Attention economy, so attention as a currency is not a new concept.

If attention is a new currency, then it would be wise not to go through life with your wallet / purse left wide open. There are those who are only too happy to relieve you of its contents.

You may well get something in exchange for your attention. Such 'rewards' might include a flash, shiny car, an adrenalin-charged film, or even a meal 'to die for'. But you will acquire these goods and experiences at a cost. The cost being reduced attention to your own needs and personal growth. As we have seen, your Life Stack will crumble if you do not pay attention to all layers, but particularly to those that form the base of the stack.

Self-discipline

Managing your own attention will, at times, be perceived as antisocial. Your 'friends' might berate you for not getting drunk / 'drugged up' with the rest of the gang. Your parents or boss may show their disappointment at certain decisions you make in respect of your life and career. Deviation from inherited religious practices will be frowned upon, particularly where such practices are woven into community life.

I am not advocating that you defy your parents, or eschew your religion, but only that you act in a manner that is consistent with your values and aspirations. The more evolved you are as a person, the more likely these values and aspirations will have the 'greater good' at their core.

Paying attention requires self-discipline. Though, self-discipline is only hard work when it cuts across those existing poor habits installed earlier in your life. Once you have aligned your habits with your intentions / purpose, you will have hard-wired self-discipline into how you live your life. It will no longer be a burden on your willpower.

The future of attention

The digital economy is delivering many benefits to us as individuals and as members of society. However, it has also taken distraction to new heights. One ping is enough to stop the great opus you are working on in its tracks. The upside of course is that you are now fully up to speed on the latest trivia associated with your social network, plus you received a little dopamine hit.

So how will the future of attention unfold? Let's look at a few scenarios:

The Wall-e scenario

This Disney film painted a scenario, whereby humans did not need to work. Consequently, they had high levels of discretionary time and money. Rather than pursue athletic or physical goals, the citizens simply consumed, and so they became obese and immobile. Their bodies simply acted as a framework for turning sensory data into addictive neurotransmitters (dopamine, etc.). In this scenario, humanity is both destroying the planet and careering towards its own extinction.

Worryingly, this scenario does appear to be playing out, as people start to live increasingly large fractions of their life online, rather than in the physical world. A general increase in obesity highlights a general disconnect from our true nature (to be hunter gatherers).

The convenience of addictive food and content is much more attractive than the inconvenience of pursuing, and preparing, food, and engaging with the real world.

The Wall-e scenario can be thought of as a dystopian version of the much vaunted (at least in the mid-twentieth century) leisure age. Though with the prospect of robots obviating the need for humans in the workplace, it will likely be much discussed in the year to come.

Again, this scenario does not have a happy ending.

Augmented cognition scenario

Advances in technology, which started with the spear, result in the convergence of humanity and technology. Wearables have become 'embeddables'; today we already have prosthetic limbs and pacemakers.

The integration of technology and neural tissue is now achievable. Our minds can be used to control, for example, the cursor on a screen, even without electronic implants.

A natural extension of this is that we see the creation of what might be called the augmented cognition industry. Those who can pay will have access to 'mind apps' that enable consumers to have instant neural access to major knowledge databases, eg., Wikipedia, Bloomberg and Facebook.

Such people will literally be better informed than the rest of us. Thus, they will likely make better decisions, and thus be better positioned to take their lives in the direction of their choice.

The use of self-awareness technologies will guide us at all layers of the Life Stack, from when we need to go for a run (including how far and how fast), through to prompts that enable us to maintain contact with loved ones. Lifestyle software agents will work in the background on our behalf to identify and bring to our attention the very best in goods and experiences that fit neatly within the constraints of our cash flow.

This software might well be integrated with gamification technology that will determine at what point we are rewarded with the identified goods and experiences.

Most likely these technologies will heighten the economic (digital) divide, where the 'haves' will enjoy great prosperity and the 'have nots' will become a kind of 'perma underclass'. Even back in the eighties, the film Wall Street highlighted that having ready-access to the right feeds gives one the power to win-big in the stock market.

This scenario is perhaps akin to a dystopian American dream. Though it is unlikely that it would be constrained to the United States.

Some of us might not see this as dystopian, particularly if we are on the right side of the digital divide. Such a perspective would be indicative that our Life Stack needs some urgent attention.

The international Occupy movement is, perhaps, a response to this scenario playing out.

Another trend taking us down the road of augmented humanity is the transhumanism movement. This is a group of people who are looking at how technology can be used to augment us physically and intellectually. Some proponents embrace the notion that death is a curable illness.

I mention transhumanism in this scenario merely to make you aware that human augmentation has its own momentum at the 'radical end', thanks to some very deep thinkers.

Whether augmented humanity is in humanity's best interests, or even nature's interests, is up for discussion, given the widening portfolio of applicable technology. I wouldn't turn my nose up at a stent, if the alternative was death. And the quality of my life has been considerably enhanced thanks to my nose-mounted vision enhancers (aka glasses).

But even these augmentations are not universally available. Rather than suppress the technological evolution, we should play a more active role in making it available to all.

In any case, this scenario is a strong possibility in respect of our future.

Au naturel scenario

We are already witnessing a pushback in respect of a dissatisfaction with modern life. The Paleo movement comes to mind. Adherents point out that, unlike our ancestors, we no longer spend hours or even days hunting down food, or huddled around camp fires. But the reality is that this is how we are wired, as this is what we have done for most of our time on the planet. Consequently, we should endeavour to replicate the lives of our hunter gatherer ancestors as much as we can, otherwise we are fighting our true nature.

Such practices might include:

- Adhering to a paleo diet, which is typically high in meat protein, vegetables, fruit, nuts and seeds.
- Wearing clothes made of natural materials.
- Striking a better balance between work and play.
- Exercising in a manner that focuses on functional movement rather than big biceps, 'buns of steel' or a 'six pack'.

In theory, by virtue of living a more paleo life, we are more likely to have less distraction issues. Our days cease to be failed attempts at keeping up with an overly ambitious 'to do' list. The associated de-materialism results in us not having to pursue the most high-paying jobs, which invariably place a very high burden on our attention.

Once our minds adjust to this less frenetic lifestyle, it may be that we rediscover mental capacities that modern life has inadvertently suppressed. Thus, rather than augmenting our mental capabilities using technology, we rekindle our dormant capabilities. This will also apply to our physical capabilities. Watch a few parkour videos to witness our 'augmentation-free' physical potential.

In terms of our mind, I have no idea what these capabilities might be. But they may include telepathy, extra sensory perception and telekinesis; to name a few popular phenomena.

Imagine living a life that is so devoid of mental clutter that we have total clarity. We see the world as it is, rather than as our mind chooses to interpret it, based on what else is festering in our working memory.

Imagine being deeply connected to your loved ones, and hypersensitive to those who mean you harm. Imagine continuously experiencing the beauty of nature because you are part of the grand design. Erich Fromm in his book, The Art of Being, articulates this perfectly.

One might argue that this is a form of spirituality (no doubt many would argue that this is a form of fanciful nonsense). A type of enlightenment whereby we see the modern world for what it is, good and bad. Being attentive, we do not divert our focus away from the less positive aspects; that would be to imprison ourselves in a fantasy world. By the same reasoning, we do not allow ourselves to be consumed by the crueller aspects of reality.

There are many laid out paths for this particular journey. Mysticism, in its various forms, appears to be striving towards human transformation, and so in turn unearthing our true potential. Yoga is an example of a mystic practice. Though many of us in the modern world see it as a tool for de-stressing after work, or addressing stiffness in our lower backs / hamstrings.

Modern life seems to have a denaturing impact on well-established (five millennia in the case of yoga) practices. Shrewd entrepreneurs have industrialised such ancient practices to meet the needs of the time-starved and stressed-out modern consumer.

Modern society is becoming increasingly open to these ancient human transformation practices. Meditation in the classroom is a recent phenomenon. Some might say that this is probably just a cheaper alternative to Ritalin than an exercise in the pursuit of what might be called 'unaided transhumanism'. Whatever the rationale, it suggests that we are realising how our mind and our attention are critical to the quality of our lives.

These scenarios are all extremes. It is more likely that future society will be a blended mix. The question then boils down to which of these scenarios will have the greatest impact on you.

Which of these are likely to be prominent in your eulogy?

- A world-class super-consumer.
  - Whose body fat will be used to heat the local sports centre for a fortnight.
- A high-achieving cyborg.
  - Whose brilliant brain is available as a download via the URL on the 'service' app.
- Lived a simple life.
  - Had time for everybody. But unfortunately died at the age of 150 whilst competing in an ironman triathlon.
    - Cause: Accident death: Felled by a driverless mountain hover-taxi.

The aim of this book is to draw your attention to your attention, particularly in respect of your life path. Understanding the dynamics associated with attention will have an empowering effect. The Life Stack (chapter 2), coupled with the Mental Worktop (chapter 6), and the Unified Attention Model (chapter 10), will hopefully help you understand all the moving parts in respect of living a purposeful life.

As the world becomes increasingly digital, there is a danger that we will be pulled along our life path in accordance with the needs of others.

Paying attention to your life has never been more important.

Ultimately life mastery is a mindset and not a goal. There will always be opportunities to fine-tune our lives. Initially, much of our attention will be spent on developing habits that provide us with firm Life Stack foundations. Eventually, that attention can be used for higher endeavours, as defined by you.

Thank you for your attention.

Appendix A: Business and Society

We, like all animals and plants, develop through what we receive from the outside world. In our case, sunlight, food and water come to mind. Our development is further tuned by paying attention to the feedback we gain from our social interactions. Immature social skills, including an inability to recognise behavior-adjusting signals, could well lead to being assaulted, or developing a reputation for being odd.

So it is in business. Corporations that fail to pay attention to the market will be oblivious to both threats and opportunities. Organisations that are most attentive will act sooner, and thus increase their chances of surviving threats or capitalising on opportunities.

Even at an individual level, an inattentive workforce will misinterpret instructions, comments and body language. As the miscommunication passes along the organisation's process chain, the difference between the initial instruction and the final action might well be substantial. In business that can be costly.

Poor communication between workers can arise for a number of reasons. Unresolved issues in their life outside work can lead to reduced cognitive capacity. Their current task might well be consuming what remains of that bandwidth. Having 'maxed out' their cognitive capacity, the worker simply cannot process any further input. There is no place left on their Mental Worktop to hold / park / queue further messages.

It may be that the culture of the organisation is one of 'busy fools'. Here people are judged on how harried they look; a sure sign they are working hard. Such cultures often celebrate multi-taskers. But as we have already seen, we are not designed for multi-tasking. Our limited mental resources are squandered in task-switching rather than task completion. Again, the likelihood of lucid communications is low.

Big data

In recent years, the term big data has been coined to highlight the increasing throughput of data that is hitting organisations. Much of it being video and social in nature. Organisations that can sift through this data and detect weak signals amongst the data noise will most likely thrive, given they can act on opportunities and threats, often when their competitors are, as yet, unaware of them.

The term data analytics is also a popular term that encompasses the tools used to turn a 'data cesspool' into valuable and visual insight.

In any case, the more you can sense what is happening in your environment, the more you can adjust to it. One consequence of the digital economy is the increasing market clock-speed. Reviewing your strategy on a quarterly or annual basis is no longer enough. Business, and business strategy, is a real-time pursuit. With this increased clock-speed comes increased volatility. With increased volatility comes increased business failure. Thus, paying attention to the market has never been more important.

Is agility the answer?

In recent years, the notion of the agile organisation has been floated. In a form of bio-mimicry, organisations are increasingly following the Darwinian principle of adaptability. So, those that adapt quickly are most likely to survive. Business agility embraces this.

In my view, agility is how you behave when the lion pounces. You can freeze, jump out of the way, or grab the gun and fire. Your agility protects you, but it is a close call. Some talk about being more anticipatory. You know there are lions in the neighbourhood, so you are constantly on the lookout for the associated signals. Whilst better than agility, it implies that lions are the only threat.
In the digital economy, threats (and opportunities) can come in all shapes and sizes, and from all directions. Overly focusing in one direction, or on one form of attack, is likely to leave you vulnerable. The best martial artists are always alert.

Apparently, samurai warriors were taught to sleep very lightly so as to never be totally off guard. My personal attempts to sleep with one eye open is very much a work in progress.

Being in an attentive state is thus the default mode for samurai warriors. Even when under attack, a laser focus on the attacker needs to be combined with a wider focus to ensure there are no further enemies on the horizon, or coming from behind.

This also applies to corporations. Organisations that do not have the capability to pay attention to their market will be vulnerable. Similarly, organisations that do not pay attention to their staff, particularly their staff's level of engagement, could well find themselves a net exporter of talent. At least until the organisation grinds to a halt. I believe we will soon see the rise of the 'attentive organisation', as a business blueprint.

It is very likely that your organisation, or even your industry, could well be disrupted by an organisation that has yet to be created. Who knows what form it might take, and what it will offer that has the effect of syphoning your client base. Given the exponential nature of technology growth, it is likely that when that organisation comes into existence it will first 'fly under the radar' for a while, and then grow very quickly.

To thrive in the digital economy, organisations need analytics tools that can pick up on weak signals indicative of something substantial. At this point in time, humans tend to be better than machines at pattern recognition, but that will change in due course.

An organisation's ability to continuously pay attention to its environment, whilst progressing its business, needs attentive leaders. And attentive leaders need to be expert at managing both their Mental Worktop and their Life Stack.

We will very likely see a significant portion of the leadership development budget being spent on attention management. A 'scatter brain' samurai ("Oh, I've forgot my sword again!") was unlikely to have a long life. Twenty first century organisations need calm, lucid and attentive leadership.

Similarly, those charged with leading society need to be equally skilled. Misalign your education system with the evolving needs of commerce, and very soon your nation is an economic backwater. In respect of war, the enemy no longer wears a different uniform, and conveniently announces their intentions by crossing your boundary. Again, this involves paying attention to what is going on both internally and externally.

Whether you are an enterprise or a nation, if you snooze, you lose. It's that simple.

The Life Stack

It will help to look at your organisation / nation from a Life Stack perspective.

- Are your people physically unhealthy?
- Are they disengaged and easily distracted?
- Are they fearful of losing their job / the environment in which they live?
- Is the culture dysfunctional?
- Are your people preoccupied by making ends meet? Does your cash flow forecast look precarious?
- Do you provide an environment where people have a sense of making professional progress?
- To what extent do your people have a life beyond their work commitments? Do you have social / sporting facilities? Or do you at least offer and encourage activities beyond work?
- Do you preside over a spiritual void, where the overriding theme is narcissism / a disregard for others? Is your commitment to making the world a better place, central to your mission statement, or is it merely a document nested in some corner of your corporate website?

These are just random examples of questions you might ask in relation to each layer.

Again, if one or more of these apply to your organisation / nation, you need to prioritise your actions such that you are always addressing the lowest Life Stack layer first.

Observations on class

Traditionally we have had three classes:
- Lower.
- Middle.
- Upper.

The lower class work to survive. The middle class work to thrive. And the upper class simply enjoy being alive. Or more specifically, the upper class are able to enjoy a variety of sensations and experiences that only the time-rich can afford.

The lower class often aspired to be middle class. And so, the middle class, in theory at least, were role models. The middle class were not just making enough money to survive, but increasingly had disposable income that enabled them to have their own home, take exotic holidays, and so on.

Today there is a new class, which is referred to as the underclass. They are unemployed with no prospects of employment. They often operate outside the confines of the official economy, and often turn to self-medication to address the feelings of purposelessness (though admittedly this approach is class-agnostic).

The working class are being automated out of employment. Unions will fight this, though the battle is lost. It is no longer the workers versus the management, it is the workers versus the robots.

The middle class are similarly finding their roles being automated, or simply 'blue collarised', in the digital economy. More significantly there is a declining need for managers. The digital economy values leaders and experts only.

Under, working and middle class need guidance on how they must adjust so as to be / remain economically-relevant in the digital age. This is the responsibility of governments. And as far as I can see, very little is being done.

Getting off my high horse, the real challenge is attention and cognitive load. The associated stress will make it very difficult for the majority of people to adjust to the new digital realities. They need help.

A homeless person cannot think about work until they have somewhere to live. An unemployed factory worker will continue to remain unemployed until they are given the skills needed to thrive economically. The middleclass, in general, needs to adjust their 'incomings to outgoings ratio' in anticipation of a bumpy journey ahead, and like the working class reskill as required.

But if we look beyond economic matters and at the Life Stack in general, we see some interesting realities. Often poor people are more generous of spirit. Conversely many wealthy people are not. So, who is better off in terms of living a life worth living?

If the poor person is living within their means, has reasonable health, a good network of friends / family, and who lives, at least in part, to serve their community, then they could be considered to be living a better life than the stressed-out executive who has all the toys, but no time to play with them, who has stabbed his way to the top and lost his loved ones in the process.

One might argue that many of us have sold our soul for economic benefit. And it is the associated spiritual void that has many of us, regardless of class, self-medicating. Businesses and societies are more likely to succeed, if they can create policies and environments that enable people to get a better balance between their economic well-being and their humanity.

Bhutan measures GNH (Gross National Happiness), rather than GDP (Gross Domestic Product). Will this change of focus turn it into an economic powerhouse? It's not clear. But if the people are happy, does it need to become an economic powerhouse? Possibly the rest of the world is playing the wrong game? And possibly, the majority of us are being forced to play this game by a handful of beneficiaries.

In summary

Businesses and societies ultimately are the sum of their people. The extent to which the people live a purposeful life will determine to what extent the associated business or society thrives.

I believe businesses and societies can achieve organisational mastery by helping their people on their own personal path to life mastery.

Perhaps, in the digital age, attention management needs to find its way onto the school curriculum. I believe the more that people understand the dynamics of attention management, the more that the associated organisations and societies will thrive.

Appendix B: Glossary

Overview

This appendix provides a summary of terms that recur throughout this book. In some cases, these terms were created to communicate the associated ideas. To avoid 'concept overload', I have also commandeered established terms. However, I have fine-tuned their definitions, again, for the purposes of communicating the ideas behind Attention Dynamics.

Attention grabber	A catch-all term to refer to anything or anyone that intentionally distracts us, usually with the intention of progressing their agenda at the cost of us pursuing ours.
Career	This is the sixth layer of the Life Stack. It embraces the notion that your working life is a progression, or path, where you are in some way better (more skilled, more valuable, more senior) at the end of it, than you were at the outset.

In the industrial era, careers tended to be constrained to one field, with a primary focus on economic survival. And, at one time, were limited to just one employer. |
| Cognitive control | This is the mental process of exerting your will on what you think about, along with how you act. So, it is another term for willpower. |

Cognitive burden	This occurs when something captures / requires your attention. This involves mental effort and so has a depleting effect on your limited supply of willpower.
Cognitive overhead	See cognitive burden.
Cosmos	It is generally a reference to everything that lies beyond the Earth, though it does, in fact, include the Earth. It is also known as the Universe.
Discretionary thought	This is a reference to an element of the Mental Worktop model. It is that element of our cognitive capacity that is available to be applied to the task at hand.
Disharmony	A situation whereby there is some degree of tension or friction. Disharmonious situations typically expend energy. 'Out of sync' dancers unnecessarily expend energy as they consciously, and constantly, try to resynchronise with their partners. Disharmony diminishes our ability to get things done.
Ego	That part of the mind that is compelled to behave in a dominant and self-centred manner.
Emotion	Emotion might be considered a neurological response to our thoughts and / or the environment.
Emotional	This the third Life Stack layer. It is focused on how we manage our emotional responses.

Environment	The world around us. The people and things that we can see and / or interact with.
Financial	This is the fifth layer of the Life Stack model. It is focused on ensuring we have enough money to survive in the modern world. It also includes having some degree of comfort that should our economic situation take a turn for the worst, we have some financial reserves to buffer us through this period. A retirement 'pot', a concept popular in the industrial era, would be an example.
Habit	An unconscious behavior that is triggered by an event, such as, a muffin, alarm clock or an act of kindness.
Habits of mind	These are the conscious mechanisms we use to embed a habit into our minds. Our path to mastery is strongly correlated to our ability to form good habits
Harmony	When two or more people, or things, are interacting in a friction-free manner.
Heart-mind	An approach promoted by Chinese philosopher Mencius, whereby you engage both your heart and mind when interacting with others.
Instinct	An instantaneous response, hardwired into our physiology, to an environmental trigger.

Lifestyle	This is the seventh layer of the Life Stack. It embraces any activity we partake in, or object we acquire, whose purpose is usually not critical to our survival. As such, lifestyle is something we can focus on, once our more fundamental needs are met.
Long-term memory	This refers to the part of our brain where we store, memories, opinions and even feelings. Unlike short-term memory, long-term memory, whilst not always one hundred percent reliable, enables us to access our memories from both the recent and distant past.
Maslow's Hierarchy of Needs	A renowned model for human motivation, created by American psychologist Abraham Maslow. It correlates neatly with the Life Stack model introduced in this book.
Mastery	This is a concept associated with self-improvement. It can be applied to any domain, for example, tennis, parenthood and 'self'. Achieving mastery status implies that, at the very least, you are well placed to help others on their path to mastery.
Meaningful	In respect of our lives, meaningful implies that there was a purpose to your existence. Perhaps you created a cure for the Zika virus, or you raised one or more socially-conscious and kind children.
Memory	A general term associated with the mind, particularly in respect of the storage and processing of our thoughts and actions.

Mental bandwidth	This is a general term that highlights our limited capacity to handle concurrent activities / thoughts.
Mental Worktop	This is a model proposed by this book to help us make better use of our minds. See also: working memory.
Mind	That is the part of our brain where thoughts take place, memories are stored and decisions are made.
Mood	A prolonged emotional state. Often the result of an accumulation of triggers.
Physical	This is the first layer of the Life Stack. Primarily associated with our physical needs, including health, nutrition, sleep and safety.
Physiology	This is a medical term relating to the functioning of our body.
Psychological	This is the second layer of the Life Stack. Primarily associated with our ability to make decisions that will serve us well.
Relationship	A term that describes how we relate to others.
Response	In the context of this book, a response is how we act when stimulated by a trigger. The response might be instinctive, habitual, or it may be consciously crafted.
Poverty	A state of being where much of your mental capacity is consumed with matters related to survival.

Purposeful	See meaningful.
Short-term memory	This is the part of our brain that holds data needed for the purposes of the current activity. Remembering a phone number long enough to 'dial' the numbers would have been a relevant industrial era example.
Social	This is fourth layer of the Life Stack. It is focused on how we engage with other people, ranging from inner family to complete strangers.
Spiritual	This is the top layer of the Life Stack. The focus is on behaving and thinking in a manner geared towards making the world a better place. It involves being kind to ourselves and to others.
Subconscious	The part of our mind we do not have direct access to. However, through gut feelings, dreams and other mechanisms, our unconscious uses its vast repository of data to inform our conscious decision making.
Stimulus	A thought or event that causes us to act in a particular way. Being 'tasered' would be an extreme example.
Trigger	See stimulus.
Unconscious	See subconscious.

Willpower	This might be considered an energy we are provided with to override our decision making, when we feel that a correction is needed. We appear to be allocated a fixed amount of willpower each day. This can be a problem when it runs out before the day has ended.
Working memory	This is the part of the brain that processes our current thoughts.
Work zone	This is a notional concept to help us think about how our working memory is typically used. The Mental Worktop model I have presented in this book subdivides working memory into four work zones.
World	This can be a reference to the planet we inhabit, or those aspects of life that in some way involve us (our world).

Appendix C: Key Themes

Overview

Here you will find the main themes / concepts / tools I have introduced in this book. They are collated such that they reflect the context in which they are relevant.

The Life Stack

- Physical.
- Psychological.
- Emotional.
- Social.
- Financial.
- Career.
- Lifestyle.
- Spiritual.

4 Key relationships

- You.
- Your relationships.
- The world.
- The cosmos.

Life-enhancing concepts

- Mastery.
- Attention.
- Confidence and courage.
- Energy.
- Goals.
- Habit.
- Kindness.
- Motivation.
- Positivity.
- Purpose.
- Values.
- Willpower.

The Mind

- Conscious mind.
- Dreams.
- Environment.
- Gut feeling.
- Habit.
- Long-term memory.
- Reflex.
- Short-term memory.
- Thought.
- Trigger.
- Unconscious mind.
- Working memory.

Mental Worktop

- Acute disharmony.
- Chronic disharmony.
- Clutter.
- Discretionary bandwidth.

Unified Attention Model

- Accelerator.
- Air conditioning.
- Boot / Trunk.
- Brakes.
- Cylinders.
- Driver.
- Engine.
- Fuel tank.
- Gears.
- Lights.
- Mirrors.
- Passengers.
- Radio.
- Steering wheel.
- Turbocharger.
- Wheels.
- Windscreen.
- Wipers.

The Physical layer

- Self-defence.
- Sleep.
- Nutrition.
- Exercise.

The Psychological layer

- Decision triage.
- Habits.
- Mindfulness.
- Willpower.

The Emotional layer

- Breathing.
- Curiosity.
- Gratefulness.

The Social layer

- Care.
- Engage.
- Maintain.
- Share.

The Financial layer

- Appreciating assets.
- Depreciating assets.
- Income.
- Income generating assets.
- Incomings.
- Outgoings.
- Save.
- Spend.

The Career layer

- Beyond Nine to Five.
- Branding.
- Competence.
- Declutter.
- Demand.
- Mastery.
- Passion.
- Qualifications.
- Skills.
- Test.

The Lifestyle Layer

- Ordered lifestyle.
- Non-existent lifestyle.
- Stimulating lifestyle.

The Spiritual Layer

- Dancing.
- Grace.
- Martial arts.
- Pay it forward.

Appendix D: References

Overview

Here is a list of external content I have referred to in this book.

The List

Oliver, J. 2007. **Affluenza.** Vermillion.

Fromm, E. 1993. **The Art of Being.** Robinson.

Kaufmann, S. L. 2015. **The Art of Grace. On moving well through life.** W. W. Norton and Company.

McCormack, A. G. 2015. **Beyond Nine to Five: Your career guide for the digital age.** Auridian Press.

Peters, S. 2012. **The Chimp Paradox: The mind management programme to help you achieve success, confidence and happiness.** Vermillion

Saul, R. 14th March 2014. **Doctor: ADHD does not exist.** Time.com

Csikszentmihalyi, M. 1998. **Finding Flow: The psychology of engagement with everyday life.** Basic Books.

De Becker, G. 2000. **The Gift of Fear: Survival signals that protect us from violence.** Bloomsbury Publishing.

Grant, A. M. 2014. **Give and Take: Why helping others drives our success.** Penguin Books

Harris, T. 2014. **How better tech could save us from distraction.** www.Ted.com.

Seligman, M. E. 2006. **Learned Optimism: How to change your mind and your life.** Vintage Books.

Miller, R. 2009. **Meditations on Violence.** YMAA Publication Center.

Robbins, A. 2014. **Money Master the Game: 7 simple steps to financial freedom.** Simon and Schuster UK.

Green, R. 2012. **Mastery.** Viking Press.

Humphreys, A. 2014. **Microadventures: Local discoveries for great escapes.** William Collins.

Mumford, G. 2015. **The Mindful Athlete. Secrets to pure performance.** Parallax Press.

Levitin, D. 2015. **The Organized Mind: Thinking straight in the age of information overload.** Penguin.

Anderson, K. 17th July 2013. **Pay It Forward with the five-minute favor.** Forbes.com

Puett, M and Gross-Loh, C. 2016. **The Path: A new way to think about everything.** Viking

Duhigg, C. 2012. **The Power of Habit: Why we do what we do and how to change.** William Heinemann.

Keltner, D. 2016. **The Power Paradox: How We Gain and Lose Influence.** Penguin.

Cialdini, R. 2016. **Pre-Suasion: A Revolutionary Way to Influence and Persuade.** Simon & Shuster.

Mullainathan, S. 2014. **Scarcity: The true cost of not having enough.** Penguin.

Wallman, J. **Stuffocation: Living more with less.** Penguin.

Kahneman, D. **Thinking Fast and Slow.** Penguin.

Crawford, M. 2016. **The World Beyond Your Head: How to flourish in an age of distraction.** Penguin.

About the Author

Ade McCormack is focused on helping people and organisations thrive in the post-industrial world. Clients engage Ade when they need a 'zoom out' view of how the world is changing, followed by 'zoom in' guidance on how they can capitalise on these changes.

Ade has worked in over 30 countries, across many industries. Clients engage Ade in many ways, including as a:

- Thought leader.
- Conference keynoter.
- Advisor and coach.

He is a former technologist, with a degree in Physics / Astrophysics.

Ade has written for a range of publications, including the Financial Times. He has written several business books, including 'Beyond Nine to Five: Your career guide for the digital age'. He has also lectured at MIT Sloan on digital leadership.

Ade is married with one son. He enjoys martial arts, dancing, parkour, and running. Running and parkour being his primary self-defence choices, closely followed by dancing.

Connect

Twitter: @ademccormack

LinkedIn: https://www.linkedin.com/in/ademccormack

Website: www.ademccormack.com

What next?

As part of Ade McCormack's work in helping individuals and organisations thrive in the digital age, he covers a variety of interrelated themes, including:

- Attention
- Innovation
- Disruption
- Transformation
- Risk
- Digital
- Robotics
- New technologies
- Neuroscience
- Geopolitics
- Anthropology
- Biology.

These themes are typically applied to practical matters, including:

- Leadership and strategy.
- Disruption and transformation.
- Talent management and human performance.
- Brand management and business development.
- Society and citizens.

The associated insights and actions can be woven into keynotes, workshops, coaching and advisory support.

Ade McCormack can be contacted via his website:

ademccormack.com

Printed in Great Britain
by Amazon